HOLLYWOOD'S DIRTIEST SECRET

Film and Culture Series

FILM AND CULTURE

A series of Columbia University Press
Edited by John Belton

For a complete list of titles, see https://cup.columbia.edu/series/film-and-culture-series

Hollywood's Dirtiest Secret

The Hidden Environmental Costs of the Movies

Hunter Vaughan

Columbia University Press   *New York*

Columbia University Press
Publishers Since 1893
New York   Chichester, West Sussex
cup.columbia.edu
Copyright © 2019 Columbia University Press
All rights reserved

Library of Congress Cataloging-in-Publication Data
Names: Vaughan, Hunter, author.
Title: Hollywood's dirtiest secret : the hidden environmental costs of our screen culture /
    Hunter Vaughan.
Description: New York : Columbia University Press, 2019. | Includes bibliographical
    references and index.
Identifiers: LCCN 2018044271 (print) | LCCN 2018050562 (ebook) |
    ISBN 9780231544153 (e-book) | ISBN 9780231182409 (cloth : alk. paper) |
    ISBN 9780231182416 (pbk. : alk. paper)
Subjects: LCSH: Motion picture industry—Environmental aspects. |
    Motion pictures—Production and direction—Environmental aspects.
Classification: LCC PN1993.5.A1 (ebook) | LCC PN1993.5.A1 V38 2019 (print) |
    DDC 791.4309—dc23
LC record available at https://lccn.loc.gov/2018044271

∞

Cover design: Lisa Hamm
Cover image (composite): © Photofest and blickwinkel/Alamy Stock Photo

Contents

Acknowledgments

This book reflects the merging of multiple lifelong passions and is the product of many years of research, reflection, and interaction with a range of generous and inspiring human beings, nonhuman animals, and natural and constructed environments. The path to this point has crossed many countries and cities, its concepts and arguments shared in various iterations both formal and informal during conferences and conversations and in classrooms. Much like the intersection between media and the environment, once one thread was pulled, it tugged a hundred different tapestries; disparate fields became united facets; and professors, filmmakers, and friends helped to open new horizons to explore and questions to consider. In short, writing this book has been an immersive and invigorating adventure, and what I present here is a project that is far from over and far from being exclusively mine.

In terms of the ongoing exchange of ideas and the development of this new field of inquiry, I am fortunate to have caught the swell of a wave just before it crested and to be a part of its current crashing. I am deeply grateful to those who laid the foundation and organized the forums for this set of inquiries, gave me opportunities to work through them in public and private, and served as important and inspiring colleagues, trailblazers, mental cavorters, and drinking companions throughout, including Nadia Bozak, Shane Brennan, Tom Conley, Sean

Cubitt, Kyle Edwards, Dan Herbert, Brian Jacobson, E. Ann Kaplan, Selmin Kara, Jeff Menne, Salma Monani, Elena Past, Constance Penley, Amy Rust, Steve Rust, Nicole Starosielski, and Graig Uhlin. I also owe much gratitude as well to a wonderful group of peers, colleagues, and friends, among them Tim Donahue, Brendan Kredell, Missy Molloy, Lauren Pendleton, Alison Powell, and Alex Zamalin.

Significant advances were made in this study and the furtherance of this field thanks to a Rachel Carson Fellowship in 2017, for which I am extremely thankful to the Rachel Carson Center, Munich, as well as to those that joined in those sessions, including Jim Schwoch, Jon Raundalen, and Alexa Weik von Mossner. Of this group, I owe a particular and profound debt to three longtime collaborators: Pietari Kääpä, whose ongoing commitment and affability continue to shape my next steps; Adrian Ivakhiv, whose incredibly generous reading of this book and riveting feedback were invaluable to its current shape; and Janet Walker, my longtime partner in crime, who has forged ahead with me from the beginning and remains a true standard bearer, never flagging in her diligent efforts to promote environmental justice and to help bring this intersecting field to institutional visibility. The many companions listed above have been part and parcel of my personal and professional morphology over this past decade, and I thank them from the bottom of my heart.

For the nuts and bolts of this achievement, which itself is only a step along a longer path, I am greatly appreciative of a number of industry professionals—including Ricou Browning Jr., Rachael Joy, Steve Galich, and Pete Zuccharini—who lent me their expertise and insight, and for the extensive archive research necessary I am grateful to Jenny Romero and the Margaret Herrick Library in Beverly Hills, California; Ned Comstock and the Doheny Memorial Library at the University of Southern California, Los Angeles; and the Harry Ransom Center at the University of Texas, Austin. I was fortunate to have completed this book while on research sabbatical from Oakland University and in the unique intellectual atmosphere of the University of Miami's Abess Center for Ecosystem Science and Policy, and I thank the faculty and researchers at the center—in particular Kenny Broad, Gina Maranto, and Lisa Johns—for their continued exchange, warm smiles, and inspired intelligence, with special thanks to Shireen Rahimi for her invaluable assistance with the images in this book. And I am profoundly grateful to the team at Columbia University Press, including John Belton and Michael Haskell, and to copy editor Annie Barva for her keen eye. And I extend my sincerest appreciation for Philip Leventhal, whose devoted editorial attention and keen guidance were essential to the book's final form.

On a more personal note, I send love and gratitude to my parents, Nicki and David Vaughan, for a childhood of rambling walks by the Chattahoochee River and summers spent hunting for sharks' teeth and assisting sea turtles in the soft sands of Florida's Atlantic coast: they provided me a childhood from which a deep appreciation for nature—and our place in it—was born. And for Meryl Shriver-Rice, my copilot, whose boundless curiosity and stimulating provocations transformed not only this book's potential but also my own perspective at many a turn, there is no way to adequately articulate my gratitude; luckily, she isn't verbal, so I don't have to try. She learned well from her father, Randy Rice, and reminds me at every step how important it is to feel the weight of rocks; these pages burn with that love of weight and materiality, the appreciation we owe to things. I dedicate this book to Meryl and, with her, to that weight—to the sands of Fernandina and Flagler Beach, the waters and waves of the Atlantic Ocean, the bird-swept peaks of the Blue Ridge and Dolomite Mountains, the magnolia branches of Atlanta and Orvieto, and the garden snails, majestic manatees, feline friends, and watchful herons that accompany us in everything we do.

HOLLYWOOD'S DIRTIEST SECRET

Introduction

The Big Picture

Just as water, gas, and electricity are brought into our houses from far
off to satisfy our needs in response to a minimal effort, so we shall be
supplied with visual or auditory images, which will appear and
disappear at a simple movement of the hand, hardly more than a sign.

—PAUL VALÉRY, "THE CONQUEST OF UBIQUITY"

THE SECRET

Hollywood's dirtiest secret is not lascivious, includes no insider power
plays, and does not come with low-resolution snapshots from a motel
room or rehab clinic. It does not involve a sex tape, a murder mystery,
executive drama, or a drug scandal. Hollywood's dirtiest secret is much
dirtier and much more secret, and we all are in on it—though we may
not know it yet.

As with any good secret, there are rumors milling about—floating
in the air, circulating in the water, sinking into the soil, rustling in the
leaves. Small, seductive traces of it are revealed occasionally, provoking
whispers . . . about how the production of James Cameron's *Titanic* decimated a Mexican sea urchin population . . . about how Danny Boyle's *The
Beach* wrecked the natural dunes of Phi Phi Island . . . about the hundreds
or thousands of *E.T.* Atari game cartridges buried in the Texas desert . . .
about Colby's casual theft of Great Barrier Reef coral on *Survivor: The
Australian Outback* . . . about the dirty mining of precious metals that
make up our smart mainframes and the amount of dirty energy necessary to fuel our Netflix binges. . . .

Like any good secret, we tune it out when we need to. Hush money is paid, and the Thai government forgives 20th Century Fox; *Survivor*'s producer makes a public apology and a vacuous commitment to the environment via *Entertainment Weekly*; carbon credits are purchased and trees are planted so that business can proceed as usual. And the guilty parties promise they will do better in the future: Paramount Pictures introduces its green-studio initiative, and Apple promises to no longer fund African civil wars and child labor by purchasing Congolese coltan. We keep buying and keep watching, but it's okay: we won't do *that* again.

This secret is the hidden environmental impact of how we make, watch, and dispose of movies. It may not be sexy, but as far as scandals go, it is huge—and it is connected to everything. It is connected to our everyday viewing, built into the hardware of digital technology, and secreted into the ideological foundations of popular visual culture. Our smart devices operate on the raw materials dug out of international conflict and the constant hum of fossil fuels to which we turn a deaf ear—deep scars in a material reality that we are increasingly distracted from, environmental and social justice transgressions from which we are given respite by the virtual forums of social media and blockbuster fantasy. We power on, choosing to convert natural resources into screen culture (film, television, video, and other digital content). This secret is connected to the social structures whereby we have tacitly, perhaps unknowingly, come to accept this distraction as a given and in doing so have agreed to the sacrifice of the real on the altar of entertainment spectacle.

In this book, I will utter this secret aloud, will violate the agreement by speaking its terms, and in doing so will take steps toward an ecological ethics—defined by Patrick Curry as "how human beings *ought* to behave in relation to non-human nature"[1]—that reframes the priorities of our screen culture. Using Hollywood history as an index for this tacit agreement—or "sociocultural contract," as I call it—this book explores how the messages and methods of mainstream cinema as well as our participation in it as a willing and eager audience have cultivated our perceptions of the environment and treatment of natural resources and how films' production and viewing practices have generated profound but unspoken modes of environmental impact. And, I argue, our entry into the digital age has only complicated this relationship, offering us new ways of understanding the natural world while also moving us farther away from it.

But, like any contract, this one can be renegotiated.

FROM THE IVORY TOWER TO THE EARTH

I should confess early on that I watch movies. I love watching movies. On my sofa, in a theater, in a classroom, on my phone, in black-and-white or color, alone or with people. Watching movies, streaming televisual series, ingesting online content—images and sounds beamed to me by satellite, snaked to me by undersea cable, flown to me in envelopes. Although I try to remain vigilant regarding the dangers of screen addiction, I do use smart technology. Hell, this book was written on a laptop. The entire reason I entered the profession of media scholarship and teaching is that I deeply appreciate—more so today than ever—the significant social power that screen culture wields. And, as a consequence, I believe it holds an ethical responsibility. This book is not an indictment of any single person or daily behavior; it is, rather, the expression of my own realization of the profound environmental ramifications of our visual culture and the complex materiality of the screen industries and infrastructures that provide for them. It is a plea for individuals to be more aware of the cultural practices we take for granted as well as a challenge to expect better from the industry and from professionals who cater to these practices.

Our images do not come from nothing, and they do not vanish into the air: they have always been generated by the earth and sun, by fossil fuels and chemical reactions, and our enjoyment of them has material consequences. Speaking both hope and anxiety, the German philosopher and cultural theorist Herbert Marcuse wrote, "Art cannot change the world, but it can contribute to changing the consciences and drives of men and women who change the world."[2] With full respect to Marcuse's humble intentions, I disagree: the way we make and use art actually *does* change the world, physically and compositionally, using its resources, draining its fluids, mining its innards, and rerouting its flows. This book is a documentation of that change.

Over the past two decades, as popular awareness of climate change and other environmental threats has risen and our daily lives have become further enveloped in the ubiquity of digital screens, a slow sea change has been brewing in the relationship between media studies, social sciences, and the humanities. We are nearing a confluence of critical and scholarly interest, coming from a variety of directions, around the intersection between media and the environment. This new field has grown from a seismic shift in ways of looking both at screen culture and at the purpose of theory and criticism, and its growing pains have in many ways been accentuated by the disciplinary and institutional tensions that exist between social sciences, humanities, and media studies. I intend here a blatant violation of that tension in the belief that environmental communication would benefit from more acknowledgment of the qualitative workings of visual culture and that environmental humanities would benefit from more grounded engagement with empirical perspectives such as sociology, psychology, and anthropology. In place of divided fields opposing each other in a war over regimented funding territories, methodological principles, and intellectual merit, I propose a bridge between these fields, one that engages with screen culture as a dynamic social force working at once through aesthetics and rhetoric, emotional appeal and cognitive-messaging strategies, and producing significant environmental impact.

Today's environmental debate is divisive, it is ideological (imprinted on beliefs so ingrained we no longer see them or question them), it is political, and it is emotional. In other words, it is the perfect canvas for the Hollywood brush. Yet as our lives become more and more bound to screen technologies, and as political divisiveness reaches new heights of volatility and aggression, film and media scholars seem to be shying away from hard stances, accepting the postpolitical turn and reframing their charge as one of industry experts and data analysts. I reject this trend and insist that film culture is socially relevant, *deeply* relevant, and that we can and should demand an ethical approach to criticism that is informed by the quantitative thoroughness of the social sciences. Though I am not trained as a social scientist and will not claim to practice those sciences here, the process of this book has drawn me farther outside the boundaries of film and media studies, arming a screen scholar with new horizons for how this field can intersect with studies of human psychology, collective cultural norms, and social behavior. What I *will* do here is attempt an accessible environmentalist study of popular films across

Hollywood history that folds conventional methods such as archival research and close textual readings into a larger portrait of how films have both shaped and reflected—and continue to shape and reflect—our relationship with the nonhuman natural world.

The environmental debate is largely cultural, and mainstream screen media is a huge factor in that—it has been for more than a century, even when not overtly discussing environmental issues. Recently, though, screen texts *are* discussing these issues, which is both good and bad, for they often do so in ways that are problematically tucked into allegories and woven into myths, piquing our concern with the comfort of vague outlines while shielding us from hard truths and demands for large-scale change. Perhaps without knowing it, our participation in popular screen culture belies a soft liberal embrace of environmentalist values, caressing our green disposition while implicitly allowing the industrial status quo to go unfettered. To tease out an example that is perhaps the crux of this book: *Avatar* (James Cameron, 2009) is at once a cautionary tale about the dangers of unbridled natural-resource use and the militant destruction of nature, but it is on a deeper material level a lesson in neoliberal greenwashing, luring us into believing that its environmental message is not presaged on a production process that was excessively impactful on the environment and a marketing strategy that is a textbook case of global capitalism. We believe that celebrating a film such as *Avatar* puts us on the right side, but it is actually implicating us in the dirty secret, allowing us to exist in the virtual while the material real becomes fuel for its fire.

In many ways, this issue is one of ignorance and of voluntary psychosis. It is a problem of the visible and, even more importantly, the invisible—we do not see who we are harming or how these practices are affecting the environment, and we routinely agree to accept the virtual as real. To recognize this choice has taken me many years. More than a decade ago, caught in the final throes of my Ph.D., I was returning home from the pubs along Oxford's cobblestones when I was struck by a throbbing glow that illuminated the night sky. I realized that this electric heartbeat came from inside one of the colleges. Winding my way inside, I discovered a full-scale film production—*The Golden Compass* (Chris Weitz, 2007)—and asked one of the crew members what they were doing. He responded that they were doing a run-through for the following day's shoot. Electrical cable writhed like a snake den; massive clusters of lamps and spotlights burned a surreal yellow blue into the night, a swirl of steam and smoke and chemical emission where air met the glass and metal apparatus; behemoth scaffoldings of iron and plastic, meant to last only a day or two, stood monstrous like industrial skeletons; and beating through it all like a heartbeat was the gentle hum of power generators. Though I had seen film shoots before and even worked on a major studio lot, I was nonetheless struck with the awe that hits most in the presence of a blockbuster production and momentarily thought, *"What incredible spectacle"*—a response that was immediately replaced by a cringe of anxiety as I did a double take, digesting the enormous use of resources and the production of waste and pollution at the service of artificially producing some magical version of the real: *"And this is only for a run-through?!"*

I shuffled this experience away and got back—afloat in the ivory tower—to writing on philosophy and the image, but that glow in the night sky continued to burn, the hum of generators faintly resonating. That work eventually became my first book, *Where Film Meets Philosophy*,[3] which argues that film can and does offer us forms of organizing information and knowledge with which to understand and express the world and that, because of this, it should be understood to hold an immense power for the construction and challenging of value systems. Although I stand by this rather romantic valuation of film's potential purpose, by the end of that project I was ready to exit the ivory tower, to get down to the earth, and to turn my attention and effort to problems of a more concrete and material nature.

This was not easy, though, because there is such a strong disconnect forged between our enjoyment of screen culture and our conscientiousness of its environmental impact. Though Hollywood is an easy scapegoat for the issues explored here, it is not necessarily even the root of the problem—it merely thrives on the problem. The problem is social and more largely cultural than one industry, one town, or one medium. It resides in our eager detachment from the material and ethical impacts of virtual experience, in the problematic balance of values according to which we have come collectively to orient cultural spectacle and the natural environment. Let us now confront the basic problem that is *our existence, as cultural beings that are part of the natural world*. It may help to convert a rather abstract cost–benefit question such as "What is the natural cost we are willing to pay to have art?" into a closer ethical confrontation of the material ramifications of specific manifestations of culture and what desires and pleasures this culture of spectacle appeals to and satisfies. Would you accept the extinction of a species of fish in exchange for your favorite movie? How about a species of rabbit? How many trees would you cut down in order to have *Transformers: Dark of the Moon* (Michael Bay, 2011) be part of our collective image-scape? How many highways worth of carbon output is it worth to make sure we have *Wedding Crashers* (David Dobkin, 2005)? Does that change if the question is about *Singin' in the Rain* (Stanley Donan and Gene Kelly, 1952), *The Godfather* (Francis Ford Coppola, 1972), *Thelma and Louise* (Ridley Scott, 1991), or *Moonlight* (Barry Jenkins, 2016)? What if the victims are human? What if they could be your grandchildren?

THE ROOTS OF THE PROBLEM

The quotation from Paul Valéry's essay "The Conquest of Ubiquity" at the beginning of this introduction is one often referenced by both artists and scholars of the digital age and has grown ever more popular with the environmental turn currently happening across academic disciplines as well as across society at large.[4] It so aptly—and so presciently—captures the way images and image culture have become as ubiquitously present and are consumed as readily as the utilities that in 1928 had already started to be taken for granted in the average Western household. Moreover, the invisible origin and instantaneity of our daily images' appearance and disappearance perfectly captures our contemporary notion of screen culture in the age of streaming: because of the ease and the hidden infrastructure of screen culture's conveyance, we mistake it as immaterial, just as we do the water in our pipes, the energy in our wires, the gas in our tanks. But we are realizing that these utilities are not immaterial or infinite. And as we come to appreciate more and more the materiality and impact of our natural-resource use, so should we that of our image use. In doing so, we must begin to fully assess the complex relationships among our screens, our natural resources, and the ecosystems, ecologies, and economies they are a part of.

The environmental turn can be seen in connection to a larger resurgence, in light of the increasing visibility of climate change threats, of an ecocentric and holistic worldview that was very much dispatched by the rise of capitalism, the Scientific Revolution, and the age of industry. In her brilliant book *The Death of Nature* (1980), Carolyn Merchant captures an epic historical shift from medieval agriculture to modern industrial capitalism as being definitively connected to our complex and anxious relationship with the natural world today:

> The Scientific Revolution of the sixteenth and seventeenth centuries has been treated by most historians as a period of intellectual enlightenment in which a new science of mechanism and mechanical world view laid the foundation for modern scientific, technological, and social programs. But, in the face of the current crisis over the depletion of natural resources Western society is once more beginning to appreciate the environmental values of the premechanical "world we have lost." Today, the ecological consequences of exploitative attitudes toward the four elements—earth, air, water, and fire—the ancient sources of life and energy, are beginning to be fully recognized.[5]

Much of what crystallized through the Scientific Revolution and the installment of market capitalism was, of course, already well set in place by the design of previous empires, the institutionalization of Christianity, and the rise of oligarchical political structures and commodity-exchange culture. Yet Merchant sharply identifies the fifteenth-century transition between organic and mechanistic models as an umbrella for complex changes in technology, social organization, and ideology that laid the foundation for our contemporary relationship with the environment. I argue here that our current shift from analog to digital models is equally as sweeping, complex, and problematic for the environment.

Though written nearly forty years ago, Merchant's book sagely heralded the imminent twenty-first-century return of ecology as reviving a holistic tradition founded on the belief—revitalized by the Romantics in the shadow of early industry, by preservationists such as John Muir in the face of American expansionism, and by a growing voice today at the threshold of the digital era—that human beings are not apart from nature or at the top of an environmental pyramid but are inextricably bound within a symbiotic fabric of the natural world. The renaissance of such ecological thinking has been expedited by a recent rise in the general awareness of environmental instability and a growing anxiety over the human impact on the rest of the natural world. Unlike the world of the fifteenth century, though, and unlike the world of 1980, our natural world today just happens to include artificial intelligence and virtual-reality avatars, drone warfare, accelerated species extinction, and dangerously rising sea levels. And in the midst of it all, movies.

In a deeper historical perspective, Merchant is apt to connect the advent of capitalism, industrial technology, and scientific rationalism as the underlying girders of our modern perceptions of the environment and of the consequent colonization and exploitation of natural resources. This argument is often adjoined to one of nature being both a cultural construct and a historical construct, a conceptual paradigm that has been crafted by human worldviews. Political and artistic discourses of the post-Renaissance centuries have merited criticism for erecting an apparatus that is as imperially raced as it is patriarchal, and we must integrate the natural environment into these overarching approaches to ideological structuring. Central to the environmental justice movement, systematic connections between social injustice and the environment have recently been framed specifically in relation to the advent of capitalism, class, race, and gender. McKenzie Wark's argument regarding labor and nature can be applied to a wider overlap between facets of social hierarchy and notions of the natural: "They are historically co-produced concepts."[6] Historically coproduced *and* historically bound to social structures of power. As such lenses indicate, current approaches to media and the environment are deeply enmeshed in other cultural studies approaches to social identity, capital, and inequality.

These perspectives belie a wider turn in the humanities and the emergence of environmentally focused studies of art, literature, and— finally—screen culture. What is generally referred to as "ecocriticism," or the study of how popular culture both represents the natural and positions us in relation to it, grew primarily out of literary studies and critical theory in the 1990s. Works by Lawrence Buell, Verena Andermatt Conley, and others focused on nodal points of American cultural history (e.g., transcendentalist philosophy and postwar social movements) as signposts for how literature and philosophy have shaped and been shaped by our relationship to the environment. The turn of the millennium witnessed a strong turn toward literary and film ecocriticism, echoing a rise in the visibility of environmental issues in popular and journalistic discourse and being met by a parallel turn in communications studies to the environment as a field of significant query.[7] And although many foundational works of screen ecocriticism focus on issues of representation in popular moving-image culture, scholars such as Adrian Ivakhiv have heralded an environmental bridge from ecocriticism to a more material focus, with writers such as Sean Cubitt, Nadia Bozak, Richard Maxwell and Toby Miller, and Nicole Starosielski moving away from issues of film representation and toward the geopolitics, industrial infrastructure, and material impact of media industries and practices.[8]

GREEN SCREENS

The first decade of the twenty-first century was marked by two important cultural surges: the rapid growth of our collective awareness and discussion of major environmental issues such as climate change and the proliferation of smart-technology devices and their central role in our daily lives. Although I critique overly optimistic claims of the symbiosis between the green revolution and the digital revolution, we cannot deny that the two are historically, technologically, and socially connected. They are emerging simultaneously, often empower one another through mechanical complexity and moral principle, and in many cases engage similar population sets and political stances.

There is no question that we live in a volatile time, where the challenges of social division and global inequality are only exacerbated by the increasing effects and risk perception of accelerated climate change. This is not an issue that can—or will—wait, and it touches our entire screen universe, from the phones in our pockets to the rovers catapulting images back to us from Mars. It is not disproportionately alarmist to state that the way social and cultural systems interact with—and position us in relation to—the environment is part of a tacit agreement we abide by every day and is part of a process of environmental destruction that is nearing a point of no return. Nor is it overly ideal to believe that although larger political decisions must be made in order to force large-scale industrial change, this change will come only at the behest of radical shifts in popular thought and collective worldview, for which screen culture could be our strongest weapon.

Many advocates, politicians, and activists appear to hold the same view, as can be seen by the recent turn to film culture as a hotbed of environmental action. The success of Al Gore and Davis Guggenheim's documentary *An Inconvenient Truth* (2006), based on Gore's multimedia lecture on climate change, not only signified that popular audiences were ready to talk about the environment but also illustrated an abundance of new uses for smart technology and screen media in our understanding and expression of the environment. Best-selling writer and activist Naomi Klein's book *This Changes Everything: Capitalism vs. the Environment* (2014) has exploded into a traveling film event and spawned a grassroots social movement;[9] similarly, historians of science Naomi Oreskes and Erik M. Conway's critique of the systematic public-relations push against climate change science and emissions regulations, *The Merchants of Doubt* (2010),[10] was adapted to the screen in 2014. Documentary and feature-fiction filmmakers continue to seek new ways to express environmental concern and to evoke ecological pathos through screen media, and the proliferation of distribution and exhibition methods made possible by cable television and the Internet has hotwired a brave new world not only of watching things but of looping screen texts to social groups and political networks.[11]

Though this book certainly offers an environmental criticism of the methods and madness of our screen culture, and though for the most part it is still business as usual in tinsel town, I also encourage a sense of optimism regarding the current green turn in American cinema. The environmental reform of Hollywood does not stop at the wallpapering of the Internet with images of Leo DiCaprio filling up his Prius at the gas pump or with the rising number of sci-fi films about environmental catastrophe. Although Mark Ruffalo's widely covered antifracking activism; Shailene Woodley's highly visible arrest at Standing Rock; Matt Damon's founding of and continued work with Water.Org; and the voicing of nature by Julia Roberts, Morgan Freeman, and others for Conservation International's *Nature Is Speaking* film series depend to varying degrees on the hierarchical institution of the star system, they are valiant attempts at the use of celebrity to solicit popular understanding and activism for environmental and social justice causes. That this is a new arena for star self-definition reinforces a growing sense of popularity in the awareness of, concern over, and desire to act on issues of climate change and environmental justice.

These voices, however, are only a part of screen culture's role in our perception of and engagement with the environment: this book is a reminder of the degree to which our ideological positioning of nonhuman nature is bound to our social norms, collective values, and interactions with screen technology. We must also remember that the increasingly frequent occurrence of extreme environmental events does not mean the same to everyone. An unsung moment in this celebrity movement took place in an improvised interruption to NBC's celebrity-heavy Hurricane Katrina relief programming in 2005, when—stepping off script and baffling Michael Myers, with whom he shared the stage—Kanye West called out the sitting U.S. president for environmental racism, staring at the camera deadpan and saying with steadfast and earnest calm, "George Bush doesn't care about black people." Kanye's brief comments were radical in their concise and accurate condemnation of the federal government's handling of the response to that natural disaster and its aftermath, in which the victims were predominately black and lower class.

The more we understand about the environmental toll of human actions, the more we also come to understand how the politics and culturing of the natural world is deeply tied—both symbolically and concretely—to the fabric of racial inequality, class stratification, colonial exploitation, and gendered objectification. What Rob Nixon terms the "slow violence" of environmental harm is meted out unequally, with its slowness being both a temporal slowness of degradation and a slowness of response due to the fact that this violence most frequently targets non-white and poorer communities and nations.[12] Far from superseding the human struggles of identity and inequity, the imminent need for environmental responsibility accentuates the need for accommodating the variant demands of social diversity. To borrow an insight from Sean Cubitt: "Ecocriticism has to get beyond the stage of special pleading for a single cause, and to consider what, uniquely, it can offer as *the* holistic mode of critical thought in the twenty-first century."[13]

ECOMATERIALISM AND ITS EXTENTS

One way to meet Cubitt's challenge is to integrate problems of representation into a more focused concern with screen culture's material costs because the materiality of this planet and its resources is something we all are bound to. In these pages, I stage an *ecomaterialist* intervention in film analysis and production-culture studies, offering an alternative history of Hollywood and, by extension and with full implication, of the audience for which it exists. By "ecomaterialist," I mean an approach that does not limit its environmental scope to the question of representation (i.e., *how nature is shown* or *how environmental issues and social groups are portrayed on screen*) but explores the material environmental impact of film practices, from the extraction of minerals to the chemical waste of its process, the centrality of natural symbolism in its marketing and crossover merchandising, and the restructuring of urban communities based on production culture ebbs and flows.

In doing so, I challenge the multitiered notion that our image culture is immaterial. As the French philosopher Paul Virilio has argued, "The cinema became the major site for a trade in dematerialization, a new industrial market which no longer produced matter but light."[14] This notion is at the center of the screen myth—a sleight of hand, a dazzle of fireworks that pleads magical illumination but is actually the product of immense amounts of resources, energy, pollution, and waste. This book turns on the house lights so as to drown out the projector, allowing us a moment to look around the theater and at one another as co-conspirators bound by a tacit social agreement to a cultural behavior of huge environmental proportions.

In this ecomaterialist framework, I reframe the life cycle of the screen text through a lens that goes beyond the parameters of the typical production/distribution/exhibition assessment, considering the film's mineral prebirth, zombie remains, wide-scale alchemy of social design, and shelf life as a tangible and symbolic object.[15] I look at the cradle-to-cradle life cycle of film culture's environmental impact: from the raw materials of screen hardware (including the environmental justice issues of mining precious metals for the manufacture of smart devices) to the on-site practices of filmmaking (including the decimation of location ecosystems caused by Hollywood shoots) to the global imperialism of e-waste disposal.

A central component of my notion of ecomaterialism is the term *materialism*, a conceptual minefield that has inspired many recent works both in the field and peripheral to it, including voices from political ecology and object-oriented ontology—in addition to its meanings in colloquial, archaeological, and environmental science vocabularies. For environmental studies, *materialism* refers to resource use, whereas for archaeologists it entails the cultural artifacts through which we can understand collective values, rituals, and social structures. In the colloquial, though, *materialistic* is a pejorative adjective used for people overly obsessed with consumer objects. Interweaving these various meanings through an environmental take on the Frankfurt School's Marxist principle of dialectical materialism and therefore insisting that the natural world be included in an understanding of historical and political events arising from contradictory social forces, the term *ecomaterialism* evokes here the social inequalities, resource exploitation, and tangibility at the heart of mainstream screen culture. I connect these understandings of screen culture—as resource use, as network of artifacts, as dialectic tension between social and ecosystemic forces, as problematic crux of our consumer habits and collective desire for spectacle— through a systematic study of mainstream film culture's practices and products.

Most recent approaches to "materialism" center around a deconstruction of the subject–object hierarchy still dominating Western worldviews and defining the value difference between human *life* and inanimate *things*, and I bring this deconstruction to bear on the relational values we have with our environment—in terms of how we use it and the bearing it has on our quality of life.[16] In *Vibrant Matter* (2010), Jane Bennett draws attention to the "vitality of matter," critiquing the ethics that resist such a turn: "my hunch is that the image of dead or thoroughly instrumentalized matter feeds human hubris and our earth-destroying fantasies of conquest and consumption." The very term *materiality* applies a sense of a flattened playing field and "draws human attention sideways, away from the ontologically ranked Great Chain of Being and toward a greater appreciation of the complex entanglements of humans and nonhumans."[17]

Bennett's influence can be seen in recent studies such as *Digital Rubbish* (2013) by Jennifer Gabrys and *A Geology of Media* (2015) by Jussi Parikka, which integrate this challenge of materialism and materiality into studies of the waste and remains of media technology. Making strange bedfellows of the archaeological, environmental, and colloquial understandings of the term *material*, the recent interest in e-waste and fossilization offers a rich perspective for the arching significance of our screen culture. In what Gabrys refers to as a "natural history" of electronics, she documents the record of dead electronics and the fossil forms in which they persist as evidence of the "materiality of electronics . . . often lost between the apparent 'virtuality' of information, the increasingly miniature scale of electronics, and the remoteness of electronic manufacture and disposal."[18] How we dispose of our screen technologies and how their carcasses continue to live with us provide varying pendants of the ideological ties between media and the environment.

Parikka engages similar notions of fossil and zombie media with questions of deep time to unearth "the specificity and agency of mediatic matter,"[19] insisting that technology be viewed as an active agent—and not merely as a tool—in our social and political configurations. I incorporate this approach into a Marxist materialism that is grounded in the praxis of capital and exploitation, including the planet itself as the participant in industrial productivity ultimately alienated from both product and profit. I embrace recent Marxist arguments waged by heralds of the "Capitalocene," challenging the popular "Anthropocene" as positing an ahistorical and abstract homogenous humanity, set teleologically across a smooth linear story of progress and awaiting a technocratic solution.[20] The problems we face in this era of accelerated climate change and environmental disruption are not simply problems of the human but are specifically problems of capitalist industry—philosophical impacts of the logic of capital and material impacts of the practice of industry, which in turn buttress the social inequalities of neoliberalism. We cannot extricate an understanding of Western media practices and ecosystem relations from the thorny tentacles of capital and should instead understand how capital shapes our various ways of relating to each other and to the environment. As such, I offer an ecomaterialism of screen culture that merges problems of technology development, media infrastructure, and resource use with problems of political economy, cultural values, and social justice.

Although insisting on a material-oriented perspective, we must not lose sight of the important social and political configurations through which natural resources are used. Accordingly, the goal of this book is to maintain a social purpose and environmental justice ethics, moving dialectically between the material impact of screen culture and reflections upon the *sociocultural contract* that makes this culture possible and that our screen texts intrinsically reaffirm at most turns. Adapted from the term Jean-Jacques Rousseau coined in his treatise on the compromise individuals make to preserve order in collective society,[21] the term *sociocultural contract* refers to the unspoken agreement made within a society as to how it will produce and value cultural attitudes, behaviors, customs, and materiality.

In this case, the agreement in question is the one regarding popular screen entertainment: what we use it for, how we generate it, how it affects us, and how this use and generation and effect reflect our fundamental valuation of the nonhuman natural world. An examination of this agreement is particularly urgent because that valuation has—according to unanimous scientific consensus—led us to an environmental precipice.[22] How has Hollywood helped us to lay a foundation for organizing our relationship to spectacle and the environment in ways that are detrimental to ecological stability, and how are these foundations being used to build new cultural customs in the digital age?

Much of this symbiosis involves our cultural production of *mythology*, a concept I return to repeatedly. The term *mythology* here refers to the collective need and cultural structuring of a symbolic register in which we can narratively and aesthetically address difficult collective anxieties and through which we both reflect and construct social norms and communal value systems. Film culture has a special place in this dynamic composition of mythology: the "dream factory" is really a mythology factory. Its assembly line extends across the planet; its delivery service is wired into our coat pockets and living rooms, penetrating our most private spaces and saturating our public ones; and its material impact is unrivaled by that of other popular arts. Moreover, its vertiginous potential as a time machine to catapult us between past and future and its bewitching blend of reality and fantasy make it an incredibly rich—and therefore dangerous—mythology factory.

In this book, I tease out this concept of mythology as one that is both fundamental and fundamentally problematic to our relationship with the environment because it allows us to mediate the natural while also rendering it in some ways unreal, be it fictionalized or virtualized—and, if unreal, consequently detached from the human experience and not worth the empathy, connection, and care that we owe it. This is the great danger of a cultural balance where spectacle becomes an end in itself. Spectacle is a binding fuse of sensation, desire, and ecology, lending itself to mating rituals and predatory tactics across a number of species; and it is perhaps in exploring the sensory expressions, collective desires, and industrial ecologies that drive spectacle that we might come closer to understanding the sociocultural contract of popular cinema. The prominence of screen spectacle in our cultural value system is problematic specifically because it manifests a collective desire to sacrifice the stability of the natural world for our entertainment, pleasure, and comfort. This problem has only grown with the proliferation of screen devices in daily use and the advent of virtual and augmented realities. The already tenuous umbilical cord that connects us to the real stretches still thinner as our ability to simulate it expands, no matter how empowering and liberating new technologies may seem—the sociocultural contract is entering a new phase, one of even dirtier industrial potential and more cleverly hidden secrets.

THE BLUEPRINT

The structure of screen mythology is pervasive and powerful and can best be revealed and most accessibly discussed in relation to popular cultural texts; for better or worse, this means examining the Hollywood blockbuster. Though not always the most artistically crafted or philosophically profound, mainstream feature films hold a special place at the center of our cultural rituals, ideological values, and existential anxieties. Films such as *Gone with the Wind* (Victor Fleming, 1939) and *Avatar* are definitive of their eras in terms of both industry practice and social zeitgeist. Hollywood's capacity as a purveyor of mythology and a shaper of worldviews as well as the vast material impact of its methods make it the necessary object of this interrogation.

In an attempt to gather the massive scope of this study into a coherent structure, I have embraced the familiarity of the natural elements as a reference point—familiar in that most global philosophies, religions, and cultures make use of some form of an elemental framework.[23] In this case, the elements provide a blueprint for historiographic and conceptual expansion, with each elementally oriented Hollywood case study ushering in a new layering of ecomaterialist study, each chapter building upon the previous one, just as the elements do not exist independently but as an interwoven whole.

Beginning with an analysis of the central role that fire and explosion play in the blockbuster tradition, chapter 1 uses the epic burning of Atlanta sequence in *Gone with the Wind* as a paradigm for connecting issues of film authorship, mythology fabrication and marketing, and philosophical questions regarding screen spectacle and the natural world. I provide a historical survey of the emergent fascination with fire in fin de siècle popular entertainment, before it became part and parcel of the film spectacle. Drawing from primary archival sources as well as from philosophical and industrial perspectives on the unique connection between fire, the moving image, and celluloid material, this chapter explores how the early structuring of creative power and extratextual discourse was integral to the formative logic of Hollywood spectacle. Furthermore, I argue that this early formative logic of Hollywood spectacle anchored popular film discourse in an aesthetic and narrative purveyance of excess and destruction, through which the material real is sacrificed on the altar of screen culture.

The pyrotechnic extravaganza of chapter 1 gets doused with artificial rain as chapter 2 turns to Stanley Donen and Gene Kelly's film *Singin' in the Rain* as a gateway for addressing natural-resource use in film production, highlighting resource materiality in screen practices from film-stock production to advertising tie-ins. An ironic behind-the-scenes mockery of Hollywood excess, *Singin' in the Rain* even reveals the resource use that drives the production of screen artifice; however, it ultimately reinforces the very values it critiques, in particular through its concrete use of natural resources and its symbolic play with water. The film's making and marketing, I argue, illuminate how film culture both intuitively and expressly quantifies and qualifies the use of natural resources. Investigating diverse sources such as the assistant director's reports and radio advertisement pitches, while also surveying the politics of water in the twentieth and twenty-first centuries, chapter 2 captures classical Hollywood at its final peak before the decline of the studio system. This snapshot of American film culture's traditional ecomaterialist logic, we will find, reveals the fundamental girders of the sociocultural contract that endure the transition to the digital era.

The way in which screen culture is emblematic of our treatment of the environment is changing as part of a global technological shift. Building upon genre as a site of mythology formation, I turn in chapters 3 and 4 to the emergence of a new genre of environmentally themed blockbuster amid the wide-scale move toward digital practice, pinpointing Jan de Bont's film *Twister* (1996) as a crucial point in that transition. Its digital dramatization of tornado-based destruction provides a crucible for digital screen culture's visualization of the invisible aspects of the environment, a signpost for how this problem of visualization ties historical, philosophical, and environmental theories of film to the coming digital age. Focusing on the connection between emergent screen technologies and the climate change debate, I explore how new screen mythologies reflect an increase in climate change awareness that has been boosted by digital technology, social media, and popular cinema—a connection that is a double-edged sword.

Building upon the myths of digital immateriality and the Scientist-Hero abundant in the making, marketing, and messages of *Twister*, chapter 4 uses *Avatar* as a case study for the ecodisaster genre's intersection between popular environmental anxiety, digital production, and the evacuation of the real. Verified self-brander and box-office record breaker with *Titanic* and again with *Avatar*, director James Cameron is also an avid pioneer of special-effects technology; moreover, as a supporter of underwater exploration, he became in June 2013 the first movie celebrity in 125 years to grace the cover of *National Geographic*, arguably the journal most responsible for shaping American popular views on the natural world.

Avatar marks the pinnacle in Hollywood's recent movement in two parallel directions: toward digital production and across the spectrum of popular environmentalism. Despite being marketed as a fully digital production with a strong environmental message, *Avatar* indulged in grotesque production excess in order to produce a film that, although seemingly progressive on the surface, merely reinforces a number of conservative ideological values. Like many recent films in the screen genre referred to in literary studies as "climate fiction" (or "cli fi") and that I dub the *ecodisaster film, Avatar* answers the anxieties of the Anthropocene by providing a fantastical escape from the very earth that we have destroyed through irresponsible industrial practices. Building upon the proliferation of digital screen mediations of the natural world, *Avatar* extols the power of digital practices to visualize ecological problems while ignoring the new imperialism established in the manufacturing, use, and disposal of new screen technologies. The sociocultural contract forged by classical Hollywood has not been restructured for the virtual era—we simply signed a multifold extension with the advent of digital technology, clicking to agree without bothering to read the fine print.

In order to acknowledge the importance both of our species' impact on the natural environment and of the environment's impact on our cultural practices, I have added a fifth element to the traditional four: the human. From institutional religious claims to early scientific cosmology to capitalist arguments for deep-sea drilling, humanity has rationalized the exploitation of nonhuman nature to the great detriment of both. Conversely, ecocritical studies of media tend to chart the human invasion of natural spaces but do not acknowledge how human culture—and, over the past century or so, screen-culture industries—have been shaped by their environmental surroundings. Arguing for the need to build bridges between media studies, environmental studies, and social sciences such as anthropology, sociology, production ethnography, and environmental communication, chapter 5 addresses how human social and cultural formations are inextricably tied to the natural environment. By assessing two specific production cultures—South Florida's underwater cinematography community and the establishment of film incentives aimed at revitalizing major urban centers such as Detroit—I explore various ways in which specific ecosystems have shaped media cultures and communities and how localized media production cultures have altered both natural and human topographies.

METHODS TO THE MADNESS

One of the great challenges—and delights—of any interdisciplinary endeavor is the need to balance various intellectual angles and analytic tools. This book is a tapestry of film and media studies, environmental lenses, and social science perspectives. It is driven by the fact that once you pull one thread on the relationship between screen culture and the environment, you feel the connectedness of countless other threads, inevitably realizing the prominence of these two grand paradigms in twenty-first-century existence. The Western world lives half in reality and half in screen-mediated virtuality, and the environment will be the defining social and geopolitical Rubik's cube for coming generations.

Ultimately, this book offers an environmental approach to film history and an interdisciplinary approach to the social organization and ecological ethics of screen culture. This environmental intervention in the Hollywood narrative must be supported as much by the existing wealth of philosophy and critical theory as by archive research, close textual reading, and analysis of secondary material. In film studies terms, this book is a historical study, involving various approaches to film-industry practice (such as authorship and genre theory); a historiography of film studies, marketing, and criticism's role in the sociocultural contract of spectacle and the environment; and a complementary practice in what Ellen Elizabeth Moore calls the "symptomatic reading" of how mainstream cinema's "environmental messages are entrenched within a capitalist framework, reinforcing a mainstream, consumerist mindset."[24] This book is also, though, a study of the society engaged in this contract and a production-culture study interested in "how media producers make culture, and, in the process, how they make themselves into particular kinds of workers in modern, mediated societies."[25]

To some extent at the mercy of methods, this study is hindered by the lack of environmental debate in American society before the 1960s, a half-century into Hollywood's reign—and by the fact that this topic is mostly absent from film texts and media studies until the 1990s. Moreover, the transparency and documentation of resource use and waste production have never been prioritized by Hollywood, nor has Hollywood ever been asked to do so. Considering that I am looking at classical Hollywood as well as at contemporary film culture, this study requires an acrobatic dexterity that, I hope, does not border on the impertinently creative in its reading between certain lines. The ability to quantify resource use and carbon dioxide emission is extremely difficult with regard to an industry so spread out and with so many diverse phases and practices, in which location scouting, studio and location shooting, digital postproduction, and various forms of distribution, marketing, and preservation are all part of the same product's lifespan. In their influential report *Sustainability in the Motion Picture Industry* for the Institute of the Environment at the University of California at Los Angeles, Charles J.

Corbett and Richard P. Turco provide excellent rubrics for assessing the environmental impact of the film and television industry. However, this report, too, concludes with an open horizon on the difficulties of calculating the impact of an industry with so many moving parts and intangible by-products.[26] Last, although strides are being made toward green film and media production, Hollywood is still an image-obsessed and spin-heavy industry with layers of lawyers and public-relations teams employed to limit access, and so my ability to learn firsthand about real change was bated and ultimately stymied by confidentiality clauses and legal-team blockades.

Beyond these issues, there are the added complexities raised by the methodological problem of assessing any causality or degree of impact that screen culture may actually have on people's ethical views and daily choices. As part of a recent rise in the field of environmental communication, Anthony Leiserowitz and others have applied social science methods to gauge the influence of blockbusters such as *The Day After Tomorrow* (Roland Emmerich, 2004) on public risk perception and behavior, relying mostly on survey-based methods to gauge films' impact on perceptions of environmental issues. Although respondents noted an increase in their awareness of climate change issues and claim that this increase would shift their future purchasing and voting decisions, such studies cannot conclusively argue for how this self-reflection may translate to actual action.[27] In his own study of *The Day After Tomorrow*, Matthew Nisbet also acknowledges the difficulty in quantifying the impact of films on daily behavior, noting further that even films with bad science details might add up to a bigger social result (in this case the conclusion that human activity is responsibility for accelerated climate change).[28]

In this book, I juggle these many discursive and methodological balls in emphasizing the argument that whether film culture dictates our every move or not, it buttresses and articulates our fundamental values and our negotiations with the world around us. Moreover, the way film culture positions and makes use of nonhuman nature is a barometer of our collective environmental ideology at a moment when this ideology must be illuminated, reflected upon, and reinvented. Entangled in this urgency, evident in this book, as in all studies of environmental media, is the problem of time, with timescales and temporalities being of particular interest and a grave challenge to environmental representation and communication. How are we to navigate the complex relationship between deep evolutionary time (roughly four and a half billion years) over which our Earth morphed into the planet we know, the relatively short time (150,000 or so years) modern humans have walked this planet, the relative-to-that short era of domesticated agriculture (approximately 12,000 years, or the majority of the Holocene period) and heavy industrial practice (about 250 years), the relative-to-all-that miniscule amount of time (60 years) since environmental science has begun to understand the impact of that industry and since the environmental social movement began in earnest, and—last—the shockingly brief period (perhaps 30 years) of heightened anxiety over, enhanced media coverage of, and central public debate of climate-related issues, which in turn have opened a cacophony of future timescales regarding just how permanent the damage we have done may be and how soon it begins to wreak serious havoc?

It is not surprising, then, that a study of popular genres and texts that deal with environmental issues would confront challenges and nuances of temporality. This book opens with a case study from classical Hollywood that casts a self-glorifying light on the spectacle of destruction in the context of a romanticized representation *of the past*. It concludes its textual case study arc with the present-day ecodisaster genre, which similarly revels in spectacular visuality but is almost uniformly set in the future—a possibly not-so-distant future of environmental dystopia. In other words, just as digital technology has come to offer us a heightened sense of information immediacy and data permanence, digital screen culture is being employed to herald the possibility of our ecosystems' and species' impermanence, projecting our rising popular anxiety over climate change onto a temporal paradigm shift from a culture of nostalgia to a culture of anticipation. Feeling helpless in the face of environmental change, we are increasingly afflicted by what E. Ann Kaplan refers to as "pre-traumatic stress disorder."[29] Although this anticipation has met the nostalgic reactionary backlash of a fiery conservatism acting in the name of American capitalism, climate change denial, and entrenched social morality (encapsulated by the slogan "Make America Great Again"), there is no question that we are witnessing a sea change in how we perceive timescales that is slowly grinding the millstone forward.

An important tenet of this sea change is the return to materiality, for materiality is the heart of where our social rituals and conceptual worldviews actually affect the natural world—ourselves included. As Hollywood celebrities join the global fight of environmental activism and the studios increasingly turn to discourses of sustainability and the environment (to save money, to rebrand themselves in a progressive light, and to sell tickets), we must demand more than the greenwashing on offer in typical industry practices. Only a serious reflection on the environmental role and effects of screen culture will prompt us to understand to what degree an overhaul is needed not only in our consumerism but in our valuation of what function art and entertainment should hold in society.

In a private conversation with activist filmmaker Louis Psihoyos, who was touring on the Oscar-winning success of *The Cove* (2009) and in the early stages of developing his impassioned film *Racing Extinction* (2015), I challenged him on the hypocrisy of practicing business as usual while being exculpated by the loophole of an environmental donation that garnered the film's certification as a "carbon-neutral film." Though pointing out that his and other productions did take strides for sustainable and environmental practice, he abashedly described the "carbon-neutral" accomplishment as akin to "buying indulgences," the Catholic tradition in which a sinner provided particular deeds or modes of penance in exchange for a lessened punishment in the afterlife. In *Racing Extinction*, Psihoyos acknowledges on camera that the worst thing a filmmaker can do for the environment is *to make a film about the environment*, evoking a catch-22 that cannot be avoided here. We will not stop making films, nor will we stop using screens, nor am I arguing for either of these outcomes. But we must—emphatically *must*—begin to adjust our focus from the surface sheen of entertainment spectacle to the hidden resource costs that produce that spectacle and the ramifications of its messages. Let those of us who watch and produce realize that both are environmental acts and demand a shift in how the natural is transformed into the cultural. Meanwhile, those of us who write must take into account the material, social, and overarching political ramifications of how our screen culture is made, consumed, preserved, and disposed. This book is intended as a step in that direction.

CHAPTER ONE

Burning Down the House

Fire, Explosion, and the Eco-ethics of Destruction Spectacle

Some say the world will end in fire,
Some say in ice.
From what I've tasted of desire
I hold with those who favor fire.

—ROBERT FROST, "FIRE AND ICE"

FIRE! FIRE! FIRE!

—BEAVIS, *BEAVIS AND BUTTHEAD*

Although my more poetic inclinations want to embrace the lyricism of Robert Frost's words as a beacon for this study, the truth is that Beavis far better represents the target audience and internal logic of mainstream American film culture. However, the pure fanaticism of Beavis's excitement when seeing fire in heavy metal music videos can be reconciled to Frost's reflection on desire, with both coming together in what French philosopher Jean Louis Schefer has referred to as "the ordinary man of cinema," a theoretical foil Schefer uses to cast aside overly esoteric methods of film theory. He explores instead a more phenomenological notion of what exactly we are connecting to, looking for, experiencing, and enjoying when we watch films.[1] According to Schefer, cinema is part of a long line of cultural practices whereby we willingly sacrifice the real on the altar of the symbolic, a cultural compulsion that pushes us to exist between the material actuality around us and an imaginary space connecting, in this case, our minds and our movies.

This desire drives us toward a symbolic fire, an incinerator of the popular-culture industry that takes the real, the wood and coal of the world, and destroys it for the entertainment of the masses; but we are also attracted like moths to the sensory brilliance of real fire, explosion, and flame as an affective and aesthetic practice. Beavis is the ultimate "ordinary man of cinema," Promethean and unbound, embodying a purely visceral and emotional exclamation of the common joy for watching things burn and blow up. His raw excitement also puts a new spin on Frost's poem, manifesting a desire that I explore here in ecomaterialist terms of the sociocultural contract whereby we collectively agree to convert material reality into destruction spectacle.

Screen culture acts as a weathervane of collective desires and values, which are laid bare for us at the height of every new movie season. On May 2, 2014, the *New York Times* Sunday edition included the publication's annual "Summer Movie Preview," mixing equal parts enthusiasm and criticism for the arrival of big-budget vacation releases. This particular year's explosive fare included such Hollywood productions as *The Amazing Spider-Man 2*, *Godzilla*, *Transformers 4*, *Fast and Furious 7*, *X-Men: Days of Future Past*, *The Expendables 3*, and the seasonally ironic *Captain America: The Winter Soldier*—all films that light up the screen with bursts of fire and flame.[2] My aim here is not to illuminate the lack of creativity in contemporary Hollywood, demonstrated by the high percentage of sequels and reboots recently occupying screens; the market logic of such a formulaic concentration does belie, however, my argument that we participate in a sociocultural contract, central to American film culture, that revolves around the spectacle of fire, explosion, and destruction. Quite simply, we like watching things blow up. We get a kick out of watching things burn. Alas, Beavis: "Fire! Fire! Fire!!!" Here, I look at the ecological ethics of the cinematic spectacle—in particular the spectacle of destruction that comes in the form of fire and explosion—from the ecomaterialist ramifications of how such spectacle is produced and marketed to the philosophical problem of its consumption and reception.

I am certainly not the first person to acknowledge the central role of spectacle in the cinematic experience. Cinema, to paraphrase Tom Gunning, began as attraction. Gunning situates the fin de siècle audience within a civilization increasingly littered with images and argues that the audience's legendary fear that August and Louis Lumière's train at La Ciotat would continue through the screen and run them over was generated less by the conviction of visual verisimilitude than by the subconscious desire to disavow the distinction between real and imaginary in the quest for spectacular thrill. In other words, the myth of an audience genuinely panicked by the oncoming train is simply that, myth; the audiences of early cinema were mesmerized less by a belief in the representation's realism than by a drive to be stimulated by the motion of images, a desire for spectacle and affect that made them willingly hand the keys over to a machinery of fantasy and a series of sensory shocks.[3]

This eager conversion of the material world into some other form is not new—only optimized by the cinematic machine. Well before film cameras rolled, Karl Marx noted ways in which the logic of capitalism turns centrally on the human transformation of nature into exchange value, describing the impact as a vaporization in which "all that is solid is melted into the air."[4] This sacrifice of the real on the altar of the symbolic has long provided a central kernel of cultural and social inquiry, and I resituate this dilemma according to an ecomaterialist framework that turns our attention to the concrete environmental ramifications of film practices.

Fire has always been central to both the material process and the symbolic magic of popular screen culture, from the hypnotizing effect of virtual dancing flames to the lore of incendiary catastrophe connected to exploding film canisters, engulfed projection booths, and grandiosely dangerous production shoots.[5] Most recently, a film fire provides the central narrative premise for the climax of Quentin Tarantino's Holocaust revenge fantasy *Inglourious Basterds* (2009), with the iconic scene being further secreted into legend by the subsequent anecdotes of how the fire stage on which the scene was shot burned out of control and nearly collapsed and killed the cast.[6]

Fire, destruction, and explosion have long been integral to the cinematic spectacle, just as they were to its cultural precursors of the late nineteenth century. In some ways, this relationship makes perfect existential sense given the newly wired electricity of a highly urbanized society: the relevance of fire-based destruction to daily life had heightened during the Industrial Revolution to the point of demanding a cathartic mode of entertainment, "a threatening yet fascinating reality" that could be reproduced, packaged, and sold.[7] This demand fed the inferno of interactive amusements developed at the turn of the century, including the transformation of Coney Island from 1897 to 1904 into a "sophisticated mass-entertainment center" that relied heavily on disaster spectacles, among the most popular of which were two fire spectacles: "Fire and Flames" and "Fighting the Fire."

These fire-spectacle reenactments involved massive sets and the employment of thousands of people (including professional firemen) and in some cases even placed spectators on set as part of the gawking crowd. Real human action and natural disaster merged to form a new kind of performance: "the fire spectacle."[8] As John Kasson writes in *Amusing the Millions*, such spectacles reflected a historically situated fascination with disaster, "a horrible delight in the apprehension that devastating tragedy had both historically and contemporaneously intruded suddenly into daily affairs."[9] This historical development of the daily presence and spectacularization of disaster coincided, of course, with the advent of cinema and became a popular motif of early screen spectacle.[10] In 1896, Thomas Edison commissioned a series of three such films: *Morning Alarm*, *Starting for the Fire*, and *Fighting the Fire*.

Biograph's film *Fighting the Flames* (1908) was in fact just a filming of one of the fire spectacles at Dreamland, a Coney Island amusement park (figure 1.1). As we will see, though, spinoffs of these amusements were not the only place for such cinematic spectacle—they were only part and parcel of a larger social familiarity with fire and destruction in the age of advanced industrialism and a cultural value process, kindled by cinema, whereby the real was transformed into screened image (figure 1.2). In ecomaterialist terms of the sociocultural contract, material resources became discounted kindling for the fire of the social desire to turn our own fears into entertainment.

Over the past century, fire has only become more central to our relationship with the environment. In *The Unnatural World*, a wide-lens survey of innovative contemporary responses to the newly emerging web of environmental problems, the science writer David Biello quotes Pauline Dube, a wildfire specialist at the University of Botswana: "The Anthropocene is truly an age of fire. . . . Thanks to humans, the whole world is now a wildfire risk."[11] Biello, *Scientific American*'s energy and environment editor, continues on to describe the existence of fire in

FIGURES 1.1 AND 1.2 The Fighting Flames Show at Coney Island and *The Life of an American Fireman* (Edwin S. Porter, 1903) capture the domestic relevance of fire catastrophe that translated to early twentieth-century popular-culture spectacles, with manufactured pyrotechnics and smoke central to the entertainments' affective power and narrative drama. *Sources*: Fighting Flames Show image courtesy of the Library of Congress. Frame capture from *Life of an American Fireman* by author.

places that did not burn before, such as Russia and Israel, due either to industrial development or to fossil-fuel exploration. He concludes: "Fire is everywhere in the world, some of it hidden inside machines small and large, some of it visible from space, vast smoke plumes fouling the atmosphere and raining ash over long distances, the red infrared glow of the blazes themselves."[12] In other words, this late-nineteenth-century condition was not a passing phenomenon, just an early spark. The same can be said for our movies.

Cut back to that list from 115 years later: *The Amazing Spider-Man 2, Godzilla, Transformers 4, Fast and Furious 7, X-Men: Days of Future Past, The Expendables 3*. . . . This batch of Hollywood releases in 2014 inspired the *Times* writer Kevin B. Lee to add to this summer movie review a study titled "Kaboom!," in which he analyzes the explosions in nine top-grossing blockbuster films over the past four decades. Lee concludes that there are two types of explosion: "dramatic" ("which have a significant narrative or emotional impact") and "decorative" ("in which explosions are deployed in a barrage, like fireball wallpaper"). Through his "Decorative Destruction Index (the number of decorative explosions divided by the total explosions per film)," Lee concludes that—relative to early films in the New Hollywood era of the blockbuster, such as *Star Wars* (George Lucas, 1977) and *Terminator 2: Judgment Day* (James Cameron, 1992)—contemporary action franchises such as pyromaniac director Michael Bay's *Transformers* reach new levels of excess (*Transformers: Dark of the Moon* [2011], for example, contains 417 total explosions, 96 percent of them being decorative).[13] In other words, in our day and age of environmental awareness and economic conservatism, blowing stuff up is more popular than ever: the fire spectacle rages on, alive and well, and no longer do we even bother with justifying it through narrative relevance.

SCREENING FIRE

As outlined in the previous section, the blaze of destruction spectacle has long been a central visual icon and driving sensory affect of the movies. This extends from the ear-popping explosions of fictional MIG airplanes in Tony Scott's film *Top Gun* (1986) to the jaw-dropping representation of real oil fields across the world. The oil-and-fire infrastructure focused on in recent documentaries such as *Crude* (Joe Berlinger, 2009) and *Gasland* (Josh Fox, 2010, 2013) has a long genealogy dating back to the early pyroprolificacy of the Lumière brothers, who sent cinematographers around the world to capture new wonders for their films, including Kamill Serf, who traveled to Azerbaijan to film the burning oil wells at Baku. Because of its ambivalent set of aesthetic characteristics— driven by the conflicting spectacle of human ingenuity, sheer natural power, and the contrast between brilliant flames and sky-choking black smoke—*Oil Wells of Baku: Close View* (Lumière, 1896) provokes a problematic spectatorial position in which we are overwhelmed by the scale of what appears at once to be a miracle and a disaster.

In their close study of this film, Robin L. Murray and Joseph K. Heumann capture the paradox of such entertainment whereby "disaster looks more like spectacle."[14] The image of flames and smoke conflates the boundary between natural disaster and manmade industry—a transgression that extends beyond the oil drilling to the cinematic spectators who are complicit in the spectacle: not only do the burning oil wells signify humanity's explosive interruption and exploitation of natural resources, but the process of watching them burn also carries deep connotations about the mediation of cinema between the viewing masses and the world outside the theater. After describing the mise-en-scène and framing of the shot, Murray and Heumann continue: "The enormity of these flaming plumes mesmerizes because their powerful blaze shocks us. But the raging flames also bring forth images of phoenixes rising from the flames and hearths stoked by Hestia, broaching the question, 'Is this beautiful?' Within the context of our Western culture, such a scene looks fabulous because it is based in a mythology in which fire and its power are associated with beautiful rebirth."[15]

We can discern in this excerpt some foundational aesthetic characteristics of the destruction spectacle as well as a problematic allegory of humanity's intervention and extraction of natural power. The "enormity" often referred to throughout the extensive shot description foreshadows the essential appeal of the blockbuster spectacle. Moreover, the evocation of the phoenix mythology is twofold. On one hand, we can see the mythology, as the authors intend it, as referring to the crude power and industrial life force being born from the flames of destruction. However, I would add that we should also understand this myth through an eco-materialist perspective on the cinema itself as a metaphor for how film culture manufactures grandiose spectacle not from nothing, but from real destruction. Real water, oil, metals, and minerals are consumed, used, transformed into images and sounds, into pure spectacle on the altar of entertainment. Though not pushing it quite this far, the authors do insist on an ecocritical reading of the film's content and connotations: "More than just spectacle, these burning oil fields, these obfuscating clouds of smoke, this general conflagration of the natural world, signify humans' rape of the landscape for personal gain—oil at any price to the natural world."[16]

Though Murray and Heumann clarify that our screen representations signify deeper issues of our interactions with the world, I would posit the real conundrum to be one that is part of a larger inquiry at the center of this chapter, a problem of the material practice and ecological ethics of the sociocultural contract's fine print regarding destruction and spectacle. What is our collective stake in this ecology between natural resource and entertainment spectacle? How do cinema and film practices engage uniquely with natural destruction? Murray and Heumann use Rahman Badalov's proclamation—"Blazing oil gushers make marvelous cinematographic material[.] . . . [O]nly cinema can capture the thick oil stream bursting forth like a fiery monster. Only cinema can display such an awesome inferno in its terrifying beauty and majesty"[17]—as an epigraph, and their study of an entire century of the oil fields genre points to the specificity of film form's privileged relationship to both spectacle and material destruction. So how, specifically, are fire and spectacle connected to the cinematographic apparatus?

This connection begins with an essential characteristic of film, the screened obsession with destruction mirroring the degree to which this medium requires the consumption of itself, its own self-annihilation, in the process of its fulfillment. Following in the technological mechanics of photography, analog film necessitates chemical reactions and makes use of degradable and unstable materials. Because its own medial specificity requires it to be run through a detrimental projection process, film has in practice been quite volatile and, ultimately, is by nature destructive of its own fabric.

Of course, environmental concerns were of little to no interest in the early decades of cinema. Concerns focused instead on the volatile chemical nature of the medium and the dangers this volatility posed as film became widely distributed, used, and stored. The medium's volatility was so problematic, in fact, that in 1926 the National Board of Fire Underwriters commissioned an article laying out safeguards and maintenance protocol as stipulated by the Motion Picture Producers and Distributers of America. Thomas McIlvaine Jr. began this study, titled "Reducing Film Fires," by pointing to the sheer immensity of film mass in use, noting that between 1922 and 1926 the feet of film used had increased from 600 million to 1.3 billion, effectively doubling in four years, 98 percent of which was flammable—flammable film being less expensive by two cents per foot. Such film decomposes at ordinary temperatures, and the gases produced in decomposition are highly explosive, McIlvaine warned, as the nitrate furnishes its own oxygen: once ignited, film, if in a roll, would even burn underwater.[18]

The medium's chemical volatility and flammability is the result of its nitrate base, a nitrocellulose strip that supports the film emulsion and is an emergent topic of interest among archivists, preservationists, and aesthetic purists. The flamboyance of nitrate film has spanned cinema lore from the 1910s to the 2010s: Robert Flaherty notoriously sparked and destroyed early footage of *Nanook of the North* (1922) with a negligent cigarette, while a nitrate fire is the basis for the aforementioned explosive climax of *Inglourious Basterds*.[19] Explosive enough to be used in munitions, highly volatile and difficult to control, nitrate was phased out of the film industry after World War II and replaced by acetate—or "safety"—stock, but the romance with nitrate has burned on.[20] Although much talk of nitrate film revolves around the aesthetic intangible that nitrate film possesses, it is clear that the nitrate obsession is in part also a romantic fascination with the risk and volatility of the medium itself. As Martin Scorcese writes in the opening lines of his foreword to Roger Smither's collected volume *This Film Is Dangerous*, "The story of nitrate is the story of the first fifty years of cinema; a brand-new art form inherently unstable and impermanent."[21]

Chemically primed to dematerialize, conventional film stock provides an ecomaterialist entry to the very base of mainstream screen culture. Moreover, the highly flammable nitrate foundation is not the only way that film is intrinsically a medium of conflagration, destruction, and waste. Its process of revelation—projection—essentially decomposes the celluloid until, if exposed long enough or close enough to the bulb's heat, it corrodes, melts, and even bursts into flames. The projection of film causes the material to deteriorate and eventually turns it into waste, just as the shooting ratio is a testament to excess and waste—the majority of cuts and shots are left on the proverbial cutting-room floor, with the films that we do see acting as a ghost memory of the images that were condemned to death.[22] Moreover, the ontological impermanence of film carries with it a metaphysical aspect as well, through which film's decomposition also fosters the gradual disappearance of the real people, places, things, and time that it had once so magically captured. Winston Wheeler Dixon gives a portrait of the historical magnitude and cause of film decay, etching out the process whereby film's deterioration takes with it an entire symbolic world, simultaneously erasing the human apparatus that created it:

> As we know, films can easily be destroyed, and 50% of all films made before 1950 no longer exist, the victims of nitrate deterioration, poor preservation, or corporate and/or private neglect. As each film ceases to exist, it takes with it the actors who performed in it, the director who staged their actions, the scenarist who plotted their conflicts, the cinematographer who recorded these staged conceits, and all the other participants in the film's creation into oblivion: merely a line, perhaps, in the Library of Congress catalogue.[23]

In addition to being curious anecdotes of screen culture's technologies, such musings heighten our understanding of the material characteristics of film in terms of its potential for volatility and explosiveness—but what about the very same tendency as it appears on the screen? What is at the social root of cinema's calling to capture grand destruction and its frequent reliance on the spectacle of fire and explosion?

THE ECO-ETHICS OF DESTRUCTION SPECTACLE

Although spectacle has always been central to the ecologies of the natural world—the performative seduction rituals of peacocks, the self-preservationist camouflaging of octopuses, and the human awe at the grandeur of mountains—only now has it been acculturated into a socio-cultural contract that values its artificial production over the raw materials and natural resources necessary for that production. As can be seen in the connection between the dangers of urbanization, Coney Island amusement park entertainments, and cinematic thrills, this contract can be traced through a genealogy that changes with technology and exhibition practices and today is fully underwritten by the popular-image industry. We have entered a historical regime of screen spectacle, which emerged with the overload of sensory—and especially visual—entertainment in the late nineteenth and early twentieth centuries and continues with the rise of 3D and IMAX exhibition formats and the emergence of virtual and augmented realities. Spectacle sits at the heart of our sociocultural contract of screen entertainment, and it is the unspoken relationship between the production of spectacular pleasure and the resources used in this pleasure production that alienates us more and more from the materiality of nature that fuels it.

Spectacle is a difficult thing to define: like grains of sand, as soon as you think you have grasped it, Michael Bay blows it up. Spectacle is both familiar enough for us to recognize and predominantly a sensory quality. To adopt the infamous phrase used by Justice Potter Stewart in reference to the obscenity of hard-core pornography, we "know it" when we "see it."[24] Spectacle is pure showing, and our engagement with it involves seeing before knowing. For the cultural historians Ben Brewster and Lea Jacobs, spectacle is dependent on the "audience's perception of the disproportion between the reality represented and the means used to represent it."[25]

This argument summarizes an important problem in any eco-ethics of spectacle, which is the public's complicity: spectacle depends on the audience's perception and approval of a disconnect between product and means of production, a participatory collusion in the sacrifice of reality, and a tacit nod toward the alternative version provided on the screen. As the French philosopher Guy Debord and the Situationists indicated four decades ago, spectacle is a collectively condoned interruption of our connection with the real—a technological interruption in the case of screen spectacle—and because it deflects our attention from the material costs of production to the surface of the virtual event, I recommend that we view spectacle as a sleight of hand that renders transparent the resources that go into the experience. Just as in other species, spectacle seduces us, lures us, and deflects us.

Along every step of development, from its narrative structuring to its marketing strategies, Hollywood spectacle casts a sheen of misdirection over the resources and waste of its practices, highlighting the technological aptitude but rendering transparent the material reality of its use. This gambit distracts us from the praxis of this technological apparatus, and we should view the environment in Marxist terms as that which is exploited in the circuit of production and consumption but never compensated, never replenished. We stand on the environment's shoulders, extract its blood, erect our effigies from its cells, and blow it up—then applaud the sheer size of the explosion and leave the carcass of our synthetic production to dribble toxic leftovers back into the soil and waterways. This cultural process of material exploitation is not simply the unilateral implementation of Hollywood malice: it requires a willing public and is part of a sociocultural contract that up to now has failed to ask, What do we collectively want from culture, and what do we accept as its price?

The "cultural politics of spectacle"[26] evoked by this question extends to a larger philosophy and sociocultural genealogy beyond the movie theater, to the theater of war that over the past century evolved from a tool of economic recovery to a remote practice in virtual murder. As Verena Andermatt Conley claims in her alternative reading of the costs and achievements of World War II, the twentieth century was structured according to an ongoing and grandiose spectacle of destruction orchestrated for the great profit of the few, history unfolding as a series of "planned and staged catastrophes by cooperative forces that delighted and profited from destruction."[27] It is actually imaginable that if billions of citizens were to turn their backs on this existential spectacle, then the producers in Hollywood would seek new content. However, the great ideological power of spectacle is that it keeps us from considering its material costs and engenders a detachment that is accentuated by the televised familiarity and the digital operation of war in the twenty-first century; we—those of us who perceive but do not experience the production of the spectacle—become detached from the actual reality of death and destruction that war produces. War is like a video game to those playing it, a movie to those watching it.[28]

Like drone bombing, film spectacle distracts the viewer from the material reality of its making—including the resources used, the natural beings affected, and the waste produced. By looking at the Hollywood blockbuster, I argue that the cultural politics of spectacle, in particular the spectacle of destruction and fire, invokes a collective catharsis, a channeling of desire to escape the real by destroying it for our viewing pleasure. The costs of this immolation—in terms of both resource consumption and psychological impact—are stacking up, though, to the point where we can no longer neglect the debt we are accruing with each screened explosion.

BREAKING BLOCKS

No genre of film or mode of production relies more or more centrally on spectacle than the blockbuster. Just as with spectacle, discourse on the blockbuster has struggled to find a cemented definition of it within film and media studies, though audiences know it when they see it. Not only is the blockbuster hard to define, but it has been understood through a stunted scholarly lens—critically dismissed due to its devotion to crowd-pleasing theatricals, intellectually vapid story lines, generic formulae, and ideological simplicity. However, Julian Stringer offers us a helpful framework: the blockbuster has "less to do with a group of artefacts than with a discourse—a loose, evolving system of arguments and readings that helps to shape commercial strategies and aesthetic ideologies."[29]

In other words, the blockbuster can be understood less in terms of what it consists of than in terms of how it is interwoven into a discursive network of production practices, textual mechanisms, and advertising strategies. This understanding aligns the blockbuster—and its guiding import of spectacle—with my attempt to go against the grain of film historiography and analysis and to posit an ecomaterialist approach that takes us beyond the problem of representation. Stringer points out that there are many ways to understand the term *blockbuster*, but I argue for an ecomaterialist interpretation: that the blockbuster is in fact an expressive mode of film culture founded on "breaking blocks," a literal destruction that takes place on the set and on the screen and that ripples across society. The blockbuster is the destruction of the real at the service of a symbolic pleasure.

The social and ethical vortex of spectacle spins exponentially from the birth of cinema forward, picking up new audiovisual media but also guarding some older, vestigial forms of entertainment—and always expanding to lay a veneer over the real wherever an unpicked pocket or market niche may be. Today's Hollywood blockbuster is financed by international conglomerates, appeals to overseas markets, and has a vast content range, including multimedia spinoffs such as theme parks and video games.[30] However, or perhaps *exactly for this reason*, the evolution of the blockbuster and large-scale cinematic spectacle is worth taking a look at in order to further develop an ecological ethics of film spectacle and an ecomaterialist perspective on Hollywood's history and practices.

The history of the blockbuster accompanies cinema's early transformation from a cultural novelty of attractions to a massive institutionalized industry. New modes of finance helped to develop a more ambitious structure of production and exhibition, thus enabling the rise of the "feature" and, supposedly even bigger and better, "specials"—the mode of product differentiation utilized by major American filmmakers such as D. W. Griffith from the mid-1910s on and a leading economic catalyst in the construction of movie palaces, the crystallization of the major studios, and the development of new film technologies.

Stretching over a century and bridging the discourse surrounding the Lumières' film *Baku Oil Fields: Close Shot* and the Decorative Destruction Index offered by the *New York Times* for the summer preview in 2014, there has always been an unspoken correlation between cinema's technological identity as the superior affective audiovisual format and the sociocultural contract of destruction spectacle. For example, in the late 1950s and 1960s, as Hollywood introduced new techniques— color film stocks, widescreen aspect ratios, and road-show exhibition tactics—to set it apart from the emergent threat of television, we again find a heightened reliance on the spectacle of destruction. But the actual practices that fabricated such screened natural disasters are troubling at best—such as Cecil B. Demille's dynamiting of his *Ten Commandments* (1923) Egypt set in the California desert, at that point the largest set ever built, to fulfill his exit contract with local landowners and to keep other filmmakers from using the set.[31] Or let us look at the John Wayne vehicle *Hellfighters* (Andrew McLaglen, 1968), a transparently masculinist celebration of flame-based spectacle for which Internet Movie Database (IMDb) gives the perfectly succinct synopsis, "The story of macho oil well firefighters and their wives."[32] In order to give the full sensory drama of these oil-well firefighters, special-effects engineers burned 350,000 gallons of diesel oil and 60,000 gallons of raw propane, producing 125-foot flames and temperatures so high they melted the director's chair.[33] In other words, the fabrication is not fake: fire in film is, at least until very recently, the ignition of real gases and the incineration of real objects— the use of real natural resources and the destruction of real things.

Despite the singular instances of anthropocentric heroism (*Hellfighters*) or conservationist education (such as Disney's *Bambi* [1942], which was so successful in advocating against forest fires that the Wartime

Advertising Council originally used Bambi as its mascot, until licensing issues pushed it to replace Bambi with Smokey the Bear[34]), onscreen destruction is often intended to serve an allegorical purpose, such as the cleansing effect of biblical apocalypse or the power vicariously experienced through the catharsis of witnessing destruction. Flames disinfect, purify, and from the ashes a phoenix will rise. Destruction and rebirth, the catharsis of symbolic demolition, and exposure to the sublime power of natural fury—fire provides us with a dynamic combination of sensory stimulation, intuitive emotional and physiological response, and allegorical significance.

This allegorical aspect is perfectly in line with the blockbuster's connection to how major Hollywood industry mechanisms such as the star system hinge on a drastic disconnect from the real. The blockbuster is the apotheosis of what separates Hollywood from "normal" America, taking the perfect bodies, bright lights, and deafening sounds and making them even more perfect, bigger, louder, more expensive, and more affectively impressive. As such, we can contextualize according to what Hollywood is selling, as emblematized by the high-concept use of fire in the film marketing, packaging, and selling of destruction spectacle. (Note that here I mean "high concept" in marketing terms, which somewhat paradoxically refers to a brand or good that is conceptually simplistic, in this case a film whose story and message can be reduced and packaged in a single image.) Let us take, for example, the marketing of a single blockbuster dynasty: the *Die Hard* series. The fairly clichéd movie posters for each film in this series illustrate to what degree the destruction spectacle hinges not only on neglecting an environmental problem of presentation but also on embracing it (figure 1.3).

The posters' focus on destruction spectacle gives a "high-concept" clarity to the generic expectations we should have of these films, but through an ecomaterialist critique I argue also that such marketing, though perhaps without full intentionality, uses the bright flames and action imagery to distract us from the paper and plastic waste that is necessary in the mass-marketing of the films. In fact, this philosophy of excess is glorified in the very regime of spectacle that built Hollywood's grandeur and mystique, and distraction from materiality and the neglect of resource cost, however intentional or unintentional, are central to the sociocultural contract of screen spectacle.

FIGURES 1.3 Bearing a tagline that perfectly encapsulates the "bigger louder brighter—HARDER" goals of the blockbuster, the poster for *Die Hard 2*—like those of its predecessor and its four sequels—places the aesthetic of fire at the center of its marketing pitch. By focusing on this, the film's ad campaign implicitly plays into Hollywood's guiding ideological premise that screen entertainment is more valuable than the resources exploded to produce it. *Source*: 20th Century Fox / Album (Alamy stock photo).

From the blitzkrieg explosions, mushroom clouds, and tumbling napalm that burrowed an essence of destruction into the imagistic memory of a century perpetually at war to the burning oil fields that would come to symbolize a planet increasingly defined by petrocultures, fire has played the elemental protagonist in the spectacle of destruction that populates our reality, our myths, and our screens. The form of this spectacle may have evolved—film to video to virtual reality—but in all cases the underlying cultural and philosophical ramifications must be addressed in ecomaterialist terms and assessed in relation to production practices.[35] Just such an examination of the Hollywood classic *Gone with the Wind* will, I hope, allow us to explore in more detail how this problem of spectacle has factored into Hollywood practice, from film-production methods to marketing strategies, and how the material and allegorical functions of natural elements and resources intersect in the complex network of our popular screen culture.

GONE WITH THE WIND

Because this book poses an intervention in Hollywood film historiography and analysis, there seems no better film for my first major case study than Victor Fleming's *Gone with the Wind* (1939), a groundbreaking precedent in blockbuster spectacle whose making has become as mythologized as the romance between Scarlett O'Hara and Rhett Butler. I use an ecomaterialist approach to reframe the mold-setting prototype and industrial exception that is *Gone with the Wind*, along with the dominant romanticizing discourses concerning spectacle and authorship that surround it.

An epic period piece about a feisty Southern heiress and a patronizing but dashing Confederate officer, *Gone with the Wind* follows Scarlett's brutal introduction to—and resilience through—adulthood amid the ravages of the Civil War and the fiery end to the plantation way of life. Seemingly the quintessential Hollywood film, *Gone with the Wind* is only so in hindsight because of the mold it set, and although it has served as the signpost for period romantic melodrama, it also offers a fascinating window onto the emergence and crystallization of certain industry practices. In his foreword to David Alan Vertrees's book *Selznick's Vision: "Gone with the Wind" and Hollywood Filmmaking*, Tom

Schatz writes: "As the field of cinema studies reaches a certain maturity, we in it continue to be confounded, indeed threatened, by an obstinate question: what are we to do with *Gone with the Wind*? The most popular and commercially successful film of all time, embraced by popular historians and journalistic critics while generally reviled by 'serious' scholars and cinephiles, *Gone with the Wind* stands as both a monument to classical Hollywood and a monumental anomaly."[36]

What makes *Gone with the Wind* so quintessential to either a reality or a perceived notion of American cinema? In *A Celebration of "Gone with the Wind,"* Adrian Turner argues, "*Gone with the Wind* is the definitive Hollywood picture. . . . It is definitive because of the circumstances of its production and promotion rather than [because of] its merits as a work of art. It is definitive because of its enormous popularity and because it is the summation of Hollywood thinking and craftsmanship at the time."[37] A combination of novel industry practice and popular success, this film can therefore help to illuminate how and where actual practice and audience reception meet in our sociocultural contract. Throughout its production, release, and multiple rereleases, the film constantly set itself apart according to the rules of blockbuster spectacle: bigger, more expensive, more impassioned, more epic, and more destructive. It was the largest and most expensive film yet made, an argument central to the film's self-branding and reception. It also received the largest amount of pre-release publicity up to that point, and I explore the relationship between fire destruction and human pleasure at the center of its marketing discourse.[38]

Before doing so, however, I want to contextualize *Gone with the Wind* historically and to introduce the dominant critical problem of authorship surrounding it. Many changes in the 1930s, both in Hollywood and in the nation as a whole, set the stage for the type of spectacle that David O. Selznick was hoping to make of Margaret Mitchell's best-selling historical-fiction novel. Although the transition to sound in 1927 had in many ways reduced the visual acrobatics of Hollywood to emphasize the dialogue-based nature of early sound film, the late 1930s saw the studios shifting to accommodate an audience in need of visual spectacle. In 1934, the organization of the Production Code Administration and the institution of the Motion Picture Production Code put an end to the lascivious sexuality of the 1920s and early 1930s, thus creating demand for a new visual stimulant to fill the screen with an antidote to the static camera of the early talkies. Moreover, the socioeconomic strains of the Depression swept a new era of escapist entertainment into the box office, while also forcing studios to attempt new modes of production economy—an economy that would prove legendary for *Gone with the Wind*. As the Depression forced many studios into receivership and the prewar period experienced increasing resource scarcity, executives and producers began to explore new methods of filmmaking that would be more sustainable and cost efficient. *Gone with the Wind* is often cited to exemplify the lavish excess of Hollywood productions, but it also partook in a process of resource recycling like no other in its time—a sustainable conflagration that became its signature event.

Its making was nevertheless a model for Hollywood spectacle, with ornate sets and costumes allowing audiences to time-travel out of the increasingly fragile end of the 1930s. This mode of historical epic, as Vivian Sobchack has pointed out, provided an "excessive parade and accumulation of detail and event" without drawing the audience's attention to the pressing anxieties of the day.[39] The most pressing of these anxieties—beyond internal economic hardship, of course—were the rising military fervor in Europe and the encroaching footsteps of world war, which evoked the memory of newsreels laden with real explosions from less than two decades earlier. Not incidentally, fire and incineration marked a number of the most successful and grandiose productions of these years, somehow foreshadowing the horrific scorched-earth mentality and visuality of the war. It was an era still resonating with the canon fire and smoke of the Great War and awaiting unprecedented destruction by fire and explosion, chain reactions of immolation that spread forward and backward in time and canvassed Hollywood's golden era. *Gone with the Wind* would thrive to a large degree because of the unprecedented spectacle of the burning of Atlanta, and both Alfred Hitchcock's *Rebecca* (1940, also produced by Selznick) and Orson Welles's *Citizen Kane* a year later would culminate in symbolic but also literal fires that would consume more or less everything that had been central to each film, from Rebecca's cursed Manderlay to Kane's precious Rosebud.

These films were also part of a large shift at this time in notions of authorship in Hollywood, and one cannot address the goals and implementation of spectacle in *Gone with the Wind* without touching on the dynamic and unique question of authorship in the making of the film.

All major studies of the film trace its creative balance and its romantic production history to the first day of shooting, the most epic and spectacular of the film's sequences and one of *the* legendary uses of pyrotechnics in Hollywood: the burning of Atlanta.

THE MYTH OF EXECUTIVE GENIUS
AND THE BURNING OF ATLANTA

There is certainly something deeply Promethean about the myth of *Gone with the Wind*'s making, its egomaniacal producer, and its setting of new precedents for on-set destruction and visual spectacle. In his foreword to Vertrees's tellingly titled book *Selznick's Vision*, Schatz adds that central to the nagging problem of *Gone with the Wind* for critics and scholars is the issue of authorship, revolving around the film's development, making, and marketing: "The key figure in this myth is, of course, David O Selznick."[40] Larger than life even then, the legend of Selznick has only inflated with time as it has been folded into and welded onto other facets of the Hollywood dream. Selznick's eventual splitting off from MGM was a pivotal moment in this visionary's ego construction, and *Gone with the Wind* was the film on which he would stake the fortune and future of Selznick International. In many ways reflecting Selznick's megalomaniacal self-image construction, the standard tale of the film's making typically includes the revolving-door list of directors and writers who cycled through at various stages, with Selznick's authoritarian control spinning the wheel. According to Gavin Lambert, "it is remarkable how Selznick, as Cukor later said, 'kept the whole thing in his head and stuck with it'"—relishing in auteur theory thirty years ahead of its time, except with the producer as auteur.[41] However, close archive research and Vertrees's reframing of the film's development and production reveal a far more collaborative process—albeit one that had little to do with the usual skill positions (director, writer) and instead led to the creation of an entirely new industry title: production designer.

Although Selznick was the driving force behind the film, from the purchase of its rights to the details of its first-run exhibition practices, the film's lavish and meticulous visual style must be credited to William Cameron Menzies—credit that was first and foremost insisted upon by Selznick himself. In a memo to Russell Birdwell and George Cukor, who was the director of the film when it first began shooting, Selznick stated, "I do not think the word 'drafting' is fair to Menzies. This term in motion picture language means simply a draftsman working under an art director. Menzies' task is a monumental one and I am anxious that he receive a fair credit. Actually what he is doing is 'designing' the picture."[42] As second assistant director Reggie Callow recounted, noting the origin of a new credit title that would become one of the Oscars' most coveted, "Production Designed by William Cameron Menzies. That's the first time the credit was given, and it was given by Selznick."[43]

The design of the film and the balance between Selznick and Menzies can be most strongly sensed in the first sequence to be shot, a shoot that took place without any of the film's stars. In fact, it was not even until the first day of the film's shooting, on the set of the burning of Atlanta on December 10, 1938, that Selznick was introduced to an English actress by the name of Vivien Leigh. Referring to the first scene shot for a film that would eventually have to be cut down to a running time of three and a half hours, Schatz claims: "Nowhere are Selznick's control and Menzies' artistry more evident than in the first scene, a narrative episode . . . which became the visual and dramatic centerpiece of the film."[44] Indeed, the production of this sequence was the most grandiose part of the film's entire shoot and would be advertised as the most expensive and spectacular scene ever filmed, becoming a visual and connotative calling card throughout the film's marketing and the critical discourse surrounding the film for decades to come.

As Schatz notes, the Atlanta fire sequence was not particularly integral to Mitchell's novel and was even downplayed in Sidney Howard's original script. Vertrees maps out the evolution of the sequence across a ten-step process, from the novel to the screen rights, synopsis, and Howard's original screenplays: "Preferring to develop dramatic characterizations rather than to exploit the spectacular potential of this episode with respect to looting and the fire, Howard allowed the wagon to proceed out of town without incident."[45] This low-key scene did not, however, fit the spectacle that Selznick had envisioned. As Annie Laurie Fuller Kurtz, wife of Wilbur G. Kurtz, a prominent southern historian and the film's technical director, wrote in her firsthand account, "Pre-viewing of 'Gone with the Wind,'" "The dramatic possibilities of this incident were suggested alike to novelist and screenwriter. It embellishes the tragic story of the fall of Atlanta as no other single incident could *do*. . . . Its lurid glare would lend the spectacular touch so necessary to motion picture interpretation."[46] In other words, the specificity of film spectacle demanded a mode of visual destruction, an actual conflagration to feed the fire of representing a love affair at such an explosive historical moment. In contrast to Howard's rather literary adaptation of the original text, Vertrees confirms (as do the archives), "Selznick recognized its [the scene's] potential for spectacle and enlisted production designer William Cameron Menzies and several screenwriters—including Ben Hecht—to embellish on what Mitchell had written."[47]

But how to produce a fire of such size and proportion and on a lot already littered with previous film sets? As Fuller Kurtz opined, "Many of the old sets would have to be removed. Rather than tear them apart piece by piece, why not burn them? And while they were burning, why not utilize the conflagration as background for the episode of the evacuation of Atlanta that wild night of Sept. 1st, 1864?"[48] Why not, indeed? The script was once again retooled by Oliver Garrett, in Vertrees words, "in time for the extensive burning of the studio's backlot on Dec 10, 1938, which was intended by production manager Raymond Klune, by Menzies, and by Wheeler to clear the way for the construction of accurate sets required for subsequent filming and to simulate the burning of Atlanta for spectacular background shots necessary for the presentation of the fire sequence."[49] It is remarkable that at this time, a half-century before the environmental movement made recycling a household term, the ultimate salesman of the industry of excess would enact such a radically sustainable process. But, like the economically driven sustainability practices and general Taylorization of early Hollywood discussed earlier, the studios' green policies were always about economy and efficiency at the base, and the burning of these classic sets killed two birds with one stone: it gave the filmmakers lumber for the fire, and it cleared out *King Kong* (Ernest B. Schoedsack and Merian C. Cooper, 1933) and *King of Kings* (Cecil B. DeMille, 1927) to make room for the epic building of Tara.

Quickly recorded into the vaunted pages of industry lore, this decision illustrates the problem of authorship surrounding the film. Whereas Gavin Lambert argues that production manager Raymond Klune suggested burning old sets—and memos confirm that Menzies and Klune worked closely on the planning and execution of the burn—Reggie

Callow attributes the recycled conflagration to Menzies. Callow's record sheds light on the actual material process:

> He [Menzies] directed the Atlanta fire, you know, for *Gone with the Wind*. Fleming wasn't even on the picture at the time. That was Menzies' idea entirely. They had these old exterior sets on the back-lot of Selznick International that they had to tear down in order to build Atlanta and Tara. So he conceived the idea to burn the old sets down with controlled fire. They put some false fronts up—very cheap false fronts—and set fire to it all, because when it's burning you don't know whether it's a western street or whether it's Atlanta or what it is. They got a special effects man—Lee Zavitz—who was the best in the business, and that's how we did it; we burned it down with controlled fire, and toward the end of shooting they just let it go and burned it all down.[50]

Meanwhile, as the shooting script was being finalized, Menzies and Klune were going through the agonizing detail of design drawings and models and rehearsing the shots.[51] During the preparations, Menzies and Klune apparently realized that even Selznick had underestimated the depth and cost of the spectacle called for. In a November memo to the producer, Menzies wrote:

> I am writing this letter in Ray Klune's presence who is rather anxious to have you realize the increased scope of this sequence over what the present script calls for. . . . The increased cost of doing it this way as against what the script actually indicated is approximately $7500.00 and he would like your approval on proceeding with it. . . . Do not misunderstand by this that we are trying to make a Chicago fire of six reels, but are merely trying to create a build for our stunt [*sic*] of the enlarged screen. At the moment we are quite encouraged with a device we are experimenting with. In any event, we are still aiming at a big pre-intermission spectacle shot.[52]

As can be seen from memos Selznick sent in the following weeks, the radical plan for the burning of Atlanta produced great anxiety in the producer, and he even came to fear its being an unnecessary indulgence.[53]

Nevertheless, Selznick was a believer in the sociocultural contract of destruction spectacle and rhetorically positioned this spectacle as part of the blockbuster's essential quality of disproportionate scale, to the point of designing a Cinerama-style camera operation that later had to be dropped from the film's exhibition plan.[54] As Vertrees reveals,

> [Selznick] wished to satisfy the "showmanship requirements of the picture," explaining to his general manager: "I feel very strongly that people have a general idea that GWTW plays against a much bigger canvas than is actually the case and that they are going to be disappointed with the intimacy of the story and with its lack of spectacle unless we give them a smashing and sensational spectacle in the fire sequence and in the ride of Rhett and Scarlett through the burning town. I feel that it will be the equivalent of the Chariot Race in *Ben Hur* [1924] and that it is our one chance, particularly since we are in color, to give them a sensational stunt."[55]

The cost and complexity were not the only issues causing hesitation and anxiety about this pyrotechnic strategy. There was also the growing realization that, contrary to Selznick's usual filming style (Callow notes that "[Selznick's] percentage of retakes was probably more than any other independent producer"[56]), the biggest, most expensive scene of the film and the first they would shoot would *not be able to have a single retake.* One take, with seven Technicolor cameras—the maximum available for lease to a studio in 1938. They would torch the world but would have only one chance to record its burning.

"SO THIS WAS HOLLYWOOD!"

The final shooting script for *Gone with the Wind* spends many pages and shots covering the Atlanta fire, though on the page the scene reads far more subtly than it views on film. For example:

Shot 220: "The glow of fire above the trees of the distant town is seen for the first time."

Shot 257: "MEDIUM CLOSE SHOT—EXPLOSIVES IN BOXCAR The fire is nearer."[57]

However, what actually happened on set and what appears on the screen created one of the great legends of American film history. For a firsthand account of what transpired, let us turn back to Annie Laurie Fuller Kurtz's "Pre-Viewing of 'Gone with the Wind'" and to the accounts given by her husband, Wilbur G. Kurtz, the film's technical director, who published various versions for venues such as the *Atlanta Journal*'s Sunday magazine. The former sets the stage of what occurred on those forty acres of backlot in Culver City, even slipping in a comment about the unique process of recycling used:

> Out front ranked a huge batter of floodlights on tall platforms, and seven cameras, three men to a machine, were trained upon the set. . . . The conflagration, technically known as a "controlled fire," was in the hands of a platoon of visiting firemen. To ensure the proper pyrotechnic effect, the ancient walls of the structures were piped with oil sprays. The torch was applied! Back of the cars a wicked tongue of flame licked upward. Foreground fires, carefully staged by the special effects men, burst into being. . . . I have been told that never before has such a three-dimensional full sized conflagration been staged in Hollywood, but then not every one has a King of Kings set and a Gone With the Wind script![58]

Kurtz himself would write unabashedly of the awe with which he beheld the spectacular production: "As for myself, I was one of those spellbound throng who watched the roaring flames devour the buildings and explode the cargoes of the boxcars. So this was Hollywood!"[59] And although perhaps no one had seen such a conflagration staged, few citizens in Culver City were accustomed to such a blaze in real life either. Kurtz further stoked the flames of the production's myth in the somewhat racist language endemic to the period:

> While the fire was confined to a limited area on the studio lot, its light could not be so restricted. . . . Such was the curiosity of the Los Angeles and Hollywood citizenry that the telephone company had a bad half-hour with the inquisitive public. Joy riders . . . felt it was worth a look. . . .

To finish up the sequence, another night session was held on the 40 acres. Some special fire effects were filmed and then the explosions were staged. Two effects were secured—one, of mere sound, and the other, a special effect of flashes . . . and since the crew didn't get around to these items until late at night, the good citizens of Culver City rang up the police station to learn what the shooting was about. They must have been relieved to find out that the Jap fleet was not bombarding Long Beach. . . . [G]reat numbers of alarmed citizens jammed emergency phone lines, believing that MGM was imperiled by flames.[60]

From firsthand accounts to later reminiscences, certain talking points remain crucial: the forty acres of the Selznick International backlot, littered with sets from Hollywood classics to be engulfed by a fire gorging on piped-in fuel; the firemen on set; and the unintended panic induced in the surrounding citizens (figure 1.4).

Lambert's poetic portrait, written some forty-five years later, is worth quoting at length because it summarizes the mixture of detail and myth

FIGURE 1.4 For the burning of Atlanta sequence in *Gone with the Wind* (Victor Fleming, 1939), the producer David O. Selznick lit an entire backlot of old sets on fire in a now-legendary day of shooting. The final Technicolor film product remains a testament to the material and symbolic significance of fire, seen here as the backdrop for Scarlett and Rhett's flight from the Union army. *Source*: Frame capture by author.

wrapped around the legend of this shoot and encapsulates the romanticism with which film critics remain enamored with this film:

The night of the 10th, the night of the fire, was cold. . . . Pipes had been run through the old sets, carrying gasoline which would ignite them, twenty-five members of the Los Angeles police department, fifty studio firemen and two hundred studio helpers were standing by with equipment and 5,000-gallon water tanks in case the flames should get out of hand. Sets of doubles for Scarlett and Rhett. . . . A special look-out platform had been built for Selznick, his mother . . . and friends. Myron [Selznick, David's brother] was expected, but had warned he might be late since he was entertaining some clients at dinner.

There was something Napoleonic in the image of the thirty-seven-year-old producer elevated on his platform, surrounded by court, waiting to give the order that would set the world on fire. However, since Myron was late, the order was delayed—like almost everything else connected with the picture. After an hour, Ray Klune told Selznick that it was impossible to keep the police and fire departments waiting any longer. Intensely nervous—what if [MGM exec Eddie] Mannix should prove right, and the highly publicized funeral pyre fail to make its impact on screen?—the producer gave his signal. Instantly the famous old sets, their wood dried for months in the California summer, began to blaze. Cukor called the first "Action!" on *Gone with the Wind*, and the doubles of Scarlett and Rhett made their escape past the burning structures of *King Kong* and *The Garden of Allah*.

As the sparks flew upward and the building began to tremble, Selznick knew that Mannix had been wrong. He turned to Raymond Klune and apologized for having doubted him. Blazing fragments soared into the darkness, and Lee Zavitz, in charge of special effects for the sequence, remembers the firemen shooting them down with their hoses, "like ducks." And to some Los Angeles residents, always fearful of natural disasters such as earthquakes and holocausts, the overpowering flow in the sky announced that the city itself was on fire. A few dozen people hastily packed suitcases, got into their cars and started driving toward the desert.[61]

From the Napoleonic producer to the outlying community's mass psychological response, Lambert reinforces the glorious legend of Selznick and hints at an intriguing extrafilmic issue unexplored regarding the film's production of destruction spectacle. These very real flames raged in a very real place, an urban space that was also part of a local ecosystem—the visual brilliance that was being preserved on film burning off an incendiary pollution hazard to add to the layer of smog blanketing Los Angeles that would become one of the best-known pockets of greenhouse gas in the world.

Once the sets were ablaze, the photography itself lasted seventy-five minutes, destined to be epic until the last frame: special-effects cinematographer Clarence Slifer related how the fiery collapse that was the background spectacle was recorded only seconds before the film negative was depleted in the camera he was operating.[62] The Benzedrine Napoleon was thrilled by the production, gushing in a letter to his wife that it was "one of the biggest thrills I have had out of making pictures" and immediately sending a memo—that night—to his professional soul mate, Jock Whitney: "YOU HAVE MISSED A GREAT THRILL. GONE WITH THE WIND HAS BEEN STARTED. SHOT KEY FIRE SCENES AT NIGHT TONIGHT AND JUDGING BY HOW THEY LOOKED TO THE EYE THEY ARE GOING TO BE SENSATIONAL. DAVID."[63]

SELLING A SPECTACLE OF FLAMES

The romanticized pyre of the Selznick International backlot consists of two major fulcra, the sequence's novel production methods and the buildup to Selznick's introduction (heated by the flames of the burning sets) to Vivien Leigh, which permeate most accounts of the shoot, even the one provided by the original movie program.[64] The double use of fire for visually brilliant destruction and as an allegory for passion became integral not only to the legend of the film's making—David Thompson would later wax, "December 10, 1938, was a grand night, with enough Technicolor flames on view to melt facts into romance"[65]—but to the marketing and reception of the film as well. Selznick's memos indicate a clear sensitivity to the language of aggression and defeat inherent in "the burning of Atlanta,"[66] especially considering the elaborate plans for the film's grand premiere in Atlanta, for which the governor of Georgia declared a state holiday and almost one million people poured into the city.[67] Nonetheless, most marketing outlets for the film focused on "the Atlanta fire" sequence, a testament to both the unprecedented magnitude of the production and the visual splendor of the final film.

The official release poster probably best known to the popular imagination, of Scarlett and Rhett embracing in the midst of flames, was the print on the lobby cards and central poster offered to theaters in the Exhibitor's Campaign Book sent out by MGM (figure 1.5).[68]

Similarly, the Campaign Book highlights a section on the film's crucial moments, and in each permutation of the book the largest and most visually central still is a composite shot with an image of passion between Rhett and Scarlett inset over the flames of Atlanta burning. The strong majority of the "For Your Lobby" posters offered to exhibitors also bore this conflated image. The symbolic marketing was rendered even more transparent when upon the film's general release the publicity service

FIGURE 1.5 Original 1939 movie poster for *Gone with the Wind*, drawing together the sensory, destructive, and symbolic power of fire. *Source*: © Film Company MGM. Photo by A.F. Archive (Alamy stock photo).

catalogs included the section "What Were the Most Memorable Scenes in GWTW?," which foregrounded (apparently neglecting Selznick's insistence) "the burning of Atlanta! Up in smoke and flames went the hopes and dreams of a proud people symbolized by the dashing Rhett and the tempestuous Scarlett!"[69] The destruction spectacle is set up here as one part of a triangular allegory, in which it stands both for the fate of the South as a whole and for the romance between Rhett and Scarlett. Regarding the latter and with an implicit sexism, it also glamorizes Rhett ("dashing," connected to hopes and dreams) while demonizing Scarlett ("tempestuous," an extension of the volatility and obscurity of smoke and flames, a natural disaster brewing).

The film's reliance on the spectacle of destruction paid off. The burning of Atlanta was identified by a Gallup poll as the film's most memorable scene,[70] and the scene was central to reviews upon the film's release, which almost uniformly connect it (the visual brilliance of the fire, the epic scale of the destruction) to the film's unprecedented budget, running time, and innovative use of technology—the necessary markers of the blockbuster and key clauses in our sociocultural contract of spectacle—while usually maintaining the fire's allegorical connection with the film's central romance. The *Hollywood Reporter*'s commentary on the press preview opened accordingly:

> This is more than the greatest motion picture which ever was made. It is the ultimate realization of the dreams of what might be done in every phase of film wizardry, in production, performance, screenwriting, photography, and every other of the multitude of technical operations which enter into the making of a picture. . . . [It] holds one spellbound from the first dazzling blaze of color to the final fadeout. . . . The tremendous sweep and dynamic power of the first half of the picture, climaxed in the staggering, awe inspiring capture and destruction of Atlanta[,] is [*sic*] so overwhelming as to leave one limp.[71]

The London film journal *Cinema* fanned the flames: "GWTW BEATS RECORD FOR SPECTACLE, STORY AND ACTING HUNDRED PER CENT. ENTERTAINMENT AND BOX-OFFICE WINNER WITHOUT PARALLEL . . . A flaming background of the American Civil War lends this tale of romantic conflict a strange earnestness, and its spectacle is always an integral part of the development."[72]

These reviews, like most, set a sort of picture-in-picture framing of the romance within the spectacle of fire and destruction, a tangling of desire and immolation in which sex and natural destruction are mutually fueling. The centrality of this symbolic cliché was not limited to the visual but was encouraged to be present in the radio ads upon the film's various releases. It proved especially central to the re-release, timed to coincide with the Civil War centennial—or, as the MGM Pressbook for 1961 exclaimed, "A SPECIAL CIVIL WAR CENTENNIAL PRESENTATION OF THE SCREEN EVENT OF THE CENTURY!" The re-release Pressbook also drew attention to "the Burning of Atlanta!," with a still of Scarlett and Rhett in the classical cheek embrace, picture-in-picture in the right corner of the train depot fire spectacle.[73]

Printed and used more than twenty years after the film's original release, this booklet makes use of identical rhetoric when it comes to natural destruction, spectacle, and material practice, even utilizing Selznick's own romanticized vision of the legendary process. According to "DAVID O. SELZNICK REMINISCES ABOUT 'GONE WITH THE WIND,'"

His "Gone With the Wind" was the genesis of the modern big-day epic spectacle. Asked about the problems inevitable in pioneering such a huge project, Selznick said, "Burning the city of Atlanta was the single biggest production problem. Atlanta, as it appeared in 1864, when it fell before General Sherman's armies, was duplicated on a 40-acre plot. Some 50 full-size buildings were constructed which subsequently were burned by the retreating Confederate troops. More than 12,000 extras played retreating soldiers and the panic-stricken populace fleeing the city. Special effects men had rigged the buildings in such a way that they would burn on signal. Some of the flames soared to a height of more than 200 feet. We used seven Technicolor cameras to film that fire scene. After all, there couldn't be a retake."

In summing up his feeling about "Gone With the Wind," Mr. Selznick stated:

"I feel that the greatest single contribution of the picture is that it gives audiences all over America an exciting awareness and dramatic understanding of the glory and greatness of this epoch in American history."[74]

Selznick's conflation of blockbuster practices, visual spectacle, and historical understanding must be read between the lines and reveals how the ongoing discourse surrounding the film utilizes the sociocultural contract of screen spectacle in order to glamorize excessive production methods. Moreover, in an implicit negation of dialectical materialism, Selznick also champions what are problematically inaccurate (or at least incomplete) historical depictions, painting the Civil War as great and glorious as opposed to an ethical and material struggle over natural resources and racist labor exploitation. Other marketing strategies echo this mythology. For example, when *Gone with the Wind* was released in 70-millimeter in 1967, the MGM Exhibitor's Campaign Book offered a number of radio announcements, including this "LIVE RADIO 60-Second Live Announcement Spot": "See David O. Selznick's overwhelming spectacle of Atlanta in flames . . . the epic clash of armies . . . and the tender romance of GONE WITH THE WIND." Connecting the film's epic themes of love and war, "One-Minute Live Announcement No. 1" anchors this axis more directly in the history it works from: "This great love story of Rhett Butler and Scarlett O'Hara begins in Tara's Halls . . . sweeps along through the awesome action of a victorious army marching to the sea . . . and takes you into Atlanta aflame, as thousands try to flee the holocaust that devours a doomed city. . . . And now—as America observes the one-hundredth anniversary of the War Between the States, you can see the picture that captures its spectacular excitement . . . its romantic intensity."[75]

The claim that the War Between the States is captured through its "spectacular excitement" and "romantic intensity" perfectly encapsulates how our sociocultural contract of screen spectacle functions through the denial of the material costs and ethical violations that actually drive much of American history. In flames of incineration and passion, Selznick and Menzies offered the destruction spectacle achieved as never before, the burning carcasses of old sets stoked by piped-in fuel and Benzedrine and guaranteed to wow the audience in an immolation of history: *Gone with the Wind* set a new precedent in lighting reality on fire in the quest for screen entertainment.

Due to its conversion of historical truth into cinematic spectacle, Edna Lim marks this film as a crucial step in the genealogy of another film that I discuss in the next chapter, though for different reasons: James Cameron's *Titanic*. *Titanic*, Lim writes, is about Hollywood; it is "the *Gone with the Wind* of its generation: history as spectacle."[76] The sets cluttering the backlot of Selznick International would not be the only things recycled in the making of this epic film; history itself would be: history sorted into the right bin, broken down, repackaged. The actual passage of events and lives becomes just another used set, dried in the southern California sun and drenched in gasoline. The sociocultural contract of screen spectacle creates its own history, a history of visual splendor that blinds us to the material resources and reality we are sacrificing on its pyre.

THE LEGACY OF DESTRUCTION

Selznick knew just how integral *Gone with the Wind* was at the time and would be to the Hollywood narrative on every level, from its production scale to its creative crediting to its grand release and unprecedented marketing campaign. When the set was finally being taken apart to be shipped to Atlanta in 1959, Selznick noted: "Tara has no rooms inside. It was just a façade. Once photographed, life here is ended. It is almost symbolic of Hollywood."[77] A perfect product of the dream factory, it was all artifice: smoke, mirrors, and fire. And yet, as stated in the re-release Pressbook in 1961, "'Gone with the Wind' was the genesis of the modern big-day epic spectacle," a self-proclaimed significance that reflected the return of road-show epics and destruction blockbusters in the late 1950s and early 1960s meant to challenge the popularity of television. Recent industry histories confirm this claim, insisting that its length and lavish design, excessive budget, and state-of-the-art production values make *Gone with the Wind* the prototype for both the postwar and New Hollywood blockbuster.[78]

Beyond such narrative, logistical, and aesthetic standards, the enduring popularity of *Gone with the Wind* would help Hollywood establish a new litmus test for film art "on the basis of continuing emotional appeal."[79] This is a perfect reflection of the sociocultural contract of screen spectacle, in which our desire for certain affective spectatorial experiences overrides the integrity of any historical or material real that might need to be sacrificed. As a consequence, *Gone with the Wind* stands as an icon for Selznick's work, for Hollywood, and for the Hollywood mythologies that manifest America's collective value system. This legacy's connection to larger structural aspects of American society is perfectly described from the outside perspective of Michelangelo Antonioni, an Italian director whose initial foray into Hollywood—*Zabriskie Point*, shot in 1970 in the United States for MGM—offers a psychedelic portrait of hippie counterculture that ends with the explosion of a decadent mansion. Matilde Nardelli excuses the director somewhat: "Clearly, Antonioni gave in to the culture of waste he experienced in America—and dug into his MGM budget."[80]

Even more telling is Antonioni's account of the experience of the explosion, which couches the spectacle of destruction in capitalist and ecomaterialist terms of consumption: "I think they must teach it at school—how to consume. And when you grow up, it gets worse, you consume much more. And since the cinema is run by grown-ups, the result is that there is a squandering of material and money such as I've never seen in Europe."[81] This mode of excess, waste, and destruction *is* taught, in every facet of American life, with screen culture being the biggest classroom available—the underlying lesson, the hidden education, regards our collective connection to the material real of the natural environment.

As can be seen through this case study of *Gone with the Wind*, even the most critically saturated films hold potential for new inquiry and analysis for the ecomaterialist scholar. My alternative narrative of the iconic spectacle of *Gone with the Wind* explores its material and discursive complexities and contradictions: a film that advertised its own excess but used an industrial scale of recycling, throwing Hollywood history and American history on the pyre of our collective search for bigger and brighter—a search, as further explored in the following chapters, that demands vast natural resources, generates unique forms of pollution and waste, and implicates an entire society.

CHAPTER TWO

"Five Hundred Thousand Kilowatts of Stardust"

Water and Resource Use in Movies and the Marketing of Nature

> Of all our natural resources water has become the most precious. By far the greater part of the earth's surface is covered by its enveloping seas, yet in the midst of this plenty we are in want. . . . In an age when man has forgotten his origins and is blind even to his most essential needs for survival, water along with other resources has become the victim of his indifference.
>
> —RACHEL CARSON, *SILENT SPRING*

Seminal to the birth of the American environmental movement, Rachel Carson's book *Silent Spring* illuminated the centrality of water in the pending battle between industrial culture and environmental stability.[1] Her prognosis was sadly not exaggerated, though she could not have foreseen the forms this battle would take in the post–Cold War era of global capitalism. Half a century after Carson's book jumpstarted public debate over the environment, the July 2013 issue of *Harper's Magazine* led with a cover story titled "Glaciers for Sale," McKenzie Funk's investigation of a "global-warming get-rich-quick" borderline Ponzi scheme to sell water in bulk from Icelandic glaciers to areas in need, including China, India, and southern California. Funk summarizes the epically dramatic role of water in the environmental anxieties of the twenty-first century as well as how human ingenuity will rise to the challenge: "Water is the medium of climate change—the ice that melts, the seas that rise, the vapor that warms, the rain that falls torrentially or not at all. It is also an early indicator of how humanity may respond to climate change: by financializing it."[2] The corporatization of this quintessential resource of the commons is perhaps best illustrated by the following statistic: as of 2015, 8 *trillion* gallons of water are used annually to make Coca-Cola products—enough to supply drinking water to a quarter of the planet.[3]

Funk's article is prescient less in its revelation of the legal loopholes attained by the white-collar burglars of high finance (news that by now is sadly redundant) than for its identification of the inflated value—both in monetary and geopolitical terms—of water. As Funk's article points out, water's economic weight and existential importance make it perhaps *the* crucial issue of the coming century, the economic and practical equivalent of, respectively, gold and oil.[4] Even mainstream Hollywood got in on the scare, with George Miller's instant cult classic *Mad Max: Fury Road* (2015) foreshadowing water as the only remaining object of value (and therefore tyranny and oppression) in a postapocalyptic dystopia, an accessible environmental justice springboard for the film's high-octane action sequences and stylized violence.

Although there is certainly some debate about such analogies—water, after all, is a naturally replenishing resource that, unlike oil, is hard to quantify as a commodity because it is difficult to transport in bulk and extremely inexpensive—there can be no question about the centrality of water to human civilization, both in practical terms and in terms of our mythologies. Because of its seeming ubiquity and its logistical importance for agriculture, transport, and nourishment, water serves as a primary industrial and diplomatic concern and provides a range of symbolic cultural functions. The world's mythologies have systematically provided an extensive allotment of water deities: those of specific bodies of water, those of specific types of water, those of water in general. Being a fundamental natural element and essential life substance, water is integral to many religions' creation myths as well as to many rituals of purification. Human civilization has relied on water for its sustenance, expansion, and ingenuity, and our species has collectively worshipped, cherished, exploited, and contaminated this natural resource as only we can.

Growing concerns about water's potential scarcity are not so much about what nature offers us but about what we offer it—what humanity does with and to this natural resource and to the atmospheric ecosystem that makes it naturally renewable. As populations grow and our resources remain finite, and as industrial production continues to leak chemicals and toxins into the air, soil, rivers, and oceans, environmental discourse is not only moving to the topics on the future tech horizon, such as alternative power, but also returning to more basic discussions concerning the raw necessities of existence. Water makes up 70 percent of the human body and, in striking proportionate congruency, nearly three-fourths of the surface area of our planet. Thales of Miletus, the pre-Socratic philosopher and an early proponent of the scientific (as opposed to mythological) explanation of natural phenomena, was not exaggerating in his argument that water is the originating principle of nature. We use water for nearly everything we do; from drinking to bathing to developing photographs to cooling Internet-server warehouses, nearly every human activity involves—if not centers on—water use. As such, it is no surprise that water has been integral to the history of film, from its basic production needs to its topics of fascination, its sublime affective force, and its inquiry into human social practices.

So it is only logical, as Funk lays out, that water is the cornerstone of climate change: "the glaciers that melt, the seas that rise, the vapor that warms, the rains that fall in droves or not at all." Not surprisingly, then, water—in particular oceanic changes, including sea-level rise and the accelerating extinction of fish species and decimation of coral reefs—has therefore become the central narrative of recent films of environmental concern, such as Louis Psihoyos's *Racing Extinction* (2015), Jennifer Baichwal and Ed Burtynsky's *Watermark* (2013), Jeff Orlowski's *Chasing Coral* (2017), and Josh Fox's *Gasland* (2010), a film about fracking that opens and closes on a river and made a sensation out of setting kitchen-sink water on fire. In this chapter, I investigate how American cinema has engaged with water, from representation to production to the surrounding network of marketing and criticism. What are some thematic and resonant ways in which water has been shown on the big screen, and how have humans been positioned in relation to it? How has water been central to the production of mainstream films, in terms of its extrafilmic consumption (from the use of water to produce film stock to the hydration of cast and crew, to the use for cooling electronics) and its textual role as setting and prop, from manufactured oceans to artificial rainfall? How do we use and affect water and waterways in our production of screen culture? These questions help to trace a philosophy of representing nature, which I carry through to a material, economic, and social analysis of our screen culture's use of and impact on water as a resource. As a consequence, I develop an ecomaterialist argument regarding the problematic environmental impact of screen culture on this precious natural resource, for which the particular focus on water in *Singin' in the Rain* as a symbolic, spectacular, and marketing tool proves greatly illuminating.

FILM PHILOSOPHY AND THE ENVIRONMENT

What would it mean to incorporate a film philosophy into this ecomaterialist exploration of cinematic production cultures? The problem of subject–object relations at the center of philosophy could be applied to mainstream cinema's representations of the environment and the relationship between human civilizations and their surrounding ecosystems. Because the philosophical underpinnings of the Scientific Revolution, the Enlightenment, and the age of positivism helped to secrete Western ideological views of the natural world according to a detachment between human subject and an object world at our service, I argue that challenging the philosophical basis of this system is central to challenging the sociocultural contract of popular screen entertainment. What are the predominant ways in which water has been made central to film texts, and how is water positioned relative to humanity in terms of configurations of subject and object? How does this positioning and organizing aesthetically ground and articulate philosophical or ideological outlooks that are tied to moral systems and their contingent structures of social injustice? What does our construction and treatment of the "natural," both explicitly on the surface and hidden in layers of aesthetic convention and poetic language, say about our fundamental environmental values?

First, let us identify a certain idealized exploration of the natural world as delineated through the romantic rendering of water-based nature, which we will find to be bound to a larger network of cultural and social dynamics, including artistic traditions, religious conventions of stewardship, and gender hierarchies. This idealized exploration is typical of what David Ingram refers to as the "Wilderness Landscape," epitomized by Robert Redford's film *A River Runs Through It* (1992), a pastoral call to arms that paralleled the filmmaker's ongoing campaign for forest conservation.[5] Set in the idyllic expanse of rural Montana, this nostalgic family drama is highlighted by the masculine respect for—and ultimate mastery of—nature, as demonstrated through the narrative fulcrum of the three male protagonists (ministerial father, good son, rebellious son) and their primary form of bonding, fly-fishing. Fly-fishing: an elegant and simple mode of tricking animals into impaling themselves on metal barbs and then of struggling against their desperate flight to yank them violently from their habitat so as to suffocate them to death. But don't forget: elegant and simple and easily romanticized.

In such a narrative, the rushing wild of wooded rivers serves as both a general aesthetic framework (the rhythmic motion of nature, flows of color and light, fractalesque curves of rivulet and bend) and a natural symbol for the dichotomy between chaos and order, a dichotomy that is manifested in the male characters' manly triumph over landscape and wildlife (figure 2.1). The representational duplicity of such a film seems as clear as it is superficial: we must respect the natural world and become one with it, and in doing so—in taming our own nature through will and reason—we must separate ourselves as the chosen subject that can master what Ingram refers to as "a beautiful, Christianized sublime."[6]

FIGURE 2.1 A fly-fishing scene in *A River Runs Through It* (Robert Redford, 1992) visually encapsulates the film's contradictory messages that nature is sacred but that its penetration, taming, and exploitation are definitive of Christian masculinity. *Source*: Frame capture by author.

Understanding the subject–object organization of this film as one that pits the action-oriented and viewing male subject apart from (and sometimes inserting him into) the passive natural object in need of taming echoes the paralleling of ecocriticism and feminism mapped out by recent scholars such as Verena Andermatt Conley. In *Ecopolitics*, Conley acutely draws a genealogy of contemporary environmental discourse back to the post-structuralist identity politics of the 1960s, claiming that the subject–object binary central to the treatment of nature is similar to the treatment of women and non-European cultures and thus linking ecocriticism to the fundamental critique—staged in feminist and postcolonial studies—of classical philosophical structures that uphold inequality and exploitation.[7] Pursuing the film-philosophical claim of *A River Runs Through It*, Ingram does not isolate the text but instead notes the connection between its underlying values and Redford's corresponding metatextual political activism for the preservation of the rivers of the Northwest United States: "In *A River Runs Through It*, then, the cinematography of natural landscape as pristine serves a wider ideological project concerning the gendered relationship between human beings and nature. In addition, the promotional campaign for the film evoked nostalgia for the cult of pristine nature in order to advocate the ecological restoration of American wild rivers."[8]

Such a message, which ultimately poses water and its contents as objects to be controlled by the human subject, is only discretely different from that presented, with equal reverence, by the nature documentary. Although Redford's film obeys the rules of cinematic verisimilitude, it does so in the registry of literary adaptation and within the genre of the memoir, which is no less structured according to a truth claim than underwater documentaries, from Jacques Cousteau and Louis Malle's *The Silent World* (1956) to the digital disrobing of the deep seas provided in hugely successful franchises such as the BBC's *The Blue Planet*. These nature documentaries are quintessential popular-media extensions of the philosophical subject–object binary at the heart of Western positivist empiricism: that we can taxonomize and categorize the universe into bits of information, which by organizing we then can control. Nature films are akin to ethnographic films, only the white Western filmmaker has replaced Nanook with a school of fish or a desert ecosystem. In particular, these films tend unanimously to be structured according to the documentary rupture between image and sound: the awe-inspiring image of natural bounty and the controlling sound of the human voice. In fact, from *The Undersea World of Jacques Cousteau* to *The Blue Planet*, this voice has conventionally been male (with the notable exception of the American Discovery Channel's airing of *Planet Earth*, which replaced David Attenborough with Sigourney Weaver), shaping meaning onto the untamed plenitude of imaged otherness.

Taming waterways and aquatic ecosystems has not of course been the sole charge of cinematic explorers—military leaders, farmers, and city planners have long wrestled with the vicissitudes of water. Moreover, water's centrality to transport, trade, and everyday life means that the ethics and politics of water use have long been a problem for collective society. The United States has a long history of feuds surrounding water rights—nowhere more so than in California, cradle of our mainstream screen industry. Marc Reisner's fascinating account *Cadillac Desert: The American West and Its Disappearing Water* (2000) fully captures the local significance of this issue, from our excessive use of water to the complex politics surrounding its use:

> As is the case with most western states, California's very existence is premised on epic liberties taken with water—mostly water that fell as rain on the north and was diverted to the south, thus precipitating the state's longest-running political wars. With the exception of a few of the rivers draining the remote North Coast, virtually every drop of water in the state is put to some economic use before being allowed to return to the sea. Very little of this water is used by people, however. Most of it is used for irrigation—80 percent of it, to be exact.[9]

The most notorious instance of this exploitation—and subsequent corruption—began simultaneously with the invention of our most popular cultural medium. Bringing to the screen one of the central ecological problems of American urbanization and expansion, Roman Polanski's film *Chinatown* (1974) uses neonoir conventions to frame a political thriller involving the southern California water wars at the dawn of the twentieth century.

The water wars were sparked in 1898 when Frederick Eaton, the mayor of Los Angeles, and Walter Mulholland, superintendent of the newly created Los Angeles Department of Water and Power, set out to secure the water rights from Owens Valley farmers so as to divert water into the Los Angeles Valley. Their vision was an expanded city, and their strategy was to provide the water as a draw to potential investors and citizens. But the closest water source was in the rural farming area of Owens Valley, and the U.S. Bureau of Reclamation already had a plan to claim that valley's water rights. Dissuaded by neither government nor decency, the ambitious duo decided the mayor should go into the countryside posing as a cattle rancher, in which guise he managed to swindle the farmers out of their land. Through personal connections with the bureau's regional engineer, Eaton and Mulholland were able to convince the bureau—and subsequently President Theodore Roosevelt—to cancel the bureau's irrigation project.

From 1908 to 1913, Mulholland directed the building of the Los Angeles Aqueduct, which spans 223 miles to a reservoir in the San Fernando Valley. The water demand was so high that Owens Valley, a natural aquifer, was reduced to a desert, and Owens Lake dried up by 1924. The decimation of their farmlands induced the Owens Valley farmers to a heightened series of guerilla actions that ended in 1927, when the Inyo County Bank, run by the financial and civic leaders of the resistance, collapsed. By 1928, Los Angeles owned 90 percent of the water in Owens Valley, and agriculture in the region was effectively dead.[10]

This valley, from which George Eastman had once taken silver to make film stock back east in order to feed Hollywood's growing demand—this ecosystem that made the city of Los Angeles and the silver screen possible—would henceforth be useful only as a desert locale to film Westerns.[11] Its story would live on, with some variations, in the neonoir classic *Chinatown*.

Chinatown's release in 1974 came just a few years after the completion in 1970 of a second aqueduct, whose diversion of surface water and pumping of groundwater essentially dried out the Owens Valley springs and began to kill off all water-dependent vegetation in the area. This desertification led to a series of lawsuits on behalf of Inyo County under the California Environmental Quality Act of 1970; in direct violation of the act, Los Angeles had never completed an Environmental Impact Report, and when forced to do so by the court, the city simply provided an inaccurate report marred by incomplete accounts of water siphoning.

It wasn't until 1991, *nearly a century* after Eaton and Mulholland hatched their elaborate scam and gave birth to the City of Angels, that Los Angeles and Inyo County came to an official agreement, the Inyo– Los Angeles Long Term Water Agreement, to regulate the pumping so as to supply water to Los Angeles without destroying all life in Inyo County. *Chinatown* casts Jack Nicholson as Jake Gittes, a hardboiled detective who gets embroiled in the water wars (temporally relocated to 1937) and a sinister plot of corruption, murder, and incest. Gittes is beaten up, falls in love, watches his beloved gunned down, and is ulti- mately a helpless witness to the environmental destruction and patri- archal violence of American capitalism, crushed under the heel of the overwhelming power of private greed in the public sphere.

Though *Chinatown* adapts the history of water and drought mainly as a backdrop (figure 2.2), the politics of water use has also been more central to film texts, and in *Ecology and Popular Film* Robin L. Murray and Joseph K. Heumann offer a diachronic study of this centrality by comparing *The River* (Pare Lorentz, 1937) and *Wild River* (Elia Kazan, 1960).[12] The former, a New Deal documentary made for the Tennessee Valley Authority (TVA), draws on the public memory of flood disasters

FIGURES 2.2 The Los Angeles Aqueduct, opened in 1905, helped to reduce Owens Lake to a giant salt flat by 1930, effectively killing agricultural business and farming in the area. The ensuing water wars between urban and rural constituents provides the historical setting for *Chinatown* (Roman Polanski, 1974), in which Jack Nichol- son stars as Jake Gittes, a detective following a murder mystery around the water- starved urbanscape of early Los Angeles, as captured by this long shot of Gittes exploring a dry riverbed. *Source*: Frame capture by author.

along the Mississippi River to evoke support for Franklin D. Roosevelt's implementation of dams to halt rising water, distribute water to the area, and generate electricity. The latter is a fictional account of the TVA by a director who in fact worked on film projects under the New Deal. Elia Kazan paints a complex, dramatized portrait of the TVA as being both the only solution to the Tennessee River's inevitable dangers and a socialist policy of big government that encroached on the land rights of the farmers in surrounding areas.

Both films, Murray and Heumann note, express a certain ambiguity about the origin, process, and consequences of such large-scale projects to tailor river flow, though they focus on different politics of the issue. Pare Lorentz's film highlights the human origins of water-based natural disaster, as our exploitation of the land has altered the very ecosystem that we must subsequently step in to control, eliciting a dichotomous eco-ethical prerogative: "Flood waters must be controlled because humans have overused lands and overdeveloped flood plains, causing damage humans can only repair by building huge dams to reroute the wild river waters."[13] Kazan's film, however, is a fictional account that is more concerned with the human problem of rural Americans being displaced by the controlled flooding caused by the TVA's dams. Although these films are very different, setting them side by side helps to show how the politics of water management is represented in both fiction and nonfiction cinema. Isolating their points of intersection, Murray and Heumann argue, "*The River* and *Wild River* stand out as films—eco-films, if you will—that explicitly address and support a viable solution (TVA dams) to consequences (flooding) of real environmental exploitation (overuse and overdevelopment of land)."[14]

Such denotative problems resurfaced in 2005 when Hurricane Katrina ravaged the Gulf Coast and New Orleans. Spike Lee's four-part HBO documentary miniseries *When the Levees Broke* (2006) pulls from the city's rich cultural tradition—and from its rather problematic history of natural disasters and racial and class inequality—in order to insist that viewers, citizens, and politicians commit Katrina to memory lest they be doomed to repeat the disastrous response to it. As Murray and Heumann point out, all of these films are connected by a certain ecofilmic genealogy: "the aftermath of the Katrina disaster also broaches issues of historical memory and cultural context like those that drive *The River*."[15]

However, the authors do not pursue a formal analysis of *how* these films present such issues and how this presentation affects the ethical nature of the films' rhetoric. Their study is based, like most ecocriticism, on the substance of representation, not on its form.

Following in the model of great documentarists such as Joris Ivens and Walter Ruttman, Lorentz unfurls a series of interconnected images that tie rivers to the land and the people around them. Meanwhile, a voiceover narrates the way in which human farming has relied upon and exploited this natural resource; the increasingly passionate narration is reflected by an accelerating rhythmic editing that heightens the images of rising floodwaters to a crescendo of emergency. Such a distribution of the sensible provides an ironic superficiality: just as in the nature documentary, the image tells us to respect nature, even while the speaking subject maintains control at all times over the film's environmental discourse. *Where the Levees Broke*—a synthetic documentary that makes use of archive footage, home movies, news reports, and direct cinema techniques—conversely relinquishes this unilateral discursive power of the voice. It instead gives over to the power of the images of environmental disaster, refracting the spoken discourse among a large number of interviewed subjects who are as diverse in identity as they are equal in the film's representation. Because this intersubjective and intertemporal format breaks down the classical subject–object hierarchy between human subject and objective nature, the river, the gulf, the rain, the victims, the politicians, and the analysts all become subjects within a polyphonic text.

Films such as *Chinatown*, *The River*, and *When the Levees Broke*, which debate the ambiguous social use and treatment of water as a natural resource as well as the civil manipulation of bodies of water, offer ethical commentaries on how we use the natural resources around us—and on how this use reflects underlying issues of environmental justice. However, the terrifying reality of natural disaster depicted in the latter two films has also born a big-budget motif that expresses popular anxieties regarding the human mistreatment of nature through a guilty suspicion that an inhumane and even vindictive natural environment may one day return the favor. From *Jaws* (Stephen Spielberg, 1975) to *Waterworld* (Kevin Reynolds, 1995) to *The Day After Tomorrow* (Roland Emmerich, 2004), the water-centric ecodisaster film positions the great unknown of the big blue as something to be feared, turning on nonhuman nature the very worst collaborations between classical philosophies of certainty, unilateral positioning of subject and object, and the base emotional reactions of ignorance and xenophobia. The monster in *Jaws* is, of course, not the water itself, but the great white shark that resides in its unprotected spaces. The reductive and overly mechanistic marine biology presented in the film (the shark as inhuman and unthinking force of pure necessity) is, in David Ingram's words, a "Cartesian view of animals as mindless machines."[16] The shark acts as a metonymic extension of the ocean, a high-concept manifestation of water and even of nature itself. Moreover, Ingram's evocation of the Cartesian anthropocentrism of human subjectivity is crucial to a film-philosophical understanding of how these films position humanity in relation to the natural world.

Larger-scale disaster movies such as *Waterworld* and *The Day After Tomorrow* catapult this anxiety—as well as its underlying anthropocentrism—into the political and scientific debate over global warming that has exploded during the past two decades. Both films offer an apocalyptic look at the extreme effects of global warming: in *Waterworld*, the polar icecaps have melted and covered almost the entire planet with water, and *The Day After Tomorrow* follows a series of water-based natural disasters (tsunami, flood, and ensuing ice age) caused by global warming. Both films provide a surface premise that human civilization has altered Earth's ecosystem and caused irreparable harm to the environment, eliciting an extreme and vengeful response from the elements; the films act as warnings to human civilization and as champions of environmental science. In both cases, the typical geopolitical enemies of the United States (eastern Europeans during the Cold War, Arab Muslims since September 11, 2001) have been replaced by an even vaster and more destructive force, and these films demonstrate that once we have made nature our enemy, carbon life forms are no match for the compound molecules made from hydrogen and oxygen.

The Day After Tomorrow is particularly intriguing because it marketed itself quite aggressively as an environmentalist film, not only for its apocalyptic warning but also for its production methods. It was the first Hollywood film to attract visibility as a "carbon-neutral production," which means that the carbon dioxide generated by its production was offset by funding environmental groups and planting trees. In other words, it did not necessarily change its methods to become more environmentally sound; it merely budgeted an institutional atonement for its sins. This irony underlies the standard operating procedure for eco-conscious production in Hollywood and is reaffirmed by the film's exploitative use of exaggerated scientific claims in order to heighten the melodrama of a special-effects-driven disaster flick. The film has been consistently criticized for an inaccurate environmental paranoia that in fact feeds into conservative critiques of climate change and the scientific consensus around it: the film, critics claim, hyperbolizes its assertions and even invalidates them because they are based on "irrational emotional arguments rather than rational and logical evidence."[17] Director Roland Emmerich's insistence that such exaggerations were intended to boost the film's dramatic appeal points to another desired goal of the ecodisaster genre: the film pulled in $528 million worldwide.

The conflicting layers of science, culture, and business involved in *The Day After Tomorrow* indicate a stark reality about Hollywood production culture, American audience complicity, and the ironic polyvalence of film discourse. The film is ultimately not an eco-friendly production, and its message is not a scientific one, but it was advertised as carbon neutral, and the grandeur of its spectacle proved enormously successful on a commercial level, catering to heightened audience fears in an age of increasing uncertainty and unpredictability regarding meteorological events and natural disasters. In order to unmask such superficially progressive texts, we must move away from the evident contradictions of representation in the filmic world and shift the debate to the practical problems of filmmaking and the discursive channels that spin textual meaning into a tapestry of ideological appeal and cross-market advertisement.

LIGHTS, CAMERA, WATER!

Film, like its users, needs water. Water is a necessary element on multiple levels throughout the life cycle of a film, from being an article of representation to an essential part in the chemical process that makes movie magic possible. And once that water goes through its system, film has to excrete the waste that remains. The recent turn to more sustainable and environmentally conscious practices has elicited some water-based solutions, such as the shift from individual disposable water bottles back to old-school collective water-cooler efficiency, which stands out as a pretty consistent "greening" initiative of mainstream studio practices. However, the real problems lie—as they often do—behind the "behind the scenes," in the processes that are not highlighted in information brochures or on greenwashed webpages.

Film's technology and industrial methods have a deep impact on this ubiquitously needed resource, tracing back to the production of the raw material itself. Eastman Kodak, which established its monopoly on the patent technology and practices of film-stock production in the early 1920s, was not only the nation's second-largest consumer of pure silver bullion (after the U.S. Mint) but also a cavernous abyss for water use and pollution. Moreover, the Kodak Park Plant in Rochester, New York, was propped strategically alongside Lake Ontario, from which it drew *more than 12 million gallons of water daily* for the annual production of 200,000 miles of film stock during the 1920s.[18] This comes to 18.56 cubic feet of water per second, or the equivalent of filling 240,000 bathtubs or 18 Olympic-size swimming pools per day.[19] Although these numbers should be placed in perspective alongside the numbers for other industrial practices that are shockingly high in their required water use (for example, it takes more than 10 gallons of water to produce one slice of bread, more than 713 gallons for one cotton T-shirt, and more than 39,000 gallons to manufacture a new car), the magnitude of consumption necessary for the production of early film stock is noteworthy.

Twelve million gallons. 12,000,000 gallons. Per day. In the 1920s. By the end of the twentieth century, when Eastman Kodak was responsible for 80 percent of the world's film supply, Kodak Park was using 35 to 53 million gallons of freshwater per day—at times more than quadruple the amount in the 1920s.[20] To put this amount in perspective, 53 million is 530,000 times the 100 gallons used per day by each resident of the United States (and 10 million to 20 million times the 2–5 gallons used daily by a resident of sub-Saharan Africa, seemingly insignificant by comparison).[21] The water use of half-a-million citizens of the U.S. viewing audience, all to make a raw cultural material—the majority of which will end up as waste on the cutting-room floor.

However, not only what goes in must be accounted for but also what comes out—and where it goes. After being siphoned off of Lake Ontario, the water used to create film was run through the Kodak plant's elaborate chemical-rinsing process and then dumped into the Genesee River, which extends through Rochester and another 157 miles down through New York and into Pennsylvania. In 1972, the federal Clean Water Act forced American factories to collect the majority of their wastewater in treatment plants. Regardless of that legislation, by the end of the century, Kodak's dumping of postproduction chemicals into the groundwater of New York made it the primary source of carcinogenic pathogens in the state, and Rochester was "ranked number one for overall releases of carcinogenic chemicals" from 1987 to 2000.[22]

And this, as they say, is just the tip of the iceberg—or, rather, just a small tip relative to the massive iceberg that is invisible to the eye, kept out of the spotlight of industry discourse. It is nonetheless symptomatic of the media industry's sleight of hand that diverts public and regulatory attention away from the sausage factory and toward the hot-dog stand. In addition to how film stock is made, though, issues of water consumption, usage, and dispersal have been central to the practice and discourse of some of American cinema's most iconic productions. The most recent Hollywood film to build its pre-release momentum and blockbuster aesthetic upon the grandiose control of water is James Cameron's epic romance *Titanic* (1997).

Garnering fourteen Academy Award nominations and eleven wins, including Best Film and Best Director, *Titanic* indisputably held the critical respect and appreciation of its industry peers. And its more than $2 billion in international profits, refueled by a 3D re-release in 2012, testifies to its commercial success as an audience favorite across generations, cultures, and formats. A parallel narrative that moves seamlessly between the titular ship's ill-fated maiden voyage in 1912 and a present-day attempt to salvage artifacts from its remains, *Titanic* offers an ironic testimony to the cold destructive power of an indifferent natural element. Explored through a romanticized vision of technology, the film's development and production were driven by extrafilmic Hollywood-style braggadocio about the excesses of production and the indulgence of spectacle, from the film's ballooning budget to the extravagant crafting of natural resources for its aquatic soundstage filming.

Much of the filming took place not in the Atlantic Ocean (where the narrative is set), but in two large water tanks temporarily built off the Pacific in the village of Popotla in Rosarito, Mexico, on a forty-acre oceanfront lot purchased by 20th Century Fox just for this production. The studio referred to the lot as the "100 days studio" due to its brief intended lifespan, and opened for business eighty-five years to the day after the original ship was launched. One tank held 17 million gallons of water, and the other held 5 million; the water culled directly from the ocean was polluted during its cycling through the production and then pumped back into local waterways. The film's creation of local jobs earned director James Cameron the Order of the Aztec Eagle from the grateful Mexican government and has inspired scholars to highlight *Titanic* as a testament to the model of transnational cultural production intended by the North American Free Trade Agreement.[23]

The Mexican film industry had recently collapsed, prompting legislation to allow 100 percent ownership of land by foreign investors to help employ out-of-work local film professionals.[24] However, although the production of *Titanic* in Mexico did bring a heightened visibility to northern Mexico as a site of cheap labor and real estate for American productions, to which Hollywood could easily relocate materials and equipment, it also had a very negative "unseen" impact on the local biosphere—"unseen" in that it was not part of Fox's marketing campaign for the film or part of the narrative being told in the trade papers, such as *Variety*, which feigned outrage and incredulity at the film's excesses in order to implicitly reaffirm Hollywood's grandeur. Popotla was cut off from the sea and local fisheries by a massive movie wall that was built to keep local citizens away, and Fox's chlorine treatment of the water on set led to the pollution of surrounding seawater, decimated the local sea urchin industry, and reduced overall fish levels by one-third.[25]

I discuss the ecosystemic problems associated with the incentives of outsourcing and the politics of runaway production in chapter 5, but I use this snapshot of *Titanic* here as an entry point to the methodological complexities of an ecomaterialist approach to the hidden costs of how films are made. We must identify the environmental issues at play in film production, find a way to theorize cinema's use of natural resources, and read between the lines of films' marketing discourse. To further develop the framework of such an alternative history and approach, I turn to Stanley Donen and Gene Kelly's classic *Singin' in the Rain* (1952).

Fade in:

INT. DARKNESS

A large warehouse door opens to reveal a couple in Extreme Long Shot, silhouetted against the outside light. Cut in to a Long Shot as they— Don Lockwood and Kathy Seldon—enter a Hollywood soundstage.

DON: This is the proper setting.

KATHY: Why, it's just an empty stage.

DON: At first glance, yes, but wait a second.

(Don turns a handle and lights flare on a backdrop: a pink and silver skyline.)

DON: A beautiful sunset.

(He pushes a lever: smoke comes out of a tube on the floor.)

DON: Mist from the distant mountains.

(He throws another lever: red overhead light, the twill of a flute.)

DON: Colored lights in a garden.

(Don takes Kathy's hand and ushers her to a ladder, which she ascends.)

DON: A lady is standing on her balcony, in a rose-trellised bower.

(Don turns a gel light on her: purple.)

DON: Flooded with moonlight. We add five hundred thousand kilowatts of stardust.

(The flute twills as Don throws a number of switches and overhead lights of white, red, and green shower down.)

DON: A soft summer breeze.

(Don turns on an industrial-sized fan and takes a step toward the ladder, pauses.)

DON: And . . . you sure look lovely in the moonlight, Kathy.

(Cut to Close-Up of Kathy, the lights in soft focus behind her.)

KATHY: Now that you have the proper setting, can you say it?

(Cut to Medium Shot of Don.)

DON: I'll try.

This pivotal scene in *Singin' in the Rain* (figure 2.3) provides the pinnacle of sincerity in a film that hinges on irony, artifice, and play. An integrated backstage musical set during Hollywood's transition from silent

FIGURE 2.3 Articulated quite explicitly during the soundstage scene from *Singin'
in the Rain* (Stanley Donen and Gene Kelly, 1952), Don Lockwood can attempt inter-
human emotional connection only in the artificial environment provided through
the excessive energy use of a Hollywood soundstage. *Source*: Frame capture by author.

to sound eras, *Singin' in the Rain* is a self-reflexive satire of the decep-
tions and hypocrisies that fuel the myths of the silver screen. Its multiple layers of meaning and performative innovation have elicited scholarship and analysis from many angles: star studies, genre theory, Hollywood
historiography, as well as more postmodern analysis of narrative self-
referentiality. At the same time, the film's Hollywood-insider premise
provides it a buffer from criticism, a sort of built-in self-analysis that
invites us to partake in its irony. However, although many would agree
with Sharon Buzzard's generalization that the backstage musical genre
"alerts the viewer[s] to the importance of their engagement as informed
spectators,"[26] we must also consider what is being hidden deeper beneath
this flattering guise. Like many methodologies, the ecomaterialist
approach struggles with access and record, attempting to wrest indirect
observation and theoretical conclusion from a black hole of information
scarcity. Yet by sifting through multiple archive collections, from the
assistant director's logs to advertisement clippings, the ecomaterialist
approach offers a much needed intervention in film history. Conversely, this method also illuminates how misleadingly intangible such
documentation appears at first sight, but how useful it can be in our
understanding of natural-resource use, treatment, and waste in film

production. Though the early 1950s lacked today's perspective on the environmental impact of human industry, the prominent use of nature and natural resources in *Singin' in the Rain*, from production to marketing to critical discourse, is as overwhelming as it is neglected by the mainstream narrative of the film's success.

In the early postwar period, a large dark cloud loomed over the Hollywood studios; actually, it was less a large dark cloud and more a bright little box. Television. Having reached their heyday in the 1920s and 1930s and proven themselves to be ample tools of wartime propaganda during the 1940s, the studios were at a crossroads. The introduction of television led to a decline in cinema attendance, and the Paramount Decree of 1948—antitrust litigation that terminated classical Hollywood's model of vertical integration and thus led to the studios' unanimous decision to divest their exhibition tier, the theaters—threatened the self-sustaining loop of studio finance and left executives grasping for solutions. Meanwhile, Senator Joe McCarthy and the House Un-American Activities Committee's political witch hunt polarized the nation—and the industry—according to the politics of conformity and paranoia.

Despite the political integrity of those members of the industry standing up to the Hollywood blacklist, though, the real goal of the American film industry was, as it always has been, to bring paying audiences into the theaters. This was a mission not lost on the executives at MGM, which was ahead of the curve in terms of market analysis. At a moment when audiences were drifting and funding was tenuous, the studio known for spectacle realized that the most guaranteed investment was to cater to the crowd, and so it employed unprecedented "survey-research techniques" to determine what audiences wanted to see.[27] MGM's wartime survey landed on musical comedies as being preferable to all other story types, and during the 1940s and early 1950s this finding led to a series of highly profitable films in this genre that would crescendo with the enormous success of *Singin' in the Rain*.

A coy and clever comedy with outrageously elaborate and kinetically impressive physical performances, *Singin' in the Rain* was a huge commercial and critical success, has consistently remained in the top ten of canonical "best" lists, and has inspired a wealth of homages both light and haunting. It is rife with wink-wink-nudge-nudge moments that lovingly parody the naive players and audiences of the dream factory's yesteryear, fooling its audiences into mistaking it for a *critical* take on Hollywood extravagance. Yet as a big-budget genre film from MGM and a showcase for its star *Singin' in the Rain* industrially reaffirms the very artifice and manipulation it critiques—even the sacrilegious use of dubbing that is so central to its narrative meaning.[28]

Despite its tongue-in-cheek revelation of the apparatus, *Singin' in the Rain* never fully overturns the artificiality of Hollywood and as such has maintained an ongoing threesome, comfortably in bed with the mainstream *and* its discontents. Although the film's narrative transparency has led many to embrace it as subversive, I would agree with Carol J. Clover's insistence that we "see the moralizing surface story of *Singin' in the Rain* as a guilty disavowal of the practices that went into its own making."[29] This disavowal is not a condemnation but a cover up, a misdirection through which the film invites us to believe in its revelation of artifice and plays upon our faith in its honesty. But what, then, is it covering up—what is the film's "guilty" secret? Through an ecomaterialist approach that uses the film's best-known scene as the kernel for exploring its rich layering of conflicting discourses, I analyze its environmental impact in terms of both its material practices as well as the larger significance of how it represents our relationship to the natural and the artificial. The ingenuity of *Singin' in the Rain* may have come from the creative minds of humans, but its execution was possible only through excessive use of natural resources (water in particular), which were managed with efficiency only to maximize the effect of spectacle. Moreover, its multivalent messages merely hint at the environmental costs of screen artifice while also reaffirming the sociocultural contract whereby we position the nonhuman natural world as expendable fuel for our popular entertainment.

Laughing at Clouds

As demonstrated in the pivotal soundstage scene quoted earlier, *Singin' in the Rain* explicitly acknowledges the grotesque amount of natural resources Hollywood uses in order to manufacture an artificial version of nature, implicating the viewer in an ironically frivolous staging of just how cavalier our film culture is with regard to framing its environmental context. Don's throwing of the "five hundred thousand kilowatts of stardust" lever is a moment of great devotion: devotion not only to Kathy but also to Hollywood's translation of natural resource into spectacle. With every step of his fabrication of a natural setting, Don's courage grows and Kathy's ears perk up, and she is wooed despite—and, in some perverse ways not very different from the audience, wooed *by*—the environmental costs of his romantic confession.

This extreme arrogance burrows to the discursive core of the film title's meaning, central to its most iconic scene: "singin' in the rain." Don Lockwood is in love (with the silver screen's potential magic, with Kathy, and with their plan to save his career and to launch hers), and this makes him impervious to the weather. In fact, more than impervious, it makes him reject the impositions of nature and even contradict them with a jovial eruption of emotion. The film's eponymous number embodies the classical Hollywood culture of excess and indifference toward the consequences of this excess and its pledged capacity to overcome the sovereign status of the elements. Don is not singing because it is raining; he is singing in spite of the rain. His "glorious feeling" and the performative spectacle that articulates it are a direct rejection and subordination of nonhuman nature. Not only is he contradicting the stereotypical emotional effect of rain (sadness), but he goes so far as to physically assault it, repeatedly kicking the rain to accentuate the glorious power of human ingenuity and the triumph of human force over the meager presence of this natural element.

Deemed more of a technical than a choreographic challenge and absent from the screenplays leading up to the shoot but ultimately included into the picture because it was deemed necessary to justify the film's title to audience satisfaction, the iconic sidewalk-singing and lamppost-swinging scene in *Singin' in the Rain* has provided no shortage of Hollywood legend and lore, some of it apocryphal or inaccurate, some of it still unfolding through new scholarship. Yet even more recent works on film and the environment seem to embrace previous narratives. In *Cinema as Weather*, Kristi McKim doubles down on seminal criticism of the film:

> Many plot-catalyzing instances of rain mimic or model our worldly response to rain. Peter Wollen considers Gene Kelly's titular *Singin' in the Rain* (Stanley Donen and Gene Kelly, 1952) sequence "the single most memorable dance number on film," and we might

reasonably claim this sequence also to be the single most exuberant embracing of cinematic weather on film. . . . Though Kathy Seldon's (Debbie Reynolds) doorfront kiss prompts Don Lockwood's (Gene Kelly) joyful swoon, the rainy weather affords Don an opportunity for jubilant transformation of his dreary environment; moreover, the puddles and the downpour offer an aural accompaniment and counterpoint to his tap dancing. Exemplified by *Singin' in the Rain*, the spontaneity and speed of rain's falling casts it as a frequent motivating agent; moreover, this acceleration and impact mimic narrative desire, as we anticipate the predictable weather response (by characters, by the mise-en-scène) and its significance to the narrative as a whole.[30]

Although the scene is indeed exuberant, such analysis reconfirms the previous narrative and performance-based readings of the film, viewing the "jubilant transformation of his dreary environment" as a remarkable externalization of Don's emotional state, more a testament to Gene Kelly's performativity than to the actual environmental praxis of the shoot.

Myth has it that Kelly nailed the song in one take, despite being nearly hysterical with fever and the lacing of the rainwater with milk to make it more visible. Such anecdotes have been disproven, though Kelly *was* increasingly feverish for the eight-day week it took to rehearse and then to shoot the scene (in multiple takes, of course), an extensive period of time that required numerous technical adjustments to perfect the faking of nature (the water, it turned out, became more visible when lit from behind) (figure 2.4). Despite the repeated accounts and in-depth investigation by very reputable scholars, each one—rife with an intellectual balance of admiration and scrutiny—offering a detailed portrait of the production of this scene in particular, not one study of this film raises what seems an obvious and disturbing line of questioning: Where did all that water come from? How was its use orchestrated and accounted for? Where does such a concern fit into the culture of spectacle and excess?[31]

In a typically romanticized account, the Arthur Freed Unit producing the film has been described as "living almost in a dream world" of limitless budget and material supply, a degree of excess worthy of MGM's reputation and demonstrated by the more than five hundred costumes

FIGURE 2.4 Far from the one-take brilliance offered by Hollywood lore, the iconic sidewalk scene in *Singin' in the Rain* required a week of rehearsal—with water running the entire time. This long shot of Kelly swinging from the lamppost offers a perfect conflation of the film's symbolic use of the natural elements: power flowing to illuminate Kelly's teeth, which he bares in a brilliant smile despite the cascade of artificial rain. *Source*: Frame capture by author Photo by author.

used in the film.[32] The "Singin' in the Rain" musical number, which originally appeared in *The Hollywood Revue of 1929* (Charles Reisner and Christy Cabanne), had been pitched without a specific locale in mind, and upon Gene Kelly's revelation—"I thought of the fun children have splashing about in rain puddles and decided to become a kid again during the number"[33]—the right space was sought for what Kelly and Donen envisioned as an innovative form of cinedance. In "Dance, Flexibility, and the Renewal of Genre in *Singin' in the Rain*," Peter N. Chumo II claims that the film moves beyond the conventions of its genre, taking this pivotal dance number into the street under the seemingly worst possible weather conditions. The characters are not trapped, he argues, by narrative or generic conventions.[34] Nor, I would add, are the cast and crew trapped by limitations of natural-resource consumption, water use, or power supply.

Where direct accounts fail to record industry history, we must turn to production-culture studies to provide us with some insights about the actual way in which artificial rain is manufactured. Kristi McKim cites Richard Rickitt's insider account of the consequences of unpredictable rainfall in *Special Effects: The History and Technique*: "The best policy . . .

is to hope for dry weather and create the perfect rain when it is called for."[35] A very generous conversation with longtime Hollywood special-effects coordinator Steve Galich illuminated some of the practicalities of such a shoot as well as the unique nature of MGM's infrastructure and relationship to Culver City.[36] For rainwork (or a "rain job"), special-effects teams typically run fire hoses to the "rain pipe" that is held in place by a thirty-ton crane; the water is supplied by large pumps set in place to take water from various sources, depending on the location of the shoot, including damned-up creeks, newly installed wells, and water reservoirs. Different cities have different policies in terms of how such practices are regulated. Because of local instances of industrial pollution—such as Lockheed Martin's decades-long chemical runoff into the San Fernando aquifer, uncovered in 1980—regulators now keep a close watch on industrial runoff in the Los Angeles River. As a result, the City of Burbank now requires Disney to catch all runoff and pump it into the sewer, which is both more hygienic and more wasteful. As Galich points out, in its heyday MGM more or less ran Culver City and laid out its studio lots around a central water tower (which is prominent and in some ways iconic in older photos of the studio) that could reach its extensive lots and soundstages.

This scene from *Singin' in the Rain* does not, of course, take place on the street in the worst of weather, as Chumo puts it, but was filmed—with highly controlled meteorology—on the East Side Street in Lot 2 of the MGM studio in Culver City, the nighttime sky simulated by draping black tarpaulin over two entire blocks (which also allowed MGM to avoid paying its technical crew overtime for night shooting). The centrality of heavy rainfall to the scene's metaphorical meaning and affective force necessitated an elaborate blend of engineering and design. Far from being achieved in one take, the scene took a day and a half to shoot and rendered the worst shooting ratio of the entire production, capping off an eight-day run of extreme resource waste. The set design specified seven puddles with two inches of water apiece, created by carving out the pavement on the lot. Over six days of rehearsal, a network of pipes using water directly from the Culver City water system ran six hours per day in order to provide for the complicated orchestration of what would become Kelly's most iconic moment, with the technical crew making adjustments to extend the scene space for Kelly's movement. Water running six hours a day for six days, just to rehearse. The star himself was meticulous in the scene's planning; for example, twenty minutes was dedicated to practicing the "cascade" effect of standing under the broken downspout, with technicians adjusting the pipes feeding the water to achieve the desired effect.

Although archival documents support the piecing together of this material production history, there is still a glaring hole in Hollywood's record when it comes to the documentation of natural-resource use. Production accounts lack a listing of the total amount of water used. Although this gap may be telling in itself, it remains difficult to gauge to what extent classical Hollywood productions such as *Singin' in the Rain* were aware of their environmental footprint, and popular discourse on green politics and sustainability were some decades on the horizon. Nevertheless, the last note on the assistant director's report on the rehearsal of this scene on July 17, 1951, written at 6:35 p.m., reads: "Company dismissed because crew was about to run into meal penalty—water pressure is low (40 lbs in Culver City) necessitates more rigging."[37] As Hugh Fordin describes in his book on the Freed Unit's years at MGM, *The World of Entertainment*, "Instead of the desired downpour, all they got was a tired drizzle, and this no matter how high they turned the control valves. All of the studio's tanks were checked."[38]

It was discovered, though, that "rigging" was not the problem—the problem was that at five o'clock in the afternoon the residents of Culver City were coming home, turning on their sprinklers, and thus triggering a drop in water pressure on the lot. That the assistant director's report notes this effect and that filming was consequently scheduled for earlier in the day imply at the very least that the filmmakers and studio were aware that water was in fact a collective natural resource that was in some way finite, limited in its supply and distribution. It is on the basis of such tangible hints that I reframe the film-about-which-seemingly-everything-has-been-written in the interest of an alternative industry history, an ecomaterialist counternarrative that challenges the cost–benefit ramifications of the Hollywood spectacle.

"The Title Should Have Been Hollywood"

The role of natural resources and the material environmental implications of Hollywood production practice extend beyond what appears on the screen and how it was put there. Those eight days on Lot 2 at MGM set the tone for how water was and is used discursively in the marketing, reception, and subsequent scholarly preservation of *Singin' in the Rain*. In *Movies About the Movies*, Christopher Ames captures the central song's underlying textual significance: "This particular number belongs to a class of popular songs that preach the power of one's outlook to overcome external obstacles, a significant theme in American popular culture. Thus the rain represents hardship, and Gene Kelly begins the number by dismissing his cab and folding up his umbrella (which he later gives away after using it as a dancing prop). Having fallen in love, Don Lockwood is made oblivious to the rain."[39] We can see here that just as this number epitomizes the film's soaring romantic gesture, it also sums up the film's tacit discourse on nature.

This scholarly focus on the "Singin' in the Rain" number echoes the majority of the critical reception of the film upon its release. Most American newspaper film reviews praised the film, in particular Kelly's performance—encapsulated by this very scene, in which only the technical virtuosity of MGM's sweeping Technicolor cinematography could match the star's lavish performance and the brilliant choreography that melded his tap dancing with the patter of the raindrops. However, perhaps *the* most influential reviewer of the time saw the film's title as misrepresentative. On March 28, 1952, *New York Times* film critic Bosley Crowther trained his blistering wit on Hollywood's newest sensation. Though noting, as did most other reviews, that Kelly's performance dominated the film and that "by far his most captivating number is done to the title song—a beautifully soggy tap dance performed in the splashing rain," Crowther insisted that the film's title "has no more to do with its story than it has to do with performing dogs." He continues with characteristic aplomb: "If anyone can tell us what all of the nonsense that goes on has to do with the title of the picture, we will buy him a new spring hat. But that doesn't make any difference, for the nonsense is generally good and at times it reaches the level of first-class satiric burlesque."[40]

What Crowther failed to identify—indeed, what he seemed to be blinded to by the film's excessively entertaining spectacle—is that the title is not in fact misplaced but rather misdirection on behalf of the film's discursive foundation. In other words, the title does not fail to bring to light what the film is really *about*; it is *we* who, being taken in by the film's subterfuge of an engaging story about movies, miss the mark and accept the comfortable metapleasure of the film's superficial self-reflexivity. The titular number is, as Ames puts it, "a song about singing in a musical about musicals in a Hollywood movie about Hollywood,"[41] and reviews of the time consistently applauded the film's self-ironic brilliance. *Variety* estimated that "the fact that Hollywood can laugh so heartily at itself, only adds to the appeal."[42] Let in on the dirty secret of how many kilowatts are used to power the film's stardust, we join Don and Kathy in their revelry of its artificial beauty. It is the viewer who, despite clear references made in the film to the absurd amount of power and resources wasted to produce the artificial spectacle that is a "movie," chooses not to register the larger ramifications of this conversion.

I would add to the *Variety* review that the film laughed heartily at itself *all the way to the bank* and that the affectionate satire is a foil meant to keep an increasingly adept and film-literate audience at bay in an era when Hollywood was reaching the end of its third act. The film's nostalgic farce regarding the transition to sound served as an allegory for the next great technical challenge that would alter Hollywood's practices immensely: television. Moreover, in 1948 the Paramount Decree had brought antitrust litigation to bear on the monolithic practices that had made classical Hollywood's golden age of such a high carat, and its legal requirement of vertical de-integration would affect—and be resisted—by MGM more than by any other studio.[43] As such, the film is a swan song to the dancing days of Hollywood and a bittersweet—though ultimately triumphant—testament to the industry's perseverance in the face of change. In a biography, Stanley Donen points out: "The title of the picture never should have been *Singin' in the Rain*. Look at the picture. It's not about the weather. The theme has nothing to do with rain. The picture is about movies. The title should have been *Hollywood*."[44]

But in response to Donen one must ask: Which Hollywood? The film's story line claims to be about the Hollywood of 1927. Yet its connotations are heavily drawn to comment on the Hollywood of 1952, in a state of profound conflict between increasing regulation and the need to refine its transparent production of spectacle—which is why the soundstage and the sidewalk scenes are so pertinent. This film, which offers so much insight into the way movies are made, encourages us to admire how much power is used to light a film set, thus asking us to absolve its waste and to justify its excess by paying our price of admission to the resultant spectacle.

In a profoundly apt cross-reference, Donen once quipped: "Jean-Luc Godard said that cinema is truth twenty-four times a second. I think cinema is lies twenty-four times a second."[45] However, the ironic sophistication of a film such as *Singin' in the Rain* lures us into forgetting that a movie about movies is still a movie; revealing that the silver screen is a canvas for untruth does not imply that *this* film itself is an untruth. In fact, much the opposite: it comes across *as the truth*, an honest confession of Hollywood's artificial ways. As such, *Singin' in the Rain* buries its own secrets under this sheen of honesty, making the material reality of its production perhaps even more difficult to discern beyond the reflective shine of the backstage musical veneer. In discussing the empty promise of the film's self-reflexivity, Rick Altman writes: "Because we are permitted 'backstage' within the film, we fail to recognize that there is no such thing as backstage in the film world, only 'onstage.' We never go behind the set but only behind the stage part of the set."[46] The Hollywood magic trick extends beyond the film text, and we look wherever it points; by drawing our attention to the hypocrisies of Hollywood, *Singin' in the Rain* distracts us from the ultimate hypocrisy whereby spectacle and waste are both practiced and celebrated in it.

"The Shower of Profits"

Despite what Donen says, the film is very much about rain, from the manufacturing of artificial rain to the use of rain in the film's convergence marketing practices, as we can discern from the production files, the Exhibitor's Campaign Book, print advertisement, and on-location anecdotes. On each of these levels, the film sells itself according to this scene and its poetic metaphor and sells many other things in conjunction. The playbill for the film goes into extensive production detail about the shooting of the sidewalk scene in order to press upon industry colleagues and audiences the ingenuity of natural-resource manipulation necessary to master the manufacturing of rainfall.[47] The marketing blitz that ensued upon the film's release revolved entirely around the theme of rain, rainwear, and rain-based puns. The Exhibitor's Campaign Book includes a

"Disk Jockey Stunt for M-G-M Records Album 'Singin' in the Rain'": a press release littered with photographs of female models, clad in designer raincoats and umbrellas, making promotional visits to prominent radio personalities. In language that blatantly encourages trading on the objectification of women for ad time, the text reads: "A pretty young model dressed in shorts complete with raincoat and umbrella appropriately lettered with copy advertising the sound-track album can get you a lot of free radio plugs."[48]

Such gratuitously exploitative tie-ins are continued in large full-page sample ads for Milliken's Dacron wool and Rain Shedder raincoats, including pictorial examples of ads in newspapers and magazines, descriptions of their goods and campaigns, and contact information for the respective companies. Opposite these clothing tie-ins is the perfect cliché of the gendered marketing of the 1950s, in an isolated box, headed in bold: "Mother's Day—May 11th." The studio marketers' advice begins by pointing out the holiday's sentimental and gift-giving propensity and then gives three major tips for tying the film into this particular event:

(a) Use star photos, plus Cyd Charisse, in all kinds of windows—flowers, candy, Western Union, perfumes, make-up, novelties, etc. (there are no special tie-in photos for the purpose).
(b) Try to get local stores to cooperate with a page of ads under a general heading—"It's Raining Mother's Day Gifts at These Stores." Include theatre ad.
(c) If you play the picture on Mother's Day, make a theatre gift of flowers to women first in line at opening performances.[49]

Such details echo the unabashedly conservative and patriarchal gender politics at play in the film's marketing discourse, as we already found with the "pretty young model" promised in the "Disk Jockey Stunt." Although this discussion is not a study of gender in advertising, it is certainly noteworthy how this problem fits into larger continuities of sexism and social inequality that plague our mainstream framings of the natural world.[50]

Such seemingly casual—but ultimately widely consequential—ideological dynamics are enmeshed in the film's discursive dependence on rain-based word play, imagery, and consumer goods and in the ways

FIGURE 2.5 These rainwear advertisements and Mother's Day instructions for marketing *Singin' in the Rain* are but part of a much larger cross-marketing campaign banking on the film's central symbolic use of rain. The emphatic athleticism of Kelly's iconic lamppost swinging, countered by the passive posture of the woman and the gender-specific strategy of the marketing suggestions, reveal the patriarchal norms deep-seated in both 1950s American society and reinforced across the history of classical Hollywood. *Source*: Courtesy of the Arthur Freed Collection, University of Southern California. Photo by author.

the Exhibitor's Campaign Book suggests to market the film based on its natural imagery, including radio slogans such as "It's as gay as a rainbow . . . bright as a cloud's silver lining . . . welcome as the sun after a spring shower! It's M-G-M's glorious-feeling, Technicolor musical— SINGIN' IN THE RAIN with a skyful of stars and a steady down-pour of song hits!"[51] *Singin' in the Rain* was selling nature as an analogy and was striking it rich. This is perhaps most abundantly clear in the film's full-page wide-release ad in the trade journal the *Exhibitor*, which opens in bold letters: **"IT WILL RAIN GOLD AT EASTER! Be ready with open dates to catch the shower of profits."**[52]

Nowhere are love or happiness mentioned, and this discourse isn't—as Donen might romantically opine—about Hollywood, unless it is about Hollywood to the degree that it is about turning natural resources and audience emotion into money. *This* is what the movie is about:

turning enormous profit through the beautification of excess and the spectacle of waste. And profit it did: costing $2,540,800 to make, *Singin' in the Rain* grossed $95,000 its opening weekend and brought in $7,665,000 during the entire run of its initial release.[53] Adjusted for today's dollar, the film raked in the equivalent of more than $200 million, making it the sixth highest-grossing film of 1952.[54] Put quite succinctly in the *New York Compass* review of March 28, 1952: "Another MGM Technicolor mu$ical i$ here, folk$."[55]

The dynamic centrality of rain to the film's big-picture strategy stretches even to the production crew's mode of celebration. The film closed production on November 21, 1951, and, as with all Freed pictures, the end of production was celebrated with a wrap party. The party was arranged on Stage 28 at MGM, as Freed recounts: "We brought the guests into the stage door and in order to get in I rigged up several pipes of rain. So, the only way you could get to the party was by taking an umbrella, which we handed out at the door and everybody walked through the rain."[56]

What a Glorious Legacy

From rehearsal to production to wrap party to playbill to multimedia publicity stunts and cross-marketing tie-ins, this film is as much about rain as it is about romance and movies. Even the film's legacy and its most famous cult tribute revolve around this scene, not the 95 percent of the film that is a Hollywood parody. A perfect illustration of the central song's profound cultural significance: when making his controversial masterpiece *A Clockwork Orange* (1971), a film that violently hinges on the disturbing psychological impact of screen culture, Stanley Kubrick chose to have his protagonist hauntingly sing this song while perpetrating a brutal assault and rape. This juxtaposition and its added layers of irony make clear that the character's antisocial aggression is in fact a source of happiness and not a wayward projection of anger—and impresses upon audiences the degree to which screen culture has helped to forge a break with the material consequences of our actions. Out of respect for Stanley Donen, Kubrick invited the director to view the scene, asking his permission to use the song in such a twisted fashion.[57] Kubrick's is not an alternative history of Donen's film; it is a future history of a humanity spoiled by excess, corrupted to the core by its cultural overvaluation of the artificial.

In *The Simpsons* season 6 whodunnit cliffhanger, "Who Shot Mr. Burns? Part 1" (1995), the malevolent Mister Burns celebrates his Machiavellian plan to block the sun and therefore force an entire town into total dependence on his nuclear power plant with a mash-up parody of Kelly's street choreography and Simon and Garfunkel's "The 59th Street Bridge Song." The show's cartoonish supervillain swings Lockwood-esque from a lamppost, singing the folk duo's classic tune, "Hello, lamppost, whatcha knowin'? / I've come to watch your *power flowing*." Evoking Lockwood's celebratory triumph over nature, Mr. Burns delights in human ingenuity's ability not only to embrace and to utilize nature but also to mimic it—one might even say to surpass it and, beneath it all, to profit from this substitution.

Though *Singin' in the Rain* stages a thoughtful critique of Hollywood with a number of memorable setups, gags, and numbers, the film's legacy is etched out by about four and a half minutes of artificial rainfall and a beaming white-toothed smile. It is telling that the popular parodies of this iconic scene choose to use it entirely against itself, to use it as part of a contradictory bricolage that implicates it in a postmodern wariness of image power and environmental waste. But this, of course, was not the film's goal; from its titular play on words to its material production to its playbill anecdotes and cross-marketing campaigns, the film hinges on the triumph of humanity over natural elements and resources, planting at the level of ideological value the crafted excess of the Hollywood spectacle. You can dig out the sidewalk until the puddles look perfect; if the water pressure drops, you can choose a better time of day to tap the tanks. As this film reinforces through its representational meanings, its production practices, and its various layers of discourse, the Hollywood spectacle is not to be limited by the frugality of nature.

CHAPTER THREE

Wind of Change

New Screen Technologies, the Visualization of Invisible Environmental Threats, and the Materiality of the Virtual

The world is closing in
Did you ever think
That we could be so close, like brothers?
The future's in the air
I can feel it everywhere
Blowing with the wind of change.

—SCORPIONS, "WIND OF CHANGE"

If a *Beavis and Butthead* quote to launch chapter 1 was not enough to date my personal rite of cultural passage, I thought I would double down here with an epic rock ballad that welcomed the new global order after the fall of the Berlin Wall in 1989 and the apparent end to the Cold War. *That* Cold War, anyway—not the ice age to come, at least according to many screen depictions of climate-change dystopia. Although perhaps not directly acknowledging the training wheels that were about to come off the turbocycle of hypercapitalism, the Scorpions' song "Wind of Change" ominously foreshadows a great change in the networking of the global population. One can read the lyrics today as heralding the age of the Internet, wherein technological innovation will once again, as it had with the telegraph and train, collapse the distance between us—or, at least, *virtually* collapse the distance between us in a digital shift in communication that is rewiring our brains and reshaping our existential dynamics. This future closing in of the world will exist in the ether, in the seeming immateriality of the digital. But what is invisible, or in the air, is not immaterial. The slow death of Soviet communism coincided with the rapid birth of the digital era, and in a little more than two decades we have crafted a hidden electronics grid in which dirty energy powers a runaway change in social behavior, cultural production and consumption, and environmental impact. And we might update the song's chorus to specify that "the children of tomorrow" dream through handheld computers, and the "wind of change" is darkened by soot and carrying aloft a medley of greenhouse emissions.

In the first two chapters, I looked at the way in which real materials and natural resources are consumed and even destroyed in the name of the Hollywood spectacle. I have focused thus far on film events, the way they were in the good old days of classical Hollywood: blockbuster productions filmed in uniquely extravagant contexts on studio lots, analog texts enshrined in the canon and entombed in the canisters of an emergent art form. Yet the epic drama of fire and the splashing romance of water that have littered our screens for more than a century are only a piece of the tapestry, and for the remainder of this book I turn to the environmental ramifications of digital practices, whose apparent immateriality is grounded less in the production event and more in the process of staging virtual spectacle.

In an age when most Americans have at least one screen on their person at all times and are connected to the Internet on a daily basis,[1] the use of natural resources and the navigation of environmental elements have become integral not only to the production practices, discursive tool kit, and sociocultural contract of popular film history but also to quotidian human behavior. The ideological centrality of our screen culture is no less poignant today than it was in the 1930s or the 1950s; only the foundations of the sociocultural contract have been shifted to new devices and methods of production and reception. As a consequence, the technology that has emerged at the center of our media practices implicates our daily lifestyle in a vast emergent network of digital imperialism, exploitation, and environmental destruction. From precious metal mines to the virtual shooting set, the online trailer, the server farm, and the digital dumping ground, a vast material industry powers our global digital screen culture.

Hollywood has wrapped us in a world of myths, none more than that of its own wizardry. As much as the romanticized myth of a racially harmonious Civil War–era South, *Gone with the Wind* manufactured a myth of the Great Showman, whose grand vision gave new magnitude to a cultural paradigm of spectacle as value. And much deeper than the shallow myth of a behind-the-scenes Hollywood where the virtue and merit of the Noble Performer triumph, *Singin' in the Rain*'s backstage self-reflexivity forged a generic myth of authenticity and honesty in a medium of artifice. Charles Baudelaire famously wrote that "the finest trick of the devil is to persuade you that he does not exist."[2] Well, the most insidious sleight of hand Hollywood has perfected is the presentation of itself as a magically conjured realm of virtual worlds, not as a product of matter—an illusion that has only been amplified with the advent of digital technology.

In addition to the Great Showman and the Noble Performer, I explore two other mythical Hollywood archetypes, the Scientist-Hero and the Visionary Explorer, archetypes I sketch against the backdrop of the emergence of computer graphics imaging (CGI) as the predominant form of Hollywood spectacle. After all, cinema has never only been an industry of pomp and circumstance—it has also been an industry of technological pioneering, with a history that must be understood as being as much the result of industrial innovations as part of an artistic genealogy. And as a tithe to this internal technological drive, mainstream film language has manufactured codes of transparency to protect the means of production and has presented no shortage of textual and advertising testaments to the glory of innovation.[3] In the Hollywood myth factory, a parallel thread has been unspooled around the romanticization of the onscreen scientist and offscreen technician, intertwining production discourse and representational meaning to characterize films driven by technological and, in particular, special-effects innovations, in which the diegetic scientist acts as a stand-in for the directorial wizard behind the filmmaking curtain.

How do these myths and practices affect the environment and further twist the coil of our sociocultural contract of screen spectacle? In this chapter, I investigate the environmental ramifications of Hollywood's technophilia, connecting the mythological mirroring between the Scientist-Hero and the special-effects wizard to the recent coup staged by digital technology. In fact, this technophilia might better be understood as both a *technofetishism*, according to which the industry's larger discursive practices and individual films' textual meaning express an obsession with technology that connotes a system of hierarchical values in which nonhuman nature is secondary or even oppositional, and a *technofascism*, through which the devices that make up the apparatus hold an authoritarian power over the messages articulated by this culture industry. These narrative, ideological, and mythological dynamics at the intersection between film and the environment are deeply woven into the emerging tapestry that is the ecodisaster genre.

SCREEN, GENRE, ENVIRONMENT

Genre studies in the 1970s used the wide-lensed social perspective of postwar structuralist method to look at how certain groups of films arrange recurrent values, themes, and narrative tropes in a systematic way. Although this systematic practice certainly serves an industrial function regarding high-efficiency studio contracting, creative streamlining, and film marketing, it also provides a social function beyond mere entertainment. Hollywood genres act as a social ritual, functioning to freeze time so as to treat a threat to the social order, transferring real historical or social problems onto one locus of events and characters in order to provide a symbolic screen resolution.[4] The details of each individual film are, to an extent, mere filler that recycles and renews the resolution according to current events, whereas the conventions of the genre form a sort of mythological design according to which we can abandon the reality of the present in order to address present anxieties in a temporally and spatially removed cultural arena.

This process occurs in different ways across different genres (and according to different timescales, as is addressed briefly in this chapter and at length in the next chapter), but the underlying negotiation is more or less consistently what Robin Wood understands as the resolution of tensions that make up American ideology.[5] Far from a uniform society of harmonious values and beliefs, Wood points out, puritanical, capitalist America is a hotbed of conflicting messages and worldviews—populism and greed, outlaws and order, whores and virgins—and film genres are prime realty where culture works through these contradictions. Couching a similar approach to genre in terms of narrative temporality and ideological crystallization, we might isolate the Western genre as providing for a "myth of national origin,"[6] a way for American screen culture to fictionally represent—construct, even—the history of the nation's formation. This particular construction of the nation's formation highlighted core American values that were increasingly being challenged as the United States became more industrialized and across the twentieth century experienced great social change and challenges to established order. The Western's portrayal of U.S. expansion across North America allowed for a past-tense reconciliation of internal contradictions, such as the contradiction between the principle of harmonious ethnic inclusion embodied by the melting-pot analogy and the nation's actual history of systematic racism and genocide.[7]

Most approaches to genre studies and cinema history emphasize how film genres adapt to meet society's changing need for mythological expression. This is not new to the twentieth century or unique to film, which inherited many of its industry and socially mythological functions from literature. In his study of literary history's reconciliation with capitalist industrialization, *The Country and the City*, Raymond Williams recognizes how the past becomes a textual canvas for escaping present anxieties across early Renaissance and late Enlightenment literature. As feudal society faced violently changing power relations, writers and readers embraced the cultural protection of temporal displacement, setting an idea and ideal of "ordered and happier past against the disturbance and disorder of the present. An idealization, based on a temporary situation and on a deep desire for stability, served to cover and to evade the actual and bitter contradictions of the time."[8] Cinema's turn in the driver's seat of this cultural process began at the apex of American industrialization, and as such it acted as a broken mirror for the collective concerns over the true costs—at first moral and now environmental—of our technological modernity.

Anyone aware of mainstream screen trends cannot ignore the emergence since 1990 of "a new generation of disaster films," focused on natural destruction and environmental dystopia.[9] I call this type of film the "ecodisaster film." In the next chapter, I explore the temporal dynamics of genre in an analysis of *Avatar*, but for now let us understand the ecodisaster film in terms not dissimilar from the Western. If the Western is the genre to mythologize America's frontier past, then the ecodisaster film is the genre geared to mythologize America's soon to be environmentally challenged future. The structural repetitions in film genres foster the emergence of thematic, technical, and ideological patterns through which filmmakers and audiences can deal mythologically— fictionally, narratively, and symbolically—with real historical issues and present-day social anxieties. Film genres allow us to project these issues and anxieties onto a screen space and to supply fictive solutions that, although granting the audience a certain comfortable sense of closure, do not actually address or change the systematic roots of these issues and anxieties in real life. In this process, a set of values is naturalized, secreted into the text as a seemingly inevitable or organic part of the problem and its solution—this is how ideology works, and popular-cultural genres are among its most loyal servants.

We can categorize genres based on certain conventions, including recurrent iconography, character types, and narrative tropes. For the ecodisaster film, the narrative tropes mostly involve a struggle between humans and nonhuman nature, and the special-effects-driven iconography is characterized by catastrophic natural disaster and dystopian civilizations. The predominant protagonist in this struggle is the Scientist-Hero, a cliché perfectly designed to act as a complementary double for the tech-savvy auteur seated in the director's chair.

A genre staple of the ecodisaster film, the (pretty much always white male) Scientist-Hero is central to the narrative structure and action of films such as *Twister* (Jan de Bont, 1996), *Titanic* (James Cameron, 2009), and *The Day After Tomorrow* (Roland Emmerich, 2004). In *The Day After Tomorrow*, this role falls to the paleoclimatologist Jack Hall (Dennis Quaid), whose findings about global warming are ignored by politicians until they are illustrated by a series of natural disasters; following superstorms across the globe as an advocate of science, Jack converts from intellectual to action hero in the quest to save his son. In *Titanic*, the Scientist-Hero is more a narrative foil: a deep-sea explorer played by Bill Paxton, whose exploration of the wreckage provokes the story told by an aged Rose—the "Jack and Rose" love story that won global audiences' hearts, which is only a flashback triggered by the underwater explorer's quest for knowledge. In *Twister*, the role falls again to Paxton but also to his romantic interest, played by Helen Hunt; Dr. Bill Harding and Dr. Jo Harding are tornado chasers and climatologists. Although the character stereotype is somewhat split between them, this divide comes along lines of conventional gender stereotypes: she embodies the passion and instinct, he is endowed with the technological genius.

In these films, directed by filmmakers standing in the vanguard of the blockbuster screen spectacle, the Scientist-Hero acts as a substitute for two figures who stand particularly tall, respectively, in textual and extrafilmic mythology: the cowboy and the special-effects wizard. Like the cowboy, the Scientist-Hero exists on the margins of mainstream order, a loner ill equipped for the proprieties of the political sphere and consequently misunderstood and even dismissed by the masses. However, he is also morally superior to the bearers of political power, and his marginalized views on law and behavior are necessary to preserve social stability. Like the Scientist-Hero, the special-effects wizard—who has been a cinematic brand since Georges Méliès brought his magic act to the silver screen in the 1890s—is a self-styled loner believing himself to have a uniquely visionary approach to film art. His craft is honed through a self-appraised scientific curiosity that connects innovations in media technology to scientifically oriented narrative content.

The ecodisaster genre hinges on the ideology of technological salvation in an age of increasing anxiety regarding the impact that human industry is having on the environment. Like the Western myth of the frontier, films in the ecodisaster genre recapitulate "myths of technological modernity, according to which America is defined as a model of modernizing progress."[10] American modernization is arguably the single biggest factor in global pollution and climate change over the past century and a half, and the technology that has driven it—plus the fetishization of this technology—has had a profound impact on Earth's ecosystem. And yet this modernization has also upheld a mythological fascination with science, nature, and technology that parallels cinema's long-building myth of the special-effects auteur as a technological master somehow responsible (as both privilege and cross to bear) for mediating the natural world. In this chapter and the next, I situate this cultural stereotype relative to a larger problem that it addresses: how to visualize or show the invisible.

In his mold-setting reception study of *The Day After Tomorrow*, Anthony Leiserowitz categorizes climate change as "a prototypical example of 'hidden hazards'—risks that, despite their serious consequences for society, generally pass unheeded until they reach disaster proportions."[11] From the chemical runoff of postwar agricultural pesticides to the methane emitted by massive cow ranches to nuclear radiation and global warming, the Anthropocene is rife with seemingly invisible environmental threats or hidden hazards. This invisibleness is a problem for filmmakers not only in terms of visualizing the unseen for movie audiences but also in terms of their own well-being while on film sets. Take, for instance, the ill-conceived John Wayne vehicle *The Conqueror* (Dick Powell, 1956), which ludicrously casts a Fu Manchu–mustachioed Wayne as Genghis Kahn. Made in the Utah desert in 1954 following a year of heavy nuclear testing that continues to haunt nearby towns today, *The Conqueror* came to be known as an "RKO radioactive feature."

The fallout literally and figuratively surrounding the film's cast and crew and the legacy of cancer that stained its proceeding decades were enough to inspire a *People* magazine story in 1980 that was recently revisited. Talking both to survivors of the film shoot and to crusaders for environmental justice in nearby St. George, Utah, the *Guardian* reporter Rory Carroll recounts how during the year preceding the shoot the U.S. Atomic Energy Commission detonated eleven bombs, including several between March and June that coated St. George and other surrounding towns in gray ash (and in the case of the 32-kiloton "Harry," later nicknamed "Dirty Harry," killed thousands of sheep).[12] According to environmental media scholar Justin Owen Rawlins, Snow Canyon, where many of the film's chase sequences were shot, acts as a natural repository for dust blown from Nevada's Yucca Flats via the Escalante Valley, thus preserving huge amounts of radioactive fallout from these tests—and yet it was somehow considered acceptable as the shooting location for a big-budget Hollywood film.[13]

Although the Atomic Energy Commission carpet-bombed the area with propaganda extolling the safety of the tests, the production crew had Geiger counters on location, and they apparently went so berserk that Wayne believed them to be broken. In the decades that followed, Wayne, leading lady Susan Hayward, director Dick Powell, and dozens of other cast and crew would die of cancer. This uncanny coincidence appears to have troubled RKO studio head Howard Hughes well into the twilight of his solitude as he bought up all of the film's prints and reputedly watched them daily. Carroll concludes: "By the time Wayne succumbed to stomach cancer in 1979, *The Conqueror* had been dubbed an RKO Radioactive Picture." As Carroll notes, the *People* article cited Robert Pendleton, director of radiological health at the University of Utah, who claimed that radioactivity from previous blasts probably lodged in Snow Canyon; the *People* article also, states Carroll, "attributed an immortal quote to a scientist from the Pentagon's nuclear defense agency: 'Please, God, don't let us have killed John Wayne.'"[14]

Carroll, Rawlins, and others, including those who survived the film shoot and family members of those who died later, acknowledge that there are many possible contributing factors to these deaths (Wayne, for example, was a four-pack-a-day smoker for decades). Nevertheless, it is a resounding testament to the environmental irony of film culture that a medium based so heavily in visuality came of age during a century that amplified and manufactured anew so many lethal but invisible environmental dangers. Let us turn now to the hidden hazard most prevalent in today's environmental discourse.

The widest-ranging and most geopolitically debated environmental problem, climate change has been a topic of popular media concern since the late 1980s, hitting the cover of *Discover* (1986) and *Time* (1989) some thirty years ago.[15] It grew into a transnational policy concern that prompted the Kyoto Protocol in 1997, which aimed to fight global warming by reducing greenhouse gas concentrations in the atmosphere to "a level that would prevent dangerous anthropogenic interference with the climate system."[16] According to the Kyoto Protocol and following a post-cosmopolitan approach to environmental justice,[17] the responsibility for this reduction falls primarily on developed nations, whose "development" over the past two centuries has resulted in the production of greenhouse gases that have altered the balance of our atmosphere and whose continued industrial emission increasingly endangers the balance of our planetary ecosystems. The original protocol had 144 nations participating; the second round had only 37, most of which came from the 28 member states of the European Union. The United States never ratified the protocol, rejected the second round, and has made clear that it will not ratify any treaty that will commit it to reducing carbon emissions—which makes sense for a political body built from the same ideological foundations and sociocultural contract as its film culture.

The degree to which we can expect legislation to affect our environmental footprint is, reasonably speaking, quite low; governments in the era of global capitalism are too beholden to financial interests in the petroleum industry, and the political system has proven firmly resistant to large-scale change on issues of environmental preservation. However, the political system has also long proven susceptible to public opinion, and public opinion is susceptible to cultural messages, which help to fuel grassroots activism and quotidian changes in attitude and even behavior.[18] Moreover, the ubiquity of image exchange on social media has provided tools for giving visual form to invisible political machinations and has been invaluable for facilitating collective activism. It is imperative to consider just how much influence screen culture has and how it can impact the public's awareness of—and support for—action regarding climate change's various issues, causes, and threats.

In "Hollywood and Climate Change," Stephen Rust offers an excellent survey of climate change cinema, a wide-ranging analysis of how "cinematic texts can and do reflect hegemonic environmental perceptions as well as the ways in which those prevailing hegemonies have shifted over time."[19] The glamorization of car culture, the spectacle of oil fields, and other extensions of our fossil fuel dependency have morphed from romantic icons of modernity into symbols of an increasingly troubling carbon footprint, a transition from spectacle to catastrophe that "underscores the degree to which cinema and its viewership can provide a useful glimpse into the shifting nuances that mark the cultural logic of ecology."[20] A symbiotic shift is occurring on the cusp of widespread environmental awareness: as the American audience develops more knowledge of and concern for global warming, profit margins for films addressing this concern are rising.[21] In the meantime, there is a growing interest in the material impact of film culture.

Charles J. Corbett and Richard P. Turco's report *Southern California Environmental Report Card 2006: Sustainability in the Motion Picture Industry*, commissioned by the Institute of the Environment and Sustainability at the University of California–Los Angeles, offers crucial insight into the ways in which—and the relative degree to which—the film and television industry generates an environmental footprint. Comparing the motion-picture industry with other major industries (aerospace, petroleum refining, apparel, hotels, semiconductor) in the Los Angeles area, the study maps out film culture's relative production of "conventional pollutants,"[22] shown as a function of the industries' profit output and as a parcel of those pollutants produced both locally (relative to both Los Angeles and California) and nationally. The same metrics are also used to show relative energy consumption and, based on fuel consumption, greenhouse gas emissions—all typically invisible aspects of resource use and pollution production.[23]

In all three cases, with the petroleum industry a rampant outlier exceeding all others (while also being of integral necessity to the others' ability to function), the basic breakdown is similar: the motion-picture industry in Los Angeles, where it is most highly centralized, produces nearly equivalent or more pollution and greenhouse gases than any of these other major industries (see figure 3.1). Note: this is only a measure of the impact of the production of screen texts, not of the infrastructure that makes and distributes films or of the hardware on which we watch them (all of which are also heavily tied to the semiconductor industry).

The traditional bar graph shown in figure 3.1 offers a basic but important statistical attempt to do something that film culture does

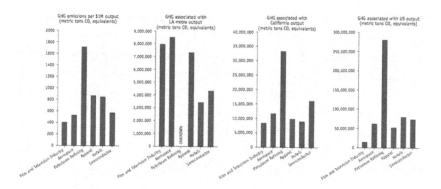

FIGURE 3.1 Greenhouse gas emissions (metric tons, carbon dioxide equivalent, annually) for selected sectors within the geographical areas indicated. *Source*: From Charles J. Corbett and Richard P. Turco, *Southern California Environmental Report Card 2006: Sustainability in the Motion Picture Industry*" (Los Angeles: Institute of the Environment, University of California at Los Angeles, 2006), figure 2, p. 8.

in other ways: *visualize* our environmental impact. And yet, as Corbett and Turco emphasize in this study, so much of the screen industries' footprint is impossible to quantify because it exists in global travel and electricity use (which has risen dramatically with the introduction and rising ubiquity of digital technology, screens, servers, and databases). Data visualization has improved greatly in visual sophistication and complexity of expression since 2006, but even today's most insightful analysts and imaginative artists cannot account for data that are not there.

Environmental crisis is forcing us into a confrontation with the sacredness of visual epistemology that film culture helped to crystallize at the end of the nineteenth century. Seeing is believing, but for the past half-century a wave of environmental studies, from Rachel Carson's work on DDT to recent climate change analysis, has emphasized the environmental and health dangers of the invisible world. As many environmental spokespeople and scientists warn, by the time we can see the effects of global warming on a large enough scale, it will be too late to reverse or even quell them. So how do we visualize the invisible? How do we render sensible that which evades our senses?

VISUALIZING THE WIND

One of the great powers of film is its ability to render the invisible visible: to bring to the surface of the screen the unseen world and to draw our attention to the significance and beauty of things we cannot—or fail to—see in everyday life.[24] This argument, used for more than a century by champions of documentary cinema, is not unique to purveyors of cinematic realism. The camera's keen ability to capture the unseen and the neglected is the driving force behind a diverse range of major film theories, including Jean Epstein's quite formalist notion of *cinégraphie*, Dziga Vertov's poetic-propagandist theory of the kino-eye, and many others.[25] Screen technology thus holds a unique potential to reveal the fine workings of the natural world and is therefore at the forefront of contemporary strategies of environmental study and messaging; however, this is not necessarily a new phenomenon, and to fully understand screen culture's place in today's perceptions of the environment, we must first trace the genealogy of this purpose.

FIGURE 3.2 The multiple-exposure study of movement by Étienne-Jules Marey (*Flight of the Pelican*, 1883) bears testament to the centrality of capturing motion to late nineteenth-century science. Marey's influence on early motion pictures is a crucial example of the role technology and communication played in early moving-image culture's attempts to record the invisible life and movement of the everyday. *Source*: Wikipedia Commons.

In fact, the visual revelation of the invisible and unseen is a central fixture of late-nineteenth-century art (e.g., the experimental painting styles of the impressionists and expressionists) and scientific technology (e.g., the anatomy of motion represented by Étienne-Jules Marey's photographic rifle), both of which greatly influenced the development of moving-image culture (figure 3.2).

It is therefore no coincidence that rendering visible and in focus the invisible aspects and objects of life was a point of particular aesthetic and symbolic fascination for early filmmakers, going back to the proto-realist Lumière brothers. Dating back to their legendary initial screening at the Grand Café in Paris on December 28, 1895, the Lumière canon consistently glorified the apparently inconsequential—or, simply, the unapparent—be it the working-class laborers in *Workers Leaving the Lumière Factory* or the wind-blown leaves in the background of *Feeding the Baby*.

Feeding the Baby is a portrait-style, thirty-second short of Auguste and Marguerite Lumière feeding their baby, Andrée, at an outdoor table. What has caught the eye of many critics since the screening of this short in 1895 is not the representation of the quotidian act of childrearing, but the hypnotizing effect of the tree leaves blowing in the background.

However, as, Kristi McKim points out, although many cinema histories note the captivating movement of the leaves, they fail to acknowledge the significance of "the weatherly motion, the invisibility which the visible leaves reveal."[26] An elemental expressivity is brought out in the moving sound-image, drawing a unique connection between this form and the sensory power of natural forces that are invisible or difficult to visualize— we must adjust our eyes to the unseen weather or elemental phenomena being revealed in these moments.

Wind in particular has long held a special place in the cinematic spectacle, as purely visual affect, narrative device, and symbolic expression for human emotion. Moreover, the filmic capture of it offers great insight and anecdote regarding how natural elements, resources, and ecosystems affect—and are affected by—film-production practices. Let's consider Victor Sjöström's film *The Wind* (1928). Sjöström, Sweden's best-known director during the silent era, was enticed by Louis Mayer to make films in the United States, where he did so under the moniker "Victor Seastrom." The Seastrom catalog includes *The Wind*, one of MGM's last silent films and, starring Lillian Gish, widely considered a masterpiece of late silent cinema. Gish plays the impoverished Letty, who moves out West to live with her cousin on a ranch. Upon her arrival, Letty becomes the object of desire for multiple local men; a point of contention between her cousin, Beverly, and his wife, Cora, whose jealousy over Letty's connection to Beverly and fondness in the eyes of their children leads Cora to exile her; and—in particular—the tortured victim of the howling winds. She tries her luck with one man, Wirt, who is married and wants her as his mistress, then with another, Lige, whom she hates. Wirt eventually returns, and, as often happens with a Gish character in the room, she accidentally shoots him, burying his body outside—a crime inevitably uncovered by the wind and ultimately absolved by the wind, which sweeps the corpse away.

The film is as characteristic of Sjöström's visual artistry as it is of Gish's emotive performance style; Adrian Danks notes that Sjöström "was always his best as a visual poet of natural forces impinging on human drama; in his films, natural forces convey drama and control human destiny."[27] In *The Book of Wind: The Representation of the Invisible*, Alessandro Nova reinforces this argument in a series of phenomenological and personal accounts of impressions left by wind in films, revolving mostly—as we saw with the popular critical narrative of rain in *Singin' in the Rain*—around notions of the natural elements as methods for externalizing character subjectivity, producing mood, and offering symbolic complement to human narratives.[28] Danks also argues, however, in slightly more ecomaterialist terms, that *The Wind* is "one of the few Hollywood films that is truly alive to the elements, to the atmosphere and physicality of place."[29] Shot on location in the Mohave Desert, where the heat could get as high as 120 degrees Fahrenheit, the film makes use of the elemental specificity of that particular ecosystem and is very much about the natural environment as a force upon the human condition.

Predating *Twister* by nearly seventy years, *The Wind* laid the foundation for the later film's elemental symbolism as well as for its method of fabricating climate spectacle: Sjöström used airplane propellers to manufacture the wind, which was made visible mostly through the rustling of human clothing and the whipping of sand. Like so many filmmakers to follow, Sjöström used the dry expansiveness and oppressive heat to force the production into a context of extreme weather experience, adding mechanical effects and human narrative to render the invisible natural forces quite visible (figure 3.3). The wind becomes a

FIGURE 3.3 In the making of Victor Sjöström's film *The Wind* (1928), jet engines were brought to the Mohave Desert to replicate strong desert winds as an extended metaphor for the emotional drama experienced by Letty (Lillian Gish), seen here battling against the elemental forces that haunt her. *Source:* Frame capture by author.

character, one that reflects the humans' emotional plight and at the same time exists well beyond and in spite of that plight: "the film," states Danks, "ultimately presents an environment that both contains and is beyond humanity (other than it can be captured here, perhaps, by a film)."[30]

This is fairly typical of Hollywood's use of wind: it is evoked symbolically as something beyond human control and yet ironically is harnessed and manufactured as something well within the control of the cinematic apparatus and twisted to the whim of our film culture. *Gone with the Wind* is just one of many films to make use of this poetic license—in its case, referring to the ephemeral nature of periods of civilization (the romanticized slave-owning plantation South is eventually "gone with the wind"). Douglas Sirk's film *Written on the Wind* (1956) applies a similar titular lyricism to the fleeting nature of human life. As is typical of Sirkian melodramas, the title also refers to the fate inscribed within social norms, against which the postwar American individual must struggle: class hierarchies, gender conformity, sexual repression— all these things are at once seemingly natural and eternal and yet are actually arbitrary, fragile, and, in the long run, impermanent. Carroll Ballard's film *Wind* (1992), about the America's Cup races of the 1980s, romanticizes the blend of man and nature in the athletic leisure pursuit of sailing. This film is about wind only so much as wind can be harnessed for human activity: the upper-class white man becomes both a part and, in understanding how to capture and use it, master of the element in this patronizing tribute to air currents emblazoned in a dazzling display of ingenuity, brawn, and cable-knit sweaters.

CAPTURING THE INVISIBLE, ENVIRONMENTAL JUSTICE, AND SOCIAL IMPACT

In fact, this understanding and utilization of wind provides a simple nature metaphor for what Richard Dyer calls human "enterprise." In *White*, Dyer uses the term *enterprise* to identify in Western literature, art, and cinema that *certain something else* supposedly possessed by the white American male that sets him apart from both the female and other races. Dyer outlines enterprise as "an aspect of both spirit itself—energy, will, ambition, the ability to think and see things through—and of its effect—discovery, science, business, wealth creation, the building of nations, the organisation of labour (carried out by racially lesser humans)."[31] This systematically racist and masculinist bedrock of American ideology is rooted in Christian mythology and is canonized in Hollywood screen culture by way of the Western,[32] which serves as a template for the ecodisaster genre. I mention this sense of enterprise, or will, here because—in *A River Runs Through It, Wind*, and many other films discussed in this book and beyond—it is embodied in the subjugation of nonhuman nature. Dominion over the environment is seen as the purview of human industriousness, an expression of (often specifically white, male, heterosexual) humans that is interwoven into heteronormative dramatic structures with underpinnings of Christian symbolism and allusion.[33]

This connection between taming the elements and the Protestant work ethic is central to the role played by the visualization of the unseen— enterprise, will, wind, air, god, good—within important structures and debates surrounding identity politics. The environmental justice movement has pushed to make problems of social justice an important component in the environmental movement as the latter rebrands itself for an era of heightened climate consequences and media visibility. However, as we will find, such issues often fall by the wayside in the attempt to dramatize global climate change for a general audience. This problem must return us to the question of visualization, popular methods of what is now called "entertainment education," and the recent ascent of the environmental spectacle.[34] Screen visualization is based on a formal specificity of the visual frame that necessitates aesthetic selections of marginalization and even exclusion and as such is deeply intertwined in the politics of representation that extend from problems of environmental justice.[35] As Shoshana Felman writes regarding the frame as a connotative process of power and exclusion, "It is precisely the imposition of a limit beyond which vision is prohibited which . . . makes possible the illusion of total *mastery* over meaning as a whole, as an unimpaired *totality*."[36]

How do we make perceptible what are in many ways invisible social and environmental problems, and how do such screen practices actually resonate with popular audiences? How does this issue of visualization affect problems of social justice? And what are the material connotations of our screen culture when we peer beyond the surface of narrative meaning and representations of nature?

Following Bill McKibben's book *The End of Nature* (1989),[37] which many see to be the first major attempt to alert a general audience to the dangers of global warming, the 1990s and early 2000s saw a spike in visibility for this issue in popular literature and on screens of various sizes, with a critical and commercial breakthrough coming in the mid-2000s. According to film trends, climate change, it would seem, can be manifested through two types of screen representation: documentary attempts to visualize climate science through forms of data visualization (as in *An Inconvenient Truth*) and the ecodisaster genre's use of CGI effects in order to show large-scale natural disasters as the narrative effect of human behaviors (as in *The Day After Tomorrow*). Though more elaborate than the bar graphs used in Corbett and Turco's report card for southern California, *An Inconvenient Truth* relies nonetheless on typical empirical iconography (bar graphs, animated illustrations, etc.) and stock imagery of polar bears, icecaps, and transport pollution. It allows us to *see* our ecological footprint in the smoke that comes out of exhaust pipes and smokestacks, and we can *see* the historical relationship between pollution and global warming in a series of spiking lines and numbers. Ecodisaster films such as *The Day After Tomorrow*, however, use the same basic formal tool (digital film) in a different type of visual register: the special effects of large-scale natural disaster, visualizing climate change through the fictionalized realization of epic consequences.

One might make the logical argument that the documentary images are real, whereas fiction films make use of false images, and yet fiction films articulate very real cultural values and social anxieties. Although their science may be soft or even outright absurd at times, such films are ostensibly working on behalf of the same mission: to educate viewers about the scale of human impact on the environment and to convince them that if action is not taken soon to reduce this impact, the results will be catastrophic. The efficacy of these attempts has been the central question in environmental communication studies and in an emerging focus on what is called "entertainment education." It is a question even taken up as the subject of Daniel Gold and Judith Helfand's documentary *Everything's Cool* (2007), which identifies Hurricane Katrina and the release of *An Inconvenient Truth* as crucial turning points in the public perception of climate change. *Everything's Cool* takes up a common struggle: how to arrive at any sort of consensus regarding the reality of climate change. This problem exists at the intersection of screen rhetoric and public risk perception and is constantly undermined by a conservative political agenda of climate change denial fueled by petroindustry dollars.[38]

The causality between screen messages and social change has long been of interest to social action groups, politicians, and parents—I refer you, among other examples, to the National Legion of Decency's century-long assault on cinema's moral substance and to the video game industry's decades-long struggle to avoid regulation of games' depictions of violence by imposing an internal ratings system—and film has been used as a conveyer of propaganda on all sides of the political spectrum. As a consequence, screen culture increasingly finds itself at the center of public debates on environmental issues such as climate change. What environmental communication expert Alison Anderson refers to as "visual politics" has taken on new force with the proliferation of televisual and Internet media and has proven integral to analyzing ecological issues, proselytizing for action groups, and even defending fossil fuel corporations. Greenpeace Communications has a full in-house studio at its main offices in Amsterdam, and, on the other side, within a month of the *Deepwater Horizon* oil spill in 2010 BP launched its first YouTube channel.[39] As such, the rise in recent commercial climate change box-office hits has stirred a renewed curiosity about how such films actually act as conduits for scientific data and social behavior, a curiosity that inspired two of the leading U.S. environmental communication scholars to pursue seminal studies of the $500 million global box-office success *The Day After Tomorrow.*

Combining reception theory with statistical survey analysis, Anthony Leiserowitz's essay "Before and After *The Day After Tomorrow*: A U.S. Study of Climate Change Risk Perception" and Matthew Nisbet's essay "Evaluating the Impact of *The Day After Tomorrow*" are only two examples of communications studies done on the controversial reception of this film.[40] I say "controversial" because the subject of these studies is another set of studies: a series of public and private surveys done on the reception of the film to gauge its impact on the scientific community and popular audience. *The Day After Tomorrow* is, of course, a fiction film that proposes a wholly exaggerated and improbable "what if" scenario of climate change apocalypse. However, as many scientists, such as

Oregon climatologist George Taylor, warned, that improbability does not mean that what the film depicts will be understood as inaccurate science: "They took a bunch of pieces of bad science and made a movie out of them. A lot of people will see this movie and mistake science fiction for fact," stated Taylor.[41] Taylor may be correct that "Hollywood should not be the source of information on climate science,"[42] but the fact remains that—as future *An Inconvenient Truth* producer Laurie David said to Al Gore at the New York premiere of *The Day After Tomorrow*[43]—popular cinema reaches more ears than scientific lectures. Although we may lament their necessity in this role, rhetorical documentaries, blockbuster films, YouTube and other viral digital platforms, and satirical television news shows such as *The Daily Show* (1996–) and *Last Week Tonight with John Oliver* (2014–) have a significant platform through which they can raise awareness for important issues.

As both Nisbett and Leiserowitz argue, the popularity of *The Day After Tomorrow* had a very real impact on the discursive place of climate change in media and the popular imagination. Media attention to climate change issues and stories increased 32 percent over its previous twelve-month average, and risk perception of climate change was heightened by the film, with watchers more likely to be concerned about the hazardous effects of global warming.[44] Moreover, those who viewed the film were more likely to alter their behaviors according to this new awareness (such as through purchasing a more fuel-efficient car), to discuss with friends and family ways to reduce global warming, to join or donate money to a global-warming group, and to express concerns to politicians or to vote according to this sensibility.[45] However, whether such claims made during a survey are followed by action is not assessed, and Leiserowitz acknowledges that, relative to the national population and even compared to the total viewers of the film (which was in the hundreds of millions), his study's sample size is insubstantial.

Nonetheless, we can conclude that if film culture doesn't alter the way people act at large, it does serve as a conduit for the discursive prevalence of environmental issues and for voices across the political spectrum. However, to attribute too much saving grace to the magic of movies is a slippery slope, one that Hollywood has lubricated for many decades. Screen culture grew not only out of the romanticism of movement and the brilliance of light but also out of the desire to capture time and to understand physics. David O. Selznick and Gene Kelly's versions of the Great Showman and the Noble Performer were rooted in the affective and poetic artistry of the apparatus, testaments to the innovative grandeur and expressive potential of moving-image arts—a grandeur and potential tied directly to Marey's photographic rifle and similar nineteenth-century experiments in scientific imagery. Cinematic showmanship has long been tied to a certain obsession with how screen technology can reveal the natural world, simultaneously conveying some brand of scientific knowledge *and* employing the elements as entertainment. In what remains of this chapter and in the next, I look at mirroring myths of the Scientist-Hero and the Visionary Explorer to tease out their centrality to the textual logic and the extratextual mythologies of films that embrace digital effects in order to narrate social anxieties and to visualize the environmental dangers that may await us in this era of accelerated climate change.

TWISTER

The second-highest-grossing film of 1996 (trailing only *Independence Day* [Roland Emmerich]), *Twister,* directed by Jan de Bont, was marketed according to a humble brag increasingly common in Hollywood: that the filmmakers' technological ambition prevented their ability to stay within an already outrageously immodest budget. Moreover, as we saw with *Gone with the Wind* and will find with *Avatar,* in the making and marketing of *Twister* there was a mirroring process whereby the regime of spectacle was directly connected to an authorial ego whose methods stirred up instant industry legend. De Bont was notoriously difficult to work with, his heated interactions compelling the original photographic crew to abandon the production five weeks into the shoot.[46] Conversely, though, the general marketing of the film fell on an analogy between the Scientist-Hero of the text and the tech-obsessed hero of the production, the director. Much of that romanticized branding is tied directly to new digital filmmaking practices and their ability to deflect our attention from the impact of the elements on set to the controlled representation of elements on screen. This new hero—auteur combination forms the narrative and industrial lynchpin of the ecodisaster genre.

A film rife with references to Hollywood's history of spectacular natural disaster, from Victor Fleming's *The Wizard of Oz* (1939) to James Cameron's *The Abyss* (1989), *Twister* self-consciously aligns itself as the standard-bearer of windswept fantasy and the emerging realm of digital effects.[47] As such, it positions itself at the helm of a genre renaissance that is cycling back to meet the demands of current environmental anxiety and to exploit the fruits on offer from new branches of CGI technology. The ecodisaster genre connects deeply to our collective cultural fascination with space, land, and encapsulation—the manner in which we have carved the planet up, defined what is human and what is environment, and determined ownership of the commons.[48] In terms of previous genres, the ecodisaster renews our fascination with the frontier, a narrative motif in which the elemental force is "presented as both lethal danger and potential source of redemption."[49] This type of dualism or dichotomy—reflecting the complicated relationship between human culture and natural environment—expresses a very real set of anxieties, but in the coding procedure of screen mythology it does so according to a fictional and formulaic narrative that provides artificial resolution where none exists in reality.

This myth construction extends to all parameters of the ecodisaster film life: the formulae of its inception and development, the aesthetics and methods of its production, and the various levels of marketing and self-branding. Even criticism of this genre tends to reaffirm the rhetorical paradigm regarding the inherent dangers of environmental decay while at the same time holding the human causes of this problem to be its only solution. In particular, this paradigm refers to the film's use of the generic convention of the Scientist-Hero. One could argue that this era of accelerated climate change has seen a rehabilitation of the scientific figure on the silver screen. In his popular science monograph on *Twister*, Keay Davidson (an award-winning popular science writer who has published in *National Geographic*, among other venues) argues that "Hollywood has a long history of portraying scientists as monsters or madmen" and concludes that *Twister* plays an important role in countering these negative stereotypes.[50] This reversal is common to the ecodisaster film, which coincides with a rising public awareness of global warming and its perilous dangers. Just as in the climate change debate, America's strong tradition of anti-intellectualism is being challenged by the celebrity status of popular scientists and the undeniably visible increase in extreme weather events and natural disasters affecting the world. We may not like what climate science is telling us, but this field is suddenly cool. As is implied in films such as *Twister* and *The Day After Tomorrow*, climatologists are the closest thing we have to a front line of defense against the menace of environmental catastrophe. However, this mode of narrative formulation is wrought with internal conflict and complexity and returns us to the unfortunately antagonistic relationship between humanity and nonhuman nature.

Twister follows the resurgent romance of Bill Harding (Bill Paxton) and his estranged wife, Dr. Jo Harding (Helen Hunt), a storm-chasing couple who have been developing "Dorothy," a new technological apparatus to set inside the eye of a tornado in order to study tornado patterns and to provide a sophisticated storm-warning system. The plot kicks off when Bill, who has moved on to the more moderate and upstanding profession of weather reporting, arrives in Oklahoma with his new love interest, Melissa (Jami Gertz), to get Jo's signature to finalize their divorce. Upon arrival, Bill discovers that Jo has built four identical Dorothy devices based on Bill's designs; however (*dun dun dunnnnnhhhh*), there is also a smug, corporate-sponsored scientist, Dr. Jonas Miller (Cary Elwes), who built his own high-tech device with aims of beating the Hardings to the punch. Bill vows to stay long enough to get a Dorothy into a twister; he and Melissa join Jo's storm-chasing crew; in constant competition with Jonas's team, they insert themselves into a series of storms with escalating peril and eventually manage to get Dorothy IV successfully up in the air; Melissa decides this life isn't for her; Bill and Jo reconcile romantically and decide to run their own storm-warning lab.

Although it is worth noting that in a genre highly given over to the gender politics of patriarchal Hollywood, *Twister* is admirable for raising the female romantic interest to the level of coprotagonist, this depiction, too, is problematic. Echoing reviews at the time, Davidson argues of Jo's character: "Hunt plays the most dynamic female scientist on film in a long time, perhaps ever." Though there are no points of comparison given (Ripley [Sigourney Weaver] in the Alien series, another franchise pitting humanity against the predatory unknown of nature, comes immediately to mind), Davidson asserts further: "For years, teachers and education experts have complained that it's hard to persuade young girls to pursue scientific careers partly because they see so few role models on TV and in films."[51] Though this argument is unsubstantiated, it is certainly true that Hollywood owes its audiences a backlog of strong and intelligent female professionals, and in terms of education entertainment this is a noble goal. Yet it is done in *Twister* with particular caveats that underline the film, the genre, and the industry's technofetishization. Although Jo is given more backstory than Bill (she is even granted the mentally subjective representation of a flashback, which shows us the tornado that killed her father, traumatized her, and inspired her life's work), *he* is ultimately the film's hero both of action and of knowledge. And it is *his* scientific savvy and especially his technological vision that achieve the epistemological taming of the elements.

This brand of hero is further complicated by the legend surrounding the protagonists' profession, one that is emblematic of a Plains approach to citizen-science, gonzo meteorology that made Paxton's portrayal iconic—so much so that upon his death in 2017 storm chasers amassed in Tornado Alley and registered a collective geographical positioning system (GPS) coordinate memorial tribute that went viral on social media (figure 3.4). In his article for *American Cinematographer* upon the film's release, David Wiener celebrates "storm chasers" as real-life action heroes, "more like Indiana Jones than weathermen." Harking back to the first storm chaser, the Englishman Dorman Newman, Wiener holds these popular scientists up as models for a sort of crowd-sourced ecology and even goes so far as to assert that "*Twister* aspires to give viewers both visceral thrills and some insights into these adventuresome souls."[52] Note that the film's goal was not to educate about scientific phenomena or to appreciate the agency of nature, but to use nature as a pretext for the crafting of a human (white American male) hero.

The environmentalist group Tapestry Institute (motto: "Reweaving the fabric of the human–nature relationship") critiques the film for its "mythic" confusion as to the role of such people in real life and its casting of the storm as a villain. "Storm spotters," as opposed to "storm chasers," are the "lay people . . . called to action when a tornado watch is issued." The site continues: "The mistaken confusion between storm chaser and storm spotter has permitted the production company to depict the film's main characters as heroes, specifically as heroic

FIGURE 3.4 Reflecting the popularity of *Twister*, Oklahoma stormchasers, coordinated by Spotter Network, provided a GPS tribute in the days following Bill Paxton's death in 2017, using new online modes of participatory digital visualization to express their collective grief. *Source*: Photograph courtesy of Spotter Network.

scientists protecting the public from dangerous tornadoes. That is not an error or an accident, either one." The site rightly identifies a cultural paradigm that asserts the scientist as hero, which implicitly and, in almost every case, explicitly casts nature as villain: "The paradigm of 'Scientist as Hero' can be expressed as mythic story very easily: a hero (who is a scientist) selflessly risks life and limb to defend others from a villain (disease, natural disaster, other organism) by using scientific knowledge and technology. In the movie 'Twister,' the scientists are in fact the heroes of the story, and tornadoes are cast in the role of villain, symbolizing nature as an enemy from which humans need to be defended by science."[53]

Such portrayals are *not* accidents but compose the dual formula of a generic trope, projecting the dramatic hero/villain structure onto the human/nature binary, which has profound connotations for how we culturally position humanity in relation to nonhuman nature. Though scholars are correct to point out that Bill and Jo's commercially funded and ethically corrupt antagonist "is alienated from redemption because of his over-reliance on technology," the film's protagonists are battling against the elements, not against him.[54] In fact, this interpretation of *Twister's* representation of technology gives into the film's most superficial ploy, a hypocrisy that Hollywood has made foundational over the decades. This ploy is one that works on the surface of the text to justify the functioning of the apparatus beneath the text, reifying technology while applying token skepticism to its dangers. Such a double standard is particularly poignant and ironic in a film, a genre, and an era so dependent on the use of—and so adamant about showcasing—new innovations in digital-effects technology.

Nonhuman nature is the villain, of course. Despina Kakoudaki describes this dramatic structure as typical of "films that revolve around natural disaster events, such as hurricanes and volcanoes, entities that have no ethics or motives and whose actions in the narrative are extreme but nonnegotiable," through which the struggle against nature necessitates the innovation of technology and, as by-product, justifies the fetishization of science and control. "In films such as *Volcano*, *Twister*, and *Dante's Peak*, the mysterious and uncontrollable workings of nature allow for the emergence of a seemingly benign state mechanism, which comes to the rescue through engaging solutions offered by science/technology along with humanistic values of courage and self-sacrifice."[55] To secrete the justification for technological control of the elements, the elements must be portrayed not only as dangerous but also as narratively and ethically in the wrong. Reviews and records of *Twister's* release focus on the filmmakers' goal "to give the tornado in their film a living malevolence," which is capitalized by de Bont's and Jack Green's frequent anthropomorphic comments about needing to direct and visualize the twister as having a villainous personality.[56]

The cognitive dissonance that runs like an ideological spine through the material practice and articulated values of this genre props up the Scientist-Hero as a mythic double for the special-effects auteur. This doubling is manifested in de Bont's repeated mention in interviews of his fascination with the destructive side of nature and his passion for new CGI abilities—*Twister* is where the two meet. Wiener quotes: "'I've always been enormously intrigued by rough weather,' Jan de Bont says. 'Lightning, hurricanes and tornadoes are the most powerful things that happen on this world. And tornadoes are so random in their destruction. They're also incredible to look at, beautiful and devastating at the same time—like in *The Wizard of Oz*. When you look at that tornado, you get mesmerized by it. When I first saw it, I thought it was real.'"[57]

These remarks require—and invite—some unpacking. First, there is the aesthetic and affective realization that extreme weather and elemental instability carry a high spectacle value, one that is further accentuated by their randomness. Because they are a product not of rationality but of chance, to capture their sublime beauty is not only to reproduce their lights and sounds and speed but also to manage to tame—and in taming to represent—their chaotic unpredictability. Second, there is de Bont's cinephilic literacy, seen in the citation of *The Wizard of Oz*, a film still today viewed as technologically precocious for its visual effects. The tornado that whisks Dorothy to Oz "mesmerizes"; it sweeps the viewers away, along with Dorothy, to that place over the rainbow, offering us the same disconnect from reality that she seeks from her Depression-era Kansas farm. And yet, third, there is the importance that the tornado seem *real*. The audiovisual verisimilitude must counterbalance the fantastical basis of the fiction with a sensory realism that is achieved through mastery of—and erasure of any trace of—the cinematographic apparatus. Much like the discourse surrounding *Twister*, de Bont's admiration for his film's CGI rendering of a sublime natural event hinges on its degree of photorealism, a connotation of digital screen style that revolves around not a reproduction of reality but a crystallization of the *illusion* of the real.

From these cursory points about how *Twister* positions and identifies nonhuman nature in narrative terms through connotations of stylistic photorealism and according to material practice, it is telling that the film's tagline upon release was "The Dark Side of Nature" (figure 3.5).[58]

MATERIAL IMPRINT OF A DIGITAL STORM

Twister, unlike *The Wizard of Oz*, does not frame its spectacle in terms of a fantastical wonderland but instead as a stark and perilous reality rendered possible by a different wonderland: the CGI wonderland of

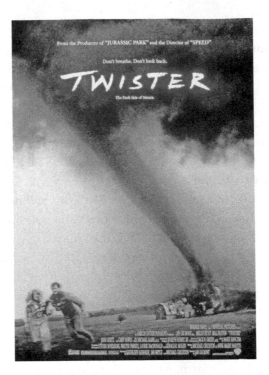

FIGURE 3.5 Referencing recent Hollywood blockbusters to contextualize itself as a CGI-effects action film, *Twister*'s (Jan de Bont, 1996) original poster features the tagline "The Dark Side of Nature"—confirming that nature is the film's villain, human beings its heroes and victims. *Source*: Entertainment Pictures (Alamy stock photo).

postproduction. De Bont remarked regarding the emergence of digital editing technologies, "A lot of people are very worried about all these new technologies. But I think it's an *incredible* tool. The possibilities you have to 'paint' an image right now are *so* enhanced. In the past, the footage was totally dependent on what the [filming] situation was like. You didn't have *time* to wait until the weather was right, until it starts raining or hailing. *We* can create rain or hail whenever we want!"[59] This comment speaks volumes to the way CGI effects not only have lent filmmakers a newly updated version of Alexandre Astruc's notion of the *camera-pen*[60] but have aided in their ongoing quest to resist the logistical impediments of nature. Let us now look at this film's formal and material praxis because it offers such an important historical bridge over the rainbow from the analog era to the digital era.

In the introduction to his book on *Twister*, Davidson makes important connections among the ecodisaster genre, the problem of stylistic realism, and cinema's greatly paradoxical responsibilities with respect to education and entertainment: "Every filmmaker who portrays a natural disaster . . . faces the same basic questions: How can this natural phenomenon, so alien to the ordinary filmgoer's experience, be rendered realistically on the screen? How can the realistic look be balanced with the audience's expectations? . . . In short, how can the silver screen do justice to the marvels of nature and, thereby, covertly educate moviegoers while overtly entertaining them?"[61] The answer to this question seemingly lay in the recent advent of computer-generated imagery.

Toyed with in the late 1970s and 1980s, CGI had its major breakout in Steven Spielberg's film *Jurassic Park* (1993), the success of which directly affected the development and production of *Twister*. Spielberg, who would receive a credit as executive producer of the latter film, ran *Twister*'s concept by the special-effects team at Industrial Light & Magic (ILM), the company started by George Lucas for creating the visual world of *Star Wars* and the effects haven that hatched the digitized dinosaurs of *Jurassic Park*. Doing what was essentially a digital test run, the ILM experts produced a simulated sample of what would be done for the majority of *Twister*, a process of live-action, analog-effect-driven filming, tightly orchestrated into a composition of preplanned digital postproduction work. *Twister*'s technological and commercial success would ultimately trailblaze the blockbuster digital era, leaving a winding path of adulation and technomanagerial romanticization. Indeed, following his questions, Davidson launches into a reification of the authenticity and potential of CGI, concluding that "any filmgoer can now undergo that unparalleled experience, thanks to the recent marriage of high-speed computers and Hollywood filmmakers."[62]

However, to understand *Twister* only as a digital film would be a horrible oversight. Although the advance planning of CGI effects should presumably have made the analog shoot less taxing, this was not the case at all—in fact, the production was heavily laden with logistical difficulties and left a trail of material excess. Having started location filming in Oklahoma in April 1995, at the height of the rainy season, the shoot encountered weather issues in its first week. These obstacles, coupled with de Bont's somewhat acerbic treatment of the crew, led to a turnover in the cinematographic team and the arrival of Jack Green, the production designer who would helm the film's visual crafting, which began with the clairvoyant use of a "'very fine-grain film' to make it easy for digital effects artists to add realistic-looking computerized images of tornadoes."[63] ILM specialists were on set to make sure that the exposed footage would match the director's planned CGI, which led to an excessive shooting ratio, the degree of which was even touted, according to the predominant Hollywood discourse of excess, as triumphant. Moreover, as Wiener notes, the shoot was done completely "wild," with no lock-down shots or preplanned camera movements,[64] which seems ironic and even self-contradictory given the orchestrated nature of CGI planning.

This is a running theme of the film's publicly glamorized shooting process, the digital aspect of which—far from working with a magical computer-generated paintbrush—necessitated further material analog-production excesses. Green was forced to adapt the predicted aesthetic palette and tonal changes, produced through the processing necessary during ILM's digital editing phase, to the unpredictable vicissitudes of Oklahoma weather, and the film's lighting proved particularly problematic. The lighting required of storm scenes led Green to pour light on the performers during extensive day exterior shoots.[65] In other words, the film was being shot on location, outdoors in Oklahoma, using natural light; but because the filmmakers wanted an artificial version of the real, they had to crank up electric lamps that could reduce the actual exposure of the human characters while making the skies look dark and stormy. Paxton recounted that the electric lamps "literally sunburned our eyeballs": both Paxton and Hunt were left temporarily blind by the artificial lighting and had to wear dark glasses and use eye drops for several days until they recovered.[66] In order to simulate one natural setting by shooting in another natural setting, energy-dependent artificial lighting was wired in—not only is this extra lighting *not* an example of digital filmmaking, but it was so intensive that *it actually burned the eyes of the film's stars.*

This was not the only ironic ecological and existential aspect of the film's on-location shoot; the comprehensive contradiction extended to the demolition of original locales in order to give the impression of real destruction. John Frazier, who was in charge of the film's special effects, was also in charge of the location set. Along with production designer Joe Nemec, Frazier supervised bulldozer crews that tore down a two-block section of an Oklahoma town. Steven Spielberg's company Amblin Entertainment, which produced the film, bought up homes and buildings in the area and then destroyed them to portray the aftermath of a tornado.[67] In a film that marketed its development and production in terms of the new era of digital painting, real buildings had to be purchased in order to be destroyed—all in order to bring to the screen the horrible menace of nature. The digital era has not protected the real from its place of honor on the altar of popular screen spectacle but has merely allowed us to fan the flames of this effigy.

In terms of actually producing the storms, the production was extremely resource intensive, industrious in its thinking but not exactly environmental. As Green recounts, "We put live rain or live hail on the actors, and later mixed in some CGI hail. We had tons of ice-chippers mounted on trucks to do traveling hail shots. There were also huge jet engines mounted on truck-trailers providing high-velocity wind to blow trees over and flatten stalks of corn."[68] The filmmakers moved seven ice trucks down to Oklahoma from Milwaukee; then crew members shoved four-hundred-pound ice blocks into a chipping machine and sprayed it over the cast to simulate a hailstorm. One forty-eight-foot flatbed truck was mounted with a 707 jet engine, which the crew aimed at the actors. Crew members also threw branches and other objects into the jet's winds to simulate hurtling tornado debris.[69] Lugging ice from Wisconsin to Oklahoma and using an absurdly massive truck to carry a jet engine: this does not sound like a digital paintbrush.

Another testament to the film's excess was its shooting ratio. As Green recounts with a noticeable hint of braggadocio regarding the storm sequence in which large farm buildings are wiped out, "We ran 13 cameras! On a shot in which a gasoline truck explodes we had between 11 and 13 cameras, including Eyemos and high-speed cameras. . . . Even if we were just doing a scene with two people talking, we still had five cameras running because of all the live special effects."[70] (I emphasize that he specifies "live special effects," not "digital effects added in post-production.") Weiner estimates that the photography crew, using that many cameras, was cranking out between ten thousand and twenty thousand feet of footage each day, which were then indiscriminately printed, as opposed to the more conventional practice of printing only what might be usable takes as gleaned from video review. As Green recalls, "We printed just about everything . . . which made dailies two or three hours long! I'd spotcheck every day, but it was just too tedious to spend all that time viewing everything."[71] They used so much film and ran so many cameras that they could not even be bothered to properly review the footage.

Similarly, in the "location" scenes (I use quotation marks because the film crew tore down the actual on-location buildings and constructed set pieces in their place), wind machines were ubiquitous. Again, Green sounds a bit proud of the excess, all in the pursuit of ecodisaster realism: "I don't know if there was a wind machine left in Hollywood. . . . We had six gasoline-driven wind machines, three or four electric wind machines, and those two huge jet engines mounted on flatbeds. It was just incredible, trying to imitate what those storms do."[72]

Gasoline, electricity, ice, jet engines . . . it is remarkable that, just as we found in *Singin' in the Rain*, the very language used in this production culture is perfectly aware of the natural resources involved and seems to scoff at the resource use necessary to mimic the same nature from which this power is derived. The most complex shot of the film involved a nonexistent (or waiting to be CGI'd) twister lifting a tractor trailer into the sky and dropping it in a fiery explosion on the highway. For the analog base of this scene, the effects crew lifted the truck with a crane; then two stunt people (standing in for Paxton and Hunt) drove a pickup truck toward the crane, where the tractor trailer, wired with explosives, hung suspended seventy-five feet in the air.

Davidson finishes this description in prose quite typical for the glorification of Hollywood spectacle, reminiscent of accounts of the burning of Atlanta in *Gone with the Wind* nearly sixty years earlier: "At a precisely specified moment, Frazier pressed a button to release the tractor-trailer. If his calculations were right, the tractor-trailer would hit the ground about 50 feet in front of the approaching stunt crew. A moment's miscalculation could kill two people. The blast came off without a hitch. That one shot cost at least $100,000" (figure 3.6).[73] Cranes, cars, explosions—all material costs for a celluloid-turned-digital scene still waiting for the complex algorithm that would spit out an image resembling a tornado.

FIGURE 3.6 *Twister*'s $100,000 shot used mostly analog film and materials, including a tractor trailer suspended by a crane and loaded with explosives, seen plummeting here in front of the pickup occupied by stunt doubles for Bill Paxton and Helen Hunt—followed, inevitably, by a spectacular explosion shot from multiple angles and produced through a combination of analog explosives and CGI cosmetics. *Source*: Frame capture by author.

Like the films I discuss in the next chapter, the cinematography and editing of *Twister*, combined with the postproduction CGI enhancement, is very much geared toward striking a balance between entertainment spectacle and stylistic realism. The film's formal strategies, moving from the exhilarating freedom of aerial helicopter shots and upbeat music to the tightly framed action sequences of the storms, interlace unsteady camera work with rapid pans and cuts to simulate the phenomenological chaos of the twister experience.[74] By placing us in the action, we are led to empathize with the humans struggling against nonhuman nature and are thus distracted from the technological and environmental materiality of the screen experience.[75]

Davidson argues that much of the film's visual realism is contingent upon what audiences are used to and expect, which comes from the proliferation of the documentation of disasters consequent of the rising accessibility of the tools of home video: "Since the early 1980s, many Americans have seen close-up videotapes of real tornadoes on TV.... [N]owadays, bouncing camera motion (the hand-held camera look) is a staple of action films; audiences *expect* it."[76] In other words, it is not the natural phenomenon that is being reproduced by *Twister*, but the post-cinematic experience of watching it on television or video. Our remove from being directly present in nature has grown by yet another entire step. As media theorist Lev Manovich has argued, digital imagery has boosted our reliance on simulation in that its authenticity is predicated not on a mimetic resemblance of the real but on a resemblance of our filmic and televisual representations of the real.[77] Analog and video are the new degree zero, and digital screen culture is merely trying to reproduce *them*. Ironically, a bit of the realism was produced through actual live-action footage; unlike viewers who would watch the tornadoes on a screen, the Oklahoma crew did in fact stumble upon twister-like storms. "There was a second unit filming as much of the real thing as possible," de Bont noted to Wiener, "but they had to keep their distance."[78] After all, *they* didn't have stunt doubles.

Though *Twister* was shot on actual film and required great material costs, the film's publicity and marketing during the shoot, the discourse surrounding it, and its place in Hollywood history are anchored in the transition from analog to digital filmmaking. It was editor Michael Kahn's first experience with nonlinear editing, in which the film is totally processed into a computer and edited digitally instead of manually working with the celluloid, adding him to a growing passenger list of maiden voyages on the S.S. *Digital*. As in many films of the past twenty years, or what we can now begin to refer to as the "digital era" of cinema, the boundless potential of CGI is being used specifically to articulate a certain environmental anxiety. Although so much of the film's discourse revolves around elemental realism—one of the film's producers, Kathleen Kennedy, claimed that "we're having to duplicate nature"[79]—it must be reiterated that from the narrative structure to the use of growling sounds in the sound mix, the film expresses an important Western paradigm that lies in the hidden depths of anthropocentric ideology: nature is a separate and dangerous thing from which humans need to be protected.[80] Moreover, this very Otherness of nature makes it our challenge to tame and our object to use: the material excess of *Twister*'s production process was justified in advance by the generic connotations of the Scientist-Hero, whose heroism comes not from protecting nature but from understanding and harnessing it.

In addition to its trailblazing use of CGI effects to buttress mainstream American screen culture's apprehension toward nonhuman nature, *Twister* was also integral to the advent of digital distribution techniques. Not only did it help to lead the transition to digitized editing, but on March 25, 1997, it became the first cinematic release on digital versatile disc (DVD); and, in a bizarre twist, some years later *Twister* was also the last film to be released in HD-DVD format before HD-DVD lost the high-definition packaging war against Blu-Ray.[81] This somewhat comically improbable detail highlights *Twister*'s connection to the environmental ramifications of digital practices that extend well beyond the production phase. As much as the green discourse surrounding the digital revolution centers on its intangibility and virtuality, it is necessary to take into consideration issues of packaging and waste as well as the energy consumption required for digital production, distribution, and maintenance. In what now reads like an endearing naivety, Davidson remarks in 1996 on the storage necessary for *Twister*: "To generate such images requires gigabytes—billions of bytes—of computer disk space, as much as one can store in dozens of small personal computers."[82] Gigabytes have given way to terabytes, but we—in many ways beholden to myths of technological salvation and the benevolent genius of film artistry—still harbor a similar sort of fascination for the grandeur of this new magic, choosing to remain blind to the new dynamics of environmental impact generated by the digital turn.

CHAPTER FOUR

Apocalypse Tomorrow

The Myth of Earth's End in the Digital Era

The previous chapters have been building historically, conceptually, and rhetorically toward a climactic crest, a wave breaking upon the shore of the twenty-first century's paradigmatic connections—and contradictions—between the digital revolution and the green revolution. At the very moment when we most need to be accountable and conscientious of the environmentally tangible, to be aware of the materiality of our cultural practice, digital technology pulls us ever farther into the ideological ether of the virtual. We increasingly exist "on the cloud," shelving our thoughts, memories, art, and records (musical, historical, and personal) in a web of virtual archives that is immediately accessible but simultaneously has the illusion of intangibility. In this chapter, I implicate the emerging green discourse of digital Hollywood in the paradoxical paradigm whereby our culture of connectivity and immediacy has promoted a reliance on server farms and similar technologies that are at once seemingly virtual and remote but in actuality are very much real and material and hold our information at the cost of vast natural-resource use and environmental disruption.[1]

Through an ecomaterialist production culture study of *Avatar* (James Cameron, 2009), I argue that this paradox holds true for the various ways in which our screen practices have transitioned from analog to digital, from celluloid film and tube televisions to binary code and online streaming. Far from a green revolution, the environmental focus of the ecodisaster film has distracted audiences from the very real material impact of digital screen practices. Mythologies—from Old Testament dominion to the Industrial Revolution's narrative of "progress" to the "freedom" guaranteed by American petro-imperialism—have long given abstract justifications for the exploitation of natural and animal resources. We can see similar structures of myth unfolding through both the ecodisaster genre and the public-relations campaign of digital entertainment. In fact, an integral step in the genealogy of this mythological trope is that which American society took in the image-blistered first half of the twentieth century and is encapsulated by the soundstage scene in *Singin' in the Rain*. This is the perfect time to return to that myth and to consider how it has morphed over the six decades that have witnessed the rise of an environmental movement in the United States and the triumph of digital technology in both entertainment industries and daily use.

TEMPORALITY, APOCALYPSE, AND THE VIRTUAL

Let us address this intersection of myths (of anthropocentrism and of digital immateriality) by drawing parallels between the ecodisaster genre's projection of social anxieties onto future worlds and the digital-culture industry's displacement of information and production into an immaterial realm. In order to do so, we must first contextualize the ecodisaster genre within the wider social function of science fiction.

Science fiction has long been the realm of the imagined beyond, both temporally and spatially—as well as technologically, biologically, and conceptually. As such, it has presented screen audiences with an opportunity to project present anxieties onto a vision of the future that is shaped by the tension between the basis of these anxieties and the core principles of the world that triggers them. Mary Shelley's novel *Frankenstein* (1818), considered by many to be the genre's urtext, articulates the Romantics' anxieties regarding early modernization and the threat of technofetishization asserted by the Industrial Revolution. *Frankenstein* was not just one person's dystopian fear but acted as a conduit for widespread tensions during that period of social and economic transition. Similarly, H. G. Wells, author of *The Time Machine* (1895) and *The War of the Worlds* (1898), was an outspoken socialist whose novels reflect a strong political fear of rampant capitalism and a widespread pacifist fear in the face of increasing global militarization.

It is not surprising that science fiction grew as a literary genre in relation to the Scientific Revolution and Enlightenment's guiding logics of rationalism and positivism. The genre's ambivalence toward the increasing presence of technology in daily life reverberated with nineteenth-century readers, just as television audiences would later embrace *The Twilight Zone* (1959–1964) and, today, *Black Mirror* (2011–). We should not consider it a coincidence that cinema's first public exhibitions occurred the same year as *The Time Machine* came out: in many ways, cinema emerged technologically to meet the needs of a modern Western subject who, through trains and telegraphs and the proliferation of visual marketing, had experienced a radically altered relationship to space and time. This modern Western subject was also a subject increasingly lured— by visual media, consumerism, and colonialism—to consume the world through the eyes.[2] The wide-scale anxiety about technology's role, expressed in Wells's popular novels, is the reaction of a fragmented human condition unfettered by the shackles of proximity and presence, inevitably at risk of losing all connection to material reality and the present moment.

This disconnection from the present is furthered by the intertemporal nature of cinema, which fossilizes light so that we might view it at a later date, disrupting our chronological connection to the present that is a fundamental stipulation of material awareness. The problematic relationship between time, technology, and humanity would remain central to the science fiction genre, which received new life with the saturated presence of postwar cinema and a network of new social anxieties regarding the fear of atomic warfare and a growing concern over environmental destruction. Nuclear proliferation was met with the proliferation of B-movie industrial units that used new drive-in and suburban multiplex exhibition modes to provide Red Scared audiences with fantastical tales of toxic fallout and assured apocalypse.

Particularly central to the body of scholarship on postwar science fiction film is the relationship between human knowledge, guilt, and temporality, with the grand destruction of World War II framing history as trauma that needs to be narrativized. The way in which cinema of the 1950s took themes of nuclear holocaust out of the historical context in which atomic energy was developed—the ahistoricization of nuclear anxiety—constitutes what Cyndy Hendershot refers to as a "paranoiac response to the cultural trauma" of nuclear destruction, the result of projecting the real into a realm of the symbolic. "Central to this ahistoricisation," she writes, "is the translation of the problem into something universal, mythological—or more appropriately, trauma becomes translated into paranoia. The world of the paranoiac is a delusory one in which historical issues are played out as mythic battles between good and evil."[3]

This paranoid response, which we see happening across the film and literature of what has popularly been dubbed "cli fi" (but which I maintain as the ecodisaster genre), results from two major factors: lack of understanding and lack of accountability. Fredric Jameson has aptly claimed that science fiction attests to capitalistic society's inability to transcend its own ideological limitations—a theme repeated via generic formulation, "over and over again to demonstrate and dramatize our incapacity to imagine the future."[4] This may well explain the genre's reliance on apocalypse, the endgame of science fiction's regurgitation of biblical and religious motifs.[5] Susan Sontag frames this "imagination of disaster" as a problem of "inadequate response," arguing that disaster in science fiction is "a sampling, stripped of sophistication, of the inadequacy of most people's response to the inassimilable terrors that infect their consciousness."[6] This response reflects not only an inability to imagine the future but also the inability to grow conceptually, which results from the inability to properly process the past, which in turn comes from both a lack of understanding and a collective immunity from responsibility.

This incapacity to process and to claim responsibility is an understandable reaction to lack of understanding, which is common among popular interpretations of complex science—a gage of our ability to understand, tame, control nature. As such, science fiction often focuses on scientific discoveries and technological inventions that are at once very difficult for the general public to understand and yet definitive of our relationship to the natural world—such as nuclear physics and the atom bomb. The attempt to represent such sublime and complex topics is necessary not only for understanding but for a sense of accountability and what this accountability says about humanity. Commenting on the accounts given by those who survived Hiroshima, Georges Bataille wrote,

"The atom bomb draws its meaning from its human origin: it is the possibility that the *hands of man* deliberately hang suspended over the future."[7] However, this extreme accountability is one from which Western capitalism and the sociocultural contract that detaches us from the material real distance the individual as much as possible. Personal accountability is replaced by romanticized notions of the scientist and technology despite the fact that similar master narratives of progress produced the very machines of the twentieth-century nightmares played out in science fiction.

SCI-FI CINEMA AND THE NEW ENVIRONMENTAL DYSTOPIA

This combination that defined the social anxiety of the Atomic Age— the dawning of understanding and the subsequent repression of guilt— has been reincarnated in the form of environmental awareness and the paralyzing fear of the human role in climate change and the current mass-extinction crisis. Not only do popular audiences not fully understand the science behind climate change, global warming, fracking, and so on, but this lack of understanding is also coupled with a stubborn refusal to fully assume responsibility for the human role in environmental destruction. Such unpredictability and the anxieties associated with it are central to the current cultural mythologies of climate change's dystopian future and the manner in which the ecodisaster genre resolves these anxieties through cathartic spectacle without necessarily critiquing the institutional causes of climate change. Though often acknowledging that human beings are responsible for ecological disaster, the ecodisaster film typically falls short of fundamentally challenging the mainstream behaviors or modes of living upon which this responsibility hinges.

The primary structural way of deflecting accountability and a genuine call for action is by projecting environmental anxiety into the future—or what E. Ann Kaplan has dubbed "pretraumatic stress syndrome (PreTSS)."[8] Instead of a distant future, though, most science fiction films—such as Stanley Kubrick's film *2001* (1968)—move only slightly into the future because doing so provides a mythological framing that remains connected to the present. Yet *2001* begins millions of years in the past, a prototype for the evolutionary time and relative staggering of timescales common in this genre: the human species has evolved over millions of years, industrial civilization has shaped the Anthropocene over only a couple of centuries, environmental concern has been a popular discourse for only a few decades . . . but the ecodisastrous apocalypse is right around the corner!

Although Kubrick's film has both direct and indirect connections to messages of deep ecology and Atomic Age technological paranoia, it does not directly address environmental problems on this planet. Richard Fleischer's film *Soylent Green*, released only five years later in 1973, does. In many ways a stock conspiracy-theory tale of a government agent who realizes that the government is corrupt (It has been making us eat *people!*), *Soylent Green*'s near future is one in which overpopulation and industrialization have caused a crisis of food and air. The film's opening credit sequence offers a phantasmagoric microcosm of the ecodisaster film: accompanying still photographs with a musical score, the credits begin with quaint sepia images of nineteenth-century rural existence; the music shifts from classical to big-band jazz as the images' content transitions into the Industrial Age. The screen gradually portrays a world more crammed with buildings, cars, people, and industrial pollution, and the editing reflects the accelerated timescale of modernization, picking up speed as the photographs gain color. The march of time gains so much momentum that eventually the screen is not big enough for only one image and, consequently, rapid wipes and split-screen techniques are used, mimicking a modern existence that is overpopulated and cluttered and, with a dizzying rapidity, burying the planet in a pile of cement, metal, automobile exhaust, factory pollution, and moving images. These images that bury the world and overload our sensory perception continue spinning away into virtuality, fooling us—just as the carbon monoxide and methane fool us, just as the invisible inputs of climate change and the invisible toxins seeping into the well water fool us—into believing that they are not real, not part of our material ecosystem. As if the images were not the intersection of naturally sourced fibers, chemical emulsions, fossilized light, and energy being streamed through power lines and exploding out a projector.

This apparently motivated connection between industrial modernization and the image—both its content and its form, with the overly busy mise-en-scène, frenetic cinematography of pans and zooms, and heightened pace of editing—is challenged later in the film. Screen representation becomes not an indicator of humanity's destruction but instead a final bastion of peace, with images of nonhuman natural beauty offered as a palliative drug in the euthanasia chamber through which population growth is controlled. A hallucinatory experience nostalgically echoing the psychedelia of the 1960s, citizens of this concrete jungle are eased into the long good-bye by the sound of pastoral classical music and images of an Earth—flowers in bloom, cascading waterfalls, meadows swaying with tall grass—that has for them disappeared or exists only as image (figures 4.1–4.3).

In many ways, this euthanasia chamber invokes Jean-Louis Baudry's description and psychoanalytic critique of the cinematographic apparatus—with the dying person standing in for the cinematic spectator and, by extension, for the slave of Plato's cave and the dreamer of Freudian regression.[9] Although I will not espouse the wholesale transposition of psychoanalysis to screen analysis, Baudry's central argument is apt: we gravitate to the virtual experience of the moving image because it offers us artificial regression to a state of subjective fluidity in which we can no longer distinguish between perception and representation—a sort of voluntary psychosis in which we confound the image and the actual. Like the slaves of Plato's cave, we, if given the choice, would opt for the comfort of the hallucination, the security of our enclosed world of flickering images.

In step with our sociocultural contract of media and the environment, this psychological regression is part of our cultural alienation of nature, assisting us to accept the substitution between actual and virtual. In other words, participating in this fundamental tenet of screen culture helps to liberate us from the real, from the material, from Earth—it mollifies us with vast euthanasia during this great Holocene extinction, the sixth great extinction this planet has experienced and the one that will be our doing. The irony of this scene in *Soylent Green* is, of course, that once we have paved over the natural world, screen images will become the only way in which we can experience that world. En route to becoming soil and soylent green (human-based food for humans), these future stand-ins for the anxieties of today opt for the virtual experience of a

FIGURES 4.1–4.3 The opening-credit sequence of *Soylent Green* (Richard Fleischer, 1973) uses rapid editing and split-screen cinematography to depict the environmental consequences of industrialization, overpopulation, and fossil-fuel dependency. In their final moments, the citizens of this industrialized world seek solace in images of the nonhuman natural world they have covered with cement (fig. 4.3). *Source*: Frame captures by author.

precinematic natural world, projected fantasies of a planet as it existed before the dawn of the moving image.

In many ways, these dying Romantics are not unlike the corpulent space citizens of Pixar's animated feature *Wall-e* (Andrew Stanton and Alan Barillaro, 2008), whose entire connection to Earth exists through simulations offered by virtual-reality sets. After centuries in the confines of an interstellar technological utopia, the spaceship-bound Americans have gradually evolved into a breed of obese screen junkies, their bone-weakened bodies planted in lounge chairs and plugged into hologrammatic screens that provide their only interactive experience (figure 4.4).

As in many science fiction films of the digital era, in *Wall-E* the virtual has supplanted the real to such an extent that it becomes the preferred register of existence—though this critique is wrapped in an undercurrent of technological fetish, such as in the film's unprecedented use of Apple hardware design as animation prototype.[10] The paradoxical critique/celebration of virtual technology offered in *Wall-e* and, we will find, in *Avatar* is not only present in science fiction narratives but also fundamental to the technofetishization surrounding digital industries and CGI filmmaking. This hypocrisy, in which cultural texts invite us to critique the dangers of the virtual even while anchoring us in the waters of its practice, is central to the updated sociocultural contract of digital screen spectacle.

FIGURE 4.4 As exemplified by this over-the-shoulder shot of a lounging virtual golfer, the future screen junkies of *Wall-e* (Andrew Stanton and Alan Barillaro, 2008) while away their spaceship life using screen technologies to simulate real experiences. *Source*: Frame capture by author.

Not coincidentally named after the term for a person's virtual alter ego, *Avatar* goes so far as to envision the virtual as a site of personal realization and environmental protection, wherein an interactive alter ego can allow one to live out one's deepest fantasies. For some, that means getting the secrets of natural-resource extraction. Set amid the twenty-second-century human colonization of a tropical moon called Pandora, the film's narrative is driven by the human quest to mine the precious unobtanium, a rare substance used in semiconducting. This imperial mining project threatens the ecosystem, traditions, and safety of the Na'vi, a blue-skinned humanoid species indigenous to Pandora. The humans navigate this environmental justice struggle by means of genetically engineered Na'vi bodies (or "avatars") that are controlled mentally by a remotely located human. Paraplegic military veteran Jake Sully is one of these remotely located humans, and his virtual interaction with the Na'vi not only permits him a hallucinogenic use of his legs but leads him to understand and to identify with the Na'vi, to fall in love and couple with a female Na'vi, and eventually to become their de facto leader in the Na'vi resistance against human colonization.

Although this chapter's analysis of *Avatar* focuses more on its production methods, it is crucial to assess the film's allegorical nature and the environmental ramifications of its temporal contortions. The liminal temporality according to which the film functions as myth is complex: (1) a film made in 2009 that reflects social anxieties concerning (2) an environment that has endured billions of years but (3) over only two centuries has been profoundly affected by the human species, to the point of raising (4) risk perception to a level of apocalyptic paranoia of what may happen within fifty years; a film (5) set in a near future that stands as (6) an allegory for the distant past, the recent past, and the present, made possible through (7) a technology whose immediacy and prioritization of the present hides the historical costs of its hardware and the ongoing consequences of its maintenance. By evoking any number of historical geopolitical scenarios, from the European conquest of the New World to the U.S. war in Iraq, *Avatar* touches on a wealth of past injustices, making it both moral lesson and cautionary tale. However, *Avatar*—like most if not all illustrative examples of the genre—folds the past into its narrative only as lingering allegory, one that is in many ways nullified by its unbounded celebration of digital possibility.

The irony of *Avatar* is that it is through Jake's virtual evacuation of the real that he manages to arrive at an ethical mode of living and ultimately then to be reborn as a real member of that alternate setting. In this genre's structures of projection and mythology, the virtual evacuation of the real is usually mirrored by a literal evacuation from Earth: on the train of *Snowpiercer* (Joon-Ho Bong, 2013), the spaceship of *Wall-e*, and the Na'vi paradise on Pandora, the ecodisaster genre offers a variety of visions for alternate living spaces once we have rendered our own planet uninhabitable. This generic trope carries the imprint of nineteenth-century Manifest Destiny ideology and the imperial motivations of the twentieth century's space race, a historical line we can draw from the American settlers' westward expansion to the marketing logic of NASA.[11] From Boeing's "Forever New Frontiers" ads to *Schoolhouse Rock*'s "Elbow Room" (an animated short that traces American expansion, from settling the western frontier to cultivating life on the moon, as a benevolent extension of the innate need to have "a little more elbow room"), popular American screen messaging has echoed the nation's sense of spatial entitlement.

These discourses draw a corollary between the frontier myth, the invasion and displacement of underdeveloped peoples, and the extraction of natural resources, feeding a paranoid anxiety regarding overpopulation and ecological danger. However, as Noël Sturgeon argues, "the danger of this extraterrestrialist environmentalist rhetoric is that it . . . sidesteps an environmental justice analysis of our problems."[12] In other words, our mythology of transplanetary existence, which has recently experienced a renaissance due to heightened awareness of climate change and fear of its impending environmental catastrophe, employs the similar ideological blindness we find in the Western, only in this case projected into the future. The ecodisaster film thus layers a set of timescales that includes the evolutionary time of mineral formation, the industrial time of extraction and consumption, the present time of ecological anxiety and political policy making, and the accelerated arrival of an unpredictable but possibly radical future.

In other words, although this genre often takes us into outer space or onto other planets, it is fundamentally a genre about Earth. And though set in the future, the films of this genre speak of the present, attempting to visualize on the screen's surface our rising anxieties regarding issues of natural-resource use, species extinction, and sea-level rise. As a popular form of mythology, this genre functions by rendering real social problems according to symbolic narrative tropes. Moreover, its technofetishization of the digital, both on screen and in wider marketing discourses, argues for the immateriality of the digital and consequently ignores the material impact of digital practices, projecting their—and our—environmental responsibility elsewhere. But these problems exist now, and digital technology is not some miraculously green network, so let us turn to the ecomaterialist paradoxes of a digital Earth.

THE DIGITAL EARTH

Our planet is not literally digital—and yet over the past two decades we have digitized it. We convert it into the digital in two crucial and simultaneous ways: (1) we carve from it the apparatus of our digital networks, using its precious metals to build hardware and its carbon fuels to power devices, weaving through its surfaces the cables and wires of our distribution systems and then returning the carcasses of our smart technology to its soil; and (2) we track and represent our ecosystems through digital media, from the sonar fish finders that accompany boats to the GPS devices that map our auto routes to the on-location shooting and postproduction computer rendering provided by digital video cameras and nonlinear editing systems. Our daily lives are increasingly woven into a series of digital devices and processes (the ubiquity of which has been dubbed the "Internet of Things") that use online connectivity to link the local and the global and to give us the impression of more efficient control over our lived spaces.[13] Similar computational devices are increasingly being integrated into the environment, with sensors orbiting the planet and planted in the soil, drifting in bodies of water and reading pollution concentrations in the air, collecting data and signaling back to both human and machine receptors for processing. The great paradox of our screen world today: It is digitized, but is it green? As Jennifer Gabrys puts it, computational technologies are becoming part of the environment, but this does not make them environmental*ist*.[14]

Fossils to Photoshop, the digital era is one born of real costs. The transition to the digital has not only produced new myths about the immateriality of screen culture (which is now stored in tiny microchips and beamed from satellites to screens that fit in your palm) but has also generated new flows of resources, labor, objects, and waste. Moreover, the new digital regime has rendered the planet and surrounding atmosphere a wired body, a conduit through which new modes of resource extraction, ecosystem analysis, information dissemination, and waste production are all tied to film and media practices. Any look at the landscape of the new millennium cannot escape the global grid of mediatized and manufactured technology that links our modes of communication, resource use, and everyday behavior. From the subterranean video displays of deepwater oil drills to the in-dash visualization of miles-per-gallon calculation in cars and remote thermostat controls such as Nest and other home-controls systems, smart technology is part and parcel of recent large-scale shifts in ecological exploration, extraction, use, and sustainability.

The materiality of digital screen technology—and, therefore, the material origin of the New Digital World Order of exploitation and environmental injustice—largely begins in precious-metal mines, operated by paramilitary groups and built around child labor, in the Democratic Republic of Congo and other African nations.[15] International scrutiny of issues related to conflict minerals in this area has swayed production toward other nations, including Brazil, China, and Australia, but the majority of tantalum reserves and production remains in Africa.[16] The materials for smart devices must then be transported to sweatshops for assembly. Probably the most notable of these labor farms are set up by Foxconn, a Taiwanese manufacturing contract firm that has factories across the globe and supplies products for major retail companies such as Apple, Hewlett-Packard, Nintendo, Nokia, Sony, and Motorola. A major benefit of being a global multinational corporation is the ability to exploit the different labor regulations and practices, unionization and pay, and import/export tariffs of different countries—exploitation that often results in horrific labor conditions.[17]

Precious metals are not the only resource integral to our digital existence, however, and the introduction of the Internet was met with sound foreboding of its environmental ramifications. From the megaphone of big business to the watchdogs of environmental groups, early reactions were laced with concern over the web's high energy demand. A report produced for the Greening Earth Society in May 1999, *The Internet Begins with Coal*, harkened the environmental toll of the coming virtual era.[18] The very same month *Forbes* magazine, usually not an arena for environmentalist rhetoric, published "Dig More Coal—the PCs Are Coming." Connecting the perilous dots of twenty-first-century e-commerce and twentieth-century energy infrastructure, Peter W. Huber launched this article thus: "SOUTHERN CALIFORNIA EDISON, meet Amazon.com. Somewhere in America, a lump of coal is burned every time a book is ordered on-line." Foreshadowing an age when Moore's Law would be expedited by the casual precedent of faster electronics speeds and larger virtual storage, but the power grid would not evolve at the same pace, Huber noted that "total demand for computational power is outrunning any efficiency gains."[19]

From daily consumer use to massive tech-industry manufacturing and operation demands, the energy toll of a wired society is staggering. Moreover, the incredible potential for storage and the supposed democratization of production and distribution empowered by our new digital tools also plays a key role in the proliferation of packaging and technological waste that is determining the tail end of the digital chain. The past twenty-five years have overflowed with social justice violations due to semiconductor and microprocessor manufacturing in the United States—for example, the proliferation of Super Fund sites from Silicon Valley's rapid development.[20]

The end of this smart-tech life cycle, which is a cradle of its own, is the digital dumping grounds of underdeveloped nations. Freighters of American e-waste deposit their contents in villages of nations such as Kenya and China, where workers—mostly child and female—pick through it, risking exposure to toxic chemicals and carcinogenic gases—a risk that greatly increases as they begin to melt the materials down in order to salvage precious metals.

In less than two decades, this practice has led to heightened levels of cancer and other disease in the vicinity of such dumping grounds, with chemicals seeping into the soil and polluting water sources, leading to birth deformities and other health disasters. Like the geopolitical and social justice connotations of coltan mining and electronics manufacturing, the waste disposal and recycling of digital media technology reeks of imperial globalization, in which wealthy societies can outsource their consumer dirty work to poorer nations, who then are further crippled through the heightened psychological and physical health detriment of unregulated practices.

This brief review of the environmental and social justice issues tied to the proliferation of digital screen technology casts light on some of the hidden social and political impacts of the smart-tech industry. The global machinery that drives our wired world is running constantly in the background of our daily cultural practices and social interactions, and mainstream screen texts are increasingly riddled with hints as to a heightening awareness of these concerns. Yet the predominant approach in Hollywood has been to champion the aesthetic and expressive potential of the digital era, thus simply casting a brighter and more colorful veil over the environmental racism and social justice implications of digital technology.

THERE BUT NOT THERE, OR THE EVACUATION OF THE REAL

The great irony of the ecodisaster genre is that—be it in the great scientist heroism of *The Day After Tomorrow*, the agrarian nationalism of *Interstellar* (Christopher Nolan, 2014), or the simplistic class commentary of *Snowpiercer*—its popularly liberal messaging is only the greenwashed tagline for a series of films at the forefront of a neoliberal digital turn. An ecomaterialist study of this genre pretty much breaks the gauge for ideological cognitive dissonance; nowhere is this more evident than James Cameron's film *Avatar*, whose artificial Na'vi environmental stewards are constructs manufactured by an excessive and wasteful dream factory reliant on industrial practices that specifically *do not* maximize their efficient use of natural resources. Despite its surface critique of the U.S. petroleum-military complex, and regardless of its fetishization of the noble savage and reductionist binary view of nature and technology, *Avatar*, in its self-obsessed mission to fully digitize, has written our sociocultural contract's next phase. This phase will be marked by the grotesque contradiction in which distinctions between the virtual and real, the digital and the material, are contorted to fit particular agendas in the exploitation of the resources and profits that drive the digital pop-culture regime. It is a film whose narrative meaning and extrafilmic discourse, despite their easily identifiable and sympathetic surface messages, are founded on the glorification of the digital revolution, hiding at all costs the profound environmental ramifications and injustices of that revolution.

In fact, the basic fallacy fundamental to the titular concept of the avatar is representative of this contradiction between surface message and material cost. There are a number of possible definitions of the term *avatar*, and my purpose here is not merely a semantic deconstruction. Though the other definitions can be addressed with equal skepticism, I focus on the one most popularly used in the digital vocabulary of virtual reality. In online virtual universes such as that of *Second Life* ("The largest-ever 3D virtual world created entirely by its users"),[21] avatars have provided an ancillary to our material existence. Not unlike the virtual identities millions of people construct for themselves through images and words on social media sites such as Facebook and Twitter, *Second Life* allows us to disappear into icons or figures—characters—of our own manufacturing that represent us in online digital arenas (figure 4.5). However, the "avatar" of *Avatar* is not an avatar at all: it is a drone, a material entity that is operated through a complex remote control. It does not exist in a virtual world, but in the material real, and the film's conflation of this difference is at the core of its neoliberal self-contradictions.

Far less akin to a *Second Life* avatar than to the bearers of destruction during the age of remote warfare, the avatar of *Avatar* is in fact a physical entity, a remote human subjectivity objectivized in the alternate manifestation of an artificial Na'vi (figure 4.7). Like a drone, this avatar is an absent presence—materially there, but whose accountability is elsewhere—and the film's inability to distinguish between drones and avatars echoes our own cultural assumption that online avatars are also not "real," even though they consist of energy and power, transferences of megabytes along a digital grid.

This duplicity of "there but not there" is a wide-reaching legacy of neocolonialism in the digital era, built through the invisible bonds of open markets and global consumerism. There but not there, this new form of digital screen-based hegemony has only been further empowered by the invisible economy of the digital (credit cards, PayPal, Square Cash) and the violence of smart wars (drone strikes, digital surveillance, cyber warfare) (figure 4.6). What we have known traditionally as cinema or film

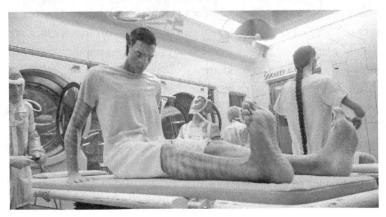

is just part of a genealogy—leading up to the present-day convergence between real and virtual—of a coexistence with screen culture in which we accept the sacrifice of the real on the altar of screen experience.

The different ways in which the digital revolution has enhanced our belief in the ability to flee the real are mirrored in contemporary industrial and cultural attempts to escape Earth. The search for other inhabitable planets (e.g., the Mars Rover missions) as well as the ego wars of maverick billionaires Elon Musk and Richard Branson to make recreational space travel a reality remind us that, as much in terms of scientific curiosity and governmental policy as in terms of general fascination, the quest to evacuate Earth has only risen with the planet's temperature.

As I discussed earlier in this chapter, this extraterrestrial drive is reflected in the generic conventions of the ecodisaster genre. These films are not limited to merely telling narratives of life beyond Earth but are equipped with a technological toolbox that makes the stylized visual creation of such worlds possible. Instead of hoping for or demanding some radical change in our approach to living on this planet, we have decided to flee it, to escape into a sensory world of digital code. Nowhere is this impulse better encapsulated than in the combination of textual and extratextual messages and contradictions of *Avatar*. In "Intergalactic Blues: Fantasy and Ideology in *Avatar*," Max Cafard offers a blistering and blustering summary of the film's paradoxical success:

> Its huge production and promotional cost of nearly $500 million is dwarfed by gross receipts of nearly $3 billion. This exceeds the GNP of at least 77 countries. Let's face it. It's the most important film in

---

FIGURES 4.5–4.7 The *Second Life* home page (fig. 4.5) presents a fully virtual online environment made up of diverse fantastical settings where users can operate digital avatars in order to interact in a fully virtual forum bereft of spatial limitations or temporal fixity. Somewhat on the opposite end of the spectrum in terms of our use of virtual technology, a shot of the war room from *Zero Dark Thirty* (Kathryn Bigelow, 2012) helps to visualize warfare as practiced since Desert Storm, dependent on the computational and representational mediation of digital technology. Far from the avatars of *Second Life*, through which people can live vicariously in an entirely virtual space, the avatars in *Avatar* (James Cameron, 2009) are based on the logic of remote drone warfare: fully material entities being controlled remotely by human operators, affecting a material ecosystem filled with real living beings. *Source*: Frame captures by author.

history. However, this is not because of the money it's raked in. A number of cinematic nullities have pulled in a huge gross. It's not because of its plot, the acting, or the directing. All of these are miserable failures. And it's certainly not because of its supposedly progressive and ecologically enlightened message. That's all a complete fake.

Avatar is the most important film in history in one precise sense. No film has ever revealed in such a spectacular way the functioning of ideology in cinema. Avatar is unsurpassed in the history of cinema in showing the ways in which ideology turns things into their precise opposite.[22]

This notion of the relationship between ideology and contradiction is central to Avatar's multilayered representational and material significance. Summarizing the film's surface political allegory, Cameron noted in interview: "We're telling the story of what happens when a technologically superior culture comes into a place with a technologically inferior indigenous culture and there are resources there that they want. . . . It never ends well."[23] And yet this film—whose cast, crew, and terabytes of digital information crisscrossed the globe many times over, passing between developed and underdeveloped nations and through fiber optic cables; whose polyphony of codes ranges from the organically botanical to the absolutely synthetic, from romanticized first-people primitivism to the cognitive allegories of the digital brain—came out quite well, with a bountiful profit and critically awarded achievement in spectacle to show for the countless material resources it claimed not to use. It had a happy ending, both onscreen and off.

Avatar is at once an attempt at political commentary, a techno-fetishizing exercise in authorial branding and a perfectly synergized manifestation of digital-era spectacle and climate-change-era marketing. A film about interstellar imperialism, wherein the greed of American petro-interests threaten the ecosystem of the resource-rich planet Pandora, Avatar is very much about the war in Iraq. Yet its narrative focus on "unobtanium" as a stand-in for the petroleum of twentieth-century capitalism is secondary to the film's larger message, which is about the cinematic potential of digital technology, of films made on the cloud. However, once again, the coltan mines, the digital dumping grounds, and the energy costs of server cinema get buried in the conversion of the real to the demands of our screen culture. Unobtanium may be a powerful allegorical fuel, but it is one that is obtained only by sacrificing the very world it is meant to be an allegory for.

AVATAR

Visualization has been a central theme in this book, in particular the paradoxes among (1) what we see on screens and the resources and processes *we don't see* yet are necessary to produce that screen spectacle; (2) emerging technological modes of *showing* the seemingly invisible fabric of environmental forces, from data-analysis platforms to televisual coverage of extreme natural occurrences to the special effects that drive the ecodisaster genre; and (3) the role that intangibility and immateriality play in the mythology surrounding the digital as hardware gets smaller and our information grid's production and maintenance get displaced to satellite and underground locations out of our line of vision. It is no surprise that *Avatar*, a film whose production and marketing so heavily relied on the ability of digital effects to visually realize a highly imagined fantasy world, would also weave into its explicit meaning a strong commentary on the importance of *seeing*. The motif of seeing serves as a central virtue for the indigenous and highly ecologically attuned Na'vi and as an ongoing parallel tenet of the film's self-definition as a beacon of Hollywood innovation.

On the narrative level, this motif serves up a rather mildly liberal book-by-its-cover lesson. In one of his many discussions of the film's overt messages, James Cameron recounted: "The film was designed as a journey of perception, as much as a physical journey in an exotic world. A fundamental idea of the film is that it is necessary to look past cultural differences, past form or skin color, to see the truth of other people, to understand them for who and what they are."[24] In his stereotypically reciprocated cynicism and distrust for the human, the Na'vi chief (and Jake's future father-in-law) dismisses the human intruder with the worst insult possible in their culture: "This alien will learn nothing . . . a rock can see more." Conversely, when Jake and Neytiri, the Na'vi princess, finally unite, her great statement of love is, "I see you." Moreover, *Avatar*'s aggressive marketing blitz and oversaturated theatrical release, which had the film opening on more screens than any movie in history and in multiple viewing formats (standard, IMAX, 3D), made it, in terms of public and private space, impossible *not* to see.[25]

And yet the film's production is rooted in an extravagant excess of visual layering and virtual imagery that disposes, to a large degree, of any ontological and perceptual connection we might have with the real, flaunting its surface spectacle while proclaiming its environmental conscience. We do not see people; we see binary-coded representations of human and Na'vi characters. We do not see a tropical planet; we see colors on a screen. We do not see an actual futuristic world; we see the virtual product of decades of dedicated special-effects technology, human labor, natural-resource use, and greenhouse emission. We do not see Pandoran fauna or melting Arctic icecaps—we see energy in the form of digital light. Contrary to its surface narrative and discursive focus on "seeing," *Avatar* is in fact a textbook case of the unseen ramifications of server cinema, a new mold for visual culture in the digital era—a film about the power of light and color to blind.

The culmination of some fifteen years' creative labor, *Avatar* stems from the CGI boom of the 1990s, which was built on the foundational computer engineering developed in academic and industrial research labs such as MIT, Harvard, Bell Labs, the Xerox Palo Alto Research Center, and the University of Utah in the 1960s and 1970s. The technologies developed in these decades made great waves in Hollywood as George Lucas's original *Star Wars* film, *A New Hope* (1977), brought not only computer effects to blockbuster cinema but also Industrial Light and Magic to the Hollywood palette. ILM was instrumental to the evolution of CGI, providing the technical skills and personnel to render the liquid-metal villain of *Terminator* 2 (James Cameron, 1984) and, in a more visually integrated fashion, the dinosaurs of *Jurassic Park* (Stephen Spielberg, 1993) less than a decade later.[26] As movie audiences of 1993 were marveling at the *mise-en-abîme* whereby *Jurassic Park* brought dinosaurs to life in a digital wonderland, Cameron was starting his own digital-effects company, Digital Domain. And by 1995 he had finished a treatment for *Avatar,* aiming to take what were merely effects and reptilian villains in *T2* and *Jurassic Park* and turn them into the entire visual world of a feature film.[27]

But Cameron is also the writer-director-producer who in 1997 unleashed the megahit *Titanic*: like Spielberg and Lucas, Cameron was well aware that effects, no matter how central to a film's making, were still just a vehicle for the human experience. So for this next step forward in computer-generated anthropocentric storytelling, Cameron was not content only to utilize motion-capture technology, in which the actors' real-time movements would produce image swarms of dots to be "solved" by a computer sixty times per second. He wanted, rather, "emotion" capture in order to *empower* (not *replace*) actors and to heighten the ability to convey the human experience. And thus his collaboration with producer Jon Landau would usher the digitally enhanced conventional romantic drama of *Titanic* into what was advertised as a "fully CGI" film, projecting the conventional romantic drama onto the generic mythology of the twenty-first century: the ecodisaster film.[28]

As Jody Duncan documented in an article published in the effects journal *Cineflex* only months after the film's release, "James Cameron described his work on *Avatar* as 'the seduction of reality,' meaning that he wanted to create an experience so detailed and textured that audiences could surrender completely to it."[29] Stephen Prince adds that visual effects always have been a seduction of reality, more so today than ever before, and are predicated not upon an impulse to betray or abandon reality but rather "to beguile it so as to draw close, study and emulate it, and even transcend it."[30] This "seduction of reality," like the sociocultural contract, is very much a paradox by which we tacitly accept the conversion of real resources into a version of the real that does not fully reject the real but "transcends" it.

This substitution of the possibly real for the real, central to screen spectatorship, is buttressed by the combination of familiar and relatable narrative tropes and an engaging visual world that, though set in a fantasyland, is rooted in familiar design, conventional perceptual cues, and easily identifiable emotional reactions. As I enumerate later in this chapter, *Avatar* was successful not because it was radically new but because it teased new topical themes of the Anthropocene and the digital out of deeply familiar content. In describing the visual construction of the Pandoran environment, flora, and fauna, Cameron and his design and production teams worked from the models of existent ecosystems: "Again, the goal was to find the alien within the familiar."[31] The familiar, in today's case, revolves around extreme anxieties regarding the human impact on the natural environment.

Avatar sets up an articulation of this environmental anxiety through both its story and its visual world. As Jody Duncan and Lisa Fitzpatrick observe in *The Making of "Avatar,"* "The Pandoran landscape is meant to communicate a vibrant, pristine, untouched, and fantastical world, one that contains the newly prized unobtanium that humans have come to mine. The Earth views, in stark contrast, depict a world in a state of ruination. Its resources depleted, the air unbreathable, its look is gritty, oppressive, monochromatic, and dark."[32]

Just as we will find that the virtuality of the Pandoran spectacle is the product of a carbon-intensive production process, it is worth noting that, in aesthetics at least, this planetary Other was just as much based on Earth as it was powered by CGI—a process ultimately handed over to the effects wizards at the New Zealand company Weta Digital. Weta's Joe Litteri, mastermind behind Peter Jackson's CGI-heavy works *King Kong* (2005) and *Lord of the Rings* (2001–2003), recounted: "Once we left the human world and went in to the jungle, we were pretty much in a CG environment the whole time."[33] And yet, though much of the film's Pandoran setting is purely digital, it was very much bound to mimetic principles. Special-effects designer Robert Stromberg noted that after a freer-flowing preliminary round of designs, "over time, we pulled back to something the audience could relate to, something that equated, to some extent, to an Earth environment."[34] This reliance on Earth—from which the film also took the energy that powered its digital production— was summarized by concept designer Dylan Cole: "We figured Earth is a better designer than we are. We couldn't design anything cooler than what already existed."[35]

CHARACTER, IDENTITY, AND THE DIGITAL FANTASY OF FUTURE REBELLION

The tension between fantasy and the real extends to the film's political message, its embodiment of the White Male Savior trope, and the recurrent emphasis on technological artistic genius and authorship central to the film's larger publicity discourse. *Avatar*'s narrative critique of colonialism for the sake of exploiting natural resources is part of a general liberal trend in Hollywood cinema toward allegories of the U.S. invasion of Iraq in 2003 and thus has a topical referent.[36] Although the film draws obvious connections between the role of corporate paramilitary interests in Iraq (e.g., Halliburton) and the military-corporate invaders of Pandora, it does so in a mythological space completely removed from the actual praxis of global petro-imperialism. In fact, this detachment is further pronounced by making sure to throw in a clear distinction between corporate greed and the noble militancy of antiterrorist armed forces. As Jake laments in the expository voiceover, in words that at once echo George W. Bush's abstract rhetoric lamenting the treatment of military veterans in the United States and denouncing the piratic nature of the occupation of Afghanistan and Iraq, "They can fix a back, but not on a vet's pension. . . . [B]ack home these guys were fighting for freedom, but here they are just hired guns working for the company."

Extending this obscurantist Manifest Destiny rubric, *Avatar* balances its nod to indigenous purity with a digitally catalyzed reliance on the White Male Savior, one that blurs lines between the white male protagonist—who exists liminally between industrialized and indigenous modes as well as between ontologically real and virtual universes—and the technological pseudogodlike filmmaker operating behind the curtain. As Sean Cubitt notes, there is a "proto-fascist ideology" at play in the film that links its "pre-destination theme" to a revenge narrative that is common in American cinema after September 11, 2001.[37] Many editorialists and critics lambasted the film for following an overly familiar White Male Savior narrative, one that follows an American white male into a non-Western civilization, where the protagonist learns the ways of the Other and ultimately becomes more attuned to that way of life than even the indigenous people, consequently becoming their leader. It is one of the more patronizing narrative tropes of liberal imperialism—liberal in its surface sensitivity to Otherness, imperialistic in the "more native than the natives" competitive spirit of American capitalism.

The White Male Savior is, of course, male, a not-insignificant detail given the Gaia-like spiritualism celebrated by the Na'vi, whom Jake ultimately both joins and leads. Building upon historical legends such as that of John Smith and Pocahontas, one of *the* foundational myths of

American national formation, *Avatar* offers a narrative of resistance that in fact reiterates rather traditional notions of heteronormativity and racial difference. As philosopher Slavoj Žižek argued in a *New Statesman* essay upon the film's release, "*Avatar*'s fidelity to the old formula of creating a couple, its full trust in fantasy, and its story of a white man marrying the aboriginal princess and becoming king, make it ideologically a rather conservative, old-fashioned film."[38]

Indeed, *Avatar*'s conventional narrative messages stand in contrast to its innovative aspects of production, a tension at the heart of the film's reception and criticism. Nodding to the film's immersive 3D effects, CGI graphics, advanced motion-capture techniques, and high-octane battles scenes, Adrian Ivakhiv points out that "the sheer spectacle of *Avatar* is what elicited the greatest interest in the early stages of the film's reception."[39] The film's extravagant visual design is breathtaking in its bursts of light and color as well as in its respect for Earth's floral systems; however, the way this design was received is problematic in its provision of a false bridge between artistic process and environmental message. Peter Jackson upholds this fallacy in his preface to *The Art of "Avatar,"* aptly titled "Suspension of Disbelief":

> This is a world with an entire ecosystem, where animal and plant life has established itself in forms both familiar and wondrous, where there are gases in the atmosphere and minerals in the ground. It is a world that has evolved over time and that abides by its own internal laws of nature and logic. But at its heart, *Avatar* is a story that speaks to a universal truth about our place in the world, and the things we value and the things we choose to destroy. It forces us to confront the issue of who we are and what we want, and to acknowledge the simple truth that, as a species, we are bound to a common fate, and so the future of humanity is in our hands. The message of this film is: Character is destiny.[40]

One of the more intriguing implications of Jackson's statement is the point that this creation of a simulated ecosystem is necessary for us to reflect on ourselves as humans. Like *Invasion of the Body Snatchers* (Don Siegel, 1956; Philip Kaufman, 1978), *2001*, and *Blade Runner* (Ridley Scott, 1982), *Avatar* is ultimately an anthropocentric film: a film about human character. And no matter how radically new the process and picture of the film are, no matter the fantasy and spectacle, no matter even the core ecological claims about the Pandoran and Na'vi organic structuring—all of these things are ultimately undercut by traditional ideological values and clichés of screen storytelling. Stemming from such narrative contradictions are a number of issues regarding the forms of representation in the film—for example, Cameron's admission (in a *Playboy* interview, fittingly!) that in order to conform to the bioaesthetic of market-group human viewers, Na'vi females were given breasts despite the fact that they are not mammals.[41]

Similarly, compromises in the film's environmental message must be acknowledged. One of the film's designers offers a poignant insight into the logic behind environmental aspects of the film's material visuality: "We wanted to convey the idea that the use of steel has become limited in this world," said Weta's creative director, Richard Taylor, "creating a need for modular components. So we created all these modular systems where, in theory, all of these gun components would clip together."[42] Although this is an impressively thought-out approach, it results in *just another way to make guns look cool*, an aestheticization of violence that suppresses the irony of representing a resource-scarce future through an excessive process of material prop construction.

However well the film may have been received by indigenous and oppressed peoples, its symbolic slippage holds only a thin veil over the ambitions of a technocratic media culture and its director's rather conservative and conventional vision.[43] Of the film as both narrative and spectacular symbolism, Cameron has stated: "It was to be an ambiguous image that could be Earth or could be Pandora . . . but an image that would, along with the voiceover, introduce the idea of a man's personal journey, a journey as much of mind as of place."[44] Jackson's words are not ill directed: *Avatar* is a film about character, about human experience, about the human experience of one human. Not about a collective indigenous messiah's journey or the plight of an invaded people, but about *a man's personal journey*, a white man's personal journey: Jake's, perhaps, or—if the discourse surrounding the film's inception, production, and marketing are any indication—Cameron's.[45]

There is no question that James Cameron has been in the vanguard of CGI filmmaking for three decades or that this technological development has dramatically altered screen culture. And the implications of digital imagery have been of central interest to screen historians and theorists, industry and technical studies, and the popular audience in general. Extending the discussion in these pages regarding mythology and temporality to the ontological aesthetics of different technological regimes, the media theorist Lev Manovich argues that the synthetic realism provided by CGI connotes a shifting temporality of the image: that photographs are of the past, whereas digital images are of the future.[46] This may be exactly why indigenous and oppressed peoples saw *Avatar* as an activist manifesto screened on their behalf: instead of an analog document of past exploitation, it offers a digital fantasy of future rebellion.[47]

SCIENCE, TECHNOLOGY, AND NATURE: ALONE TOGETHER

The shift to digital has had not only major material and political ramifications but also profound personal and social consequences. Sociologists and psychologists such as Sherry Turkle have provided a wealth of insightful qualitative and quantitative analysis of how the rise of smart-screen technology has deteriorated our sense of community and place.[48] This technology, which is meant to enhance our ability to connect and to communicate, is in fact alienating us—from each other and from the world around us. As a consequence, Turkle points out, smart devices, social media, and virtual reality have provided "a space for the emergence of a new state of the self, itself, split between the screen and the physical real, wired into existence through technology."[49] The cognitive dissonance created by this push and pull of digital media and technology use, at once seemingly miraculous and riddled with unexpected traps, has triggered a set of new psychological anxieties and social problems and is linked to a contemporary crisis in the human connection to nature. *Avatar* is driven by a similar cognitive dissonance between science and nature, a tension between ethics and technology that is played out both within the text and across its lengthy and resource-intensive production and release.[50]

The love/hate relationship with science and technology has long been one of the defining internal contradictions of science fiction. This is evident in *Twister*, which sets up a "good science" (the protagonists' pursuit of understanding nature is based on either emotional or altruistic goals) and a "bad science" (that derived through the capitalistic pursuit of fame and profit). *Avatar* pushes this relationship further, positing the technology of the American corporate imperialists as negative in contrast to the Na'vi primitivism, with the synthesis of the two—the avatar technology—as something at once both invasive and the only possible salvation for white and blue folk alike. Beyond this, the studio used its multimedia marketing platform to extol the virtues of the film's digital innovations. In fact, if one combines the film's textual and extrafilmic messages, each character's use of technology is ambiguous—the only "good" science appears to be practiced by Cameron himself.

In his tellingly lucid assessment of *Avatar*'s core messages, Peter Jackson—Cameron's heir apparent to the CGI throne and Cameron's predecessor in collaborating with Weta Digital—writes that *"Avatar* is a fascinating mix of drama and science."[51] The film works overtime to frame this tension differently both within and beyond the text. First, the technofetishism illustrated by the avatar technology is curbed by Jake's affected simplicity. Jake insists in the opening voiceover that, as opposed to his scientist brother, he is just a "dumb drunk." However, this stylistic device (the voiceover) counters such a deprecation, asserting Jake as the film's speaking subject and the viewer's point of identification. Moreover, through the technology of the avatar (which itself is strangely disconnected from the petroculture that has driven the human search for unobtanium), Jake transcends the scientific benevolence of anthropology and connects to the pretechnological purity embodied by the Na'vi. Beyond the film text, Cameron and the film's marketers feast upon a gluttonous cake-and-eat-it-too scenario through which the cast used the privileges of international transport to prep during a return-to-nature trip to the mountains of Hawaii. The film exploited similar petrotravel and material production to stage a doubly excessive filming process of both analog and digital registers and banked on the hidden environmental costs of energy production and smart-technology use to launch a server-supported campaign of the film as a visionary manifestation of digital brilliance and environmental altruism.

Let's take the first part first, beginning with the film's messages. *Avatar* hinges on two primary textual tensions regarding nature, science, and technology. The first tension, manifest in the use of a virtual corollary in the physical world—a neurodigitally controlled avatar that is physically superior to human beings—mirrors the film viewer's dualistic relationship to the image and, increasingly, to the digital screen experience. We both live through that experience and are removed from its consequences. *Avatar* offers a convenient resolution to this dualism at the end. Ultimately, it is Jake's ability to move beyond his own materiality, by using the avatar technology to inhabit an alternate and artificial body, that allows him to reconcile the sinister nature of his purpose on Pandora—a mythological reconciliation that is neither possible to us nor should be sought because it is our very materiality and the materiality of our actions and habits that we should account for, reflect upon, and change.

The second central locus of tension is the Pandoran forest, in which the trees are organically linked in a way that evokes at once nineteenth-century transcendentalism and twenty-first-century cognitive psychology. As the film's design artists noted, the visual stylization of the floral system provides a florescent glow that is meant, "in a subtle way," as a link between all living things, one that is also represented by the Na'vi tradition of bonding with a flying mountain banshee. However, the grid of the Pandoran ecosystem not only is meant to reference Eastern and First Nation spiritual philosophies but also explicitly provides today's viewers with an analogy between organic ecosystems and online interactivity. This analogy is elucidated by the tragic anthropologist Dr. Grace Augustine, portrayed by Sigourney Weaver, as she marvels at the connected intuition and spirituality between soil, trees, and Na'vi: "It's a network. It's a global network, and the Na'vi can access it. They can upload and download data" (figure 4.8).

Supported by a visual corollary between computer wires and the trees' luminescent strands, the language here (especially "global network") builds an implicit connection between the Na'vi utopian naturalism and the Digital World Order of networked neocolonialism, harkening to the ideological sales pitch of connectedness—that being able to upload and download data at will is the benevolent goal of the Information Age.

That the holistic Pandoran ecosystem is like a basic Internet server is at once exemplary of the film's multifaceted fetishization of digital

FIGURE 4.8 On *Avatar*'s fictional Pandora, the Na'vi plug into the Tree of Souls in a conflated analogy for both pretechnological spiritualism and twenty-first-century wired existence. This high-angle long shot mimics a sort of tribal ritual, updating the romanticized cliché of closer-to-nature Otherness for the viewers of the digitally connected era. *Source*: Frame capture by author.

technology and, not disconnected from this, typical of the filmmakers'— and the film's champions'—selectively and strategically metaphorical register. The problematic core of this conflated analogy, especially in connection to the film's celebration of virtual avatars in the story and of digital technology in the publicity process, only empowers *Avatar* to further obscure the issue of materiality, a complication at the heart of our neglect of the environmental consequences of the digital age. In this vein, Mark Bartlett argues:

> The avatar is then far more than a CGI wonder. It is a visualization of the impossibility of setting presence in opposition to representation, or effectivity in opposition to its simulacrum. It is precisely in this sense that *Avatar* is a radical, politically committed animated spectacle about being an animated spectacle about radical political commitment. It is not just the film's structure and content, but also its materiality, that are self-reflexive; it must be understood not merely as science fiction narrative or an ethnographic animated documentary, but also an allegory for the technocultural state of life and death today.[52]

This analysis belies a misguided anthropological understanding of "materiality" (misguided in that it cannot be an ethnographic or anthropological study of a fictional and invented species—it can merely emulate the form and methods of ethnography and anthropology). Moreover, the film's (and this argument's) sense of materiality is in fact lacking the vision to realize that the film's practice is the opposite of self-reflexive. Quite to the contrary, the excess of the film's dual analog/digital production, saturation distribution, and multiformat exhibition reaffirm exactly the same resource ideology that its villains perpetuate through violent colonization.

Many accolades of the film extend from the familiar-but-different fantastical analogy of its visual and conceptual world, which I have already observed to be the root of its aesthetic conception. Indeed, the film's verisimilitude, its fantasy world, and its surface messages are made possible by a blanket mistaking of metaphor for fact, of analogy for reality. From production to text to marketing, this is the quintessential danger of mythology, especially when its technofetishism is wrapped in a shroud of pseudoscientific referentiality. For example, the Na'vis' superhuman physique and prowess "are believable," Bartlett asserts, "because their bones are made of 'naturally occurring carbon fibre,' a concept itself believable because all life we know of is constructed of carbon molecules."[53] And yet this is merely a premise of the story world: the Na'vi are not made out of carbon, but out of motion-censored binary code and lumens, energy current and precious metals. Bartlett continues: "In general, *Avatar* is believable because every 17.28 gigabyte minute so exquisitely crafts a fascinating tension between familiarity and otherness".[54]

Of particular interest to my reading is the acknowledgment here of the film's byte size, which like so many similar analyses is threaded here into praise for the film while skirting the reality of the film's making. Yet even Bartlett demands: "How, then, are we to understand today's social relations as a phantasmagoric form of relation between *things*, when each minute of *Avatar*'s 162 minutes occupies 17.28 gigabytes of storage and required a 10,000 square foot render farm with 4000 servers using one of the most powerful supercomputers in existence and 900 people to produce?"[55] Excellent question—in order to address it, let us look now at how the film was actually made.

Avatar's realization would include incredible innovations in digital filmmaking. However, for the "first completely CGI film ever made," it used a great deal of real material and partook in an exhaustively resource-intensive process. In fact, an analog model was necessary for almost every part of the finalized digital imagery because the model served as the bridge from concept to animation. As Duncan and Fitzpatrick observe, Taylor and the Weta team started not with designs but with *ideas*: "ideas about Na'vi social structure, their cultural reference points, their lineage, and their religion. . . . When the key cultural and societal questions had been answered, Weta Workshop began to design Na'vi weapons, living quarters, and clothing, building samples even of those items that would only be created in CG."[56]

This excess of doubled production—once according to traditional methods of analog material production and again according to the energy-driven digital methods—extended to all areas of the film's mise-en-scène, including props, costumes, and settings. The film's New Zealand costume designer, John Harding, recounts: "We could have just done a drawing and given it to digital, and said, 'This is it. Make this.'" However, "a drawing wouldn't have told the CG artists how that garment would hang, what its weight was, how it would move in the wind. All of that is information you can't expect a technician in a darkened room in front of a green screen to know from a drawing."[57] So early designs were instead followed by traditional manufacture, which was then used as raw material for digital effects.

Duncan and Fitzpatrick detail the first step of the process according to the creative philosophy of the film's science fiction guidelines: "The designers used laser-cutting technique, atypical cutting patterns, and exotic gauzy materials, to construct hundreds of sample garments that would look as if they hadn't been made on Earth by human hands. 'We used a lot of fine rayon and silk combinations in beautiful, twisted weaves to get something that almost floats,' said Harding."[58] The irony, of course, is that the garments *were* made on Earth by human hands, but this labor (and the natural resources) that rendered them possible must be hidden within a Pandoran mythos that is a simulation of natural landscapes and constructed nature that must use natural resources in order to produce its artificial version . . . of nature.

Since *Avatar's* inception, its goal was always a CGI production, but the process for achieving this goal was the opposite of immaterial; although it was billed as a virtual production process that was "*better* than shooting live action,"[59] it required an enormous amount of nonvirtual (i.e., "real") manufacturing. Even the "virtual" production had a "real" footprint from the beginning: the original concept was sent to ILM, which rendered a forty-second scene—forty seconds that required vast amounts of electricity, hardware, and transport fuel. But this wasn't the extent of the film's material resource use. As producer Jon Landau points out, "Just like on a normal production . . . we had to hire a construction crew. But instead of hiring people with hammers and nails like you would normally do, we hired computer artists, and these artists had to create our world in the computer for us before we could go to the virtual-production stage."[60] What Landau does not clarify here is that it was not one or the other: they hired *both*, did *both*. In order to assist the real human cast and crew on this virtual production, the team manufactured what visual-effects artist Nolan Murtha refers to as "digital assets," such as a

FIGURE 4.9 In this "making of" video, we can see the material reality behind the screen spectacle and self-branded digital immateriality of *Avatar*. As revealed here, the film, while at the vanguard of many technological innovations in digital film-making, relies heavily on analog production materials (human actors, props and décor, three-dimensional set space) in combination with the energy-dependent and resource-heavy digital infrastructure that converts these analog people and objects to digital content. *Source*: Frame capture by author.

large-slope structure for human actors to walk uphill—so that their body language would look accurate when their setting was replaced by a CGI hill in postproduction.[61]

The shoot in fact took place in multiple phases, beginning with motion capture in Los Angeles and then moving to Wellington, New Zealand, for live-action photography. Much of its hybridized production took place in the Volume, a massive warehouse in Los Angeles converted into a motion-capture stage. It was there that the actors were strapped to wires and headsets that would chart their facial expressions to be processed digitally and projected onto their blue CGI counterparts. Despite the range of its geographical and ontological registers, though, Cameron maintained a very hands-on approach, operating a virtual camera in the Volume and a 3D camera in Wellington—two cameras that he helped to design for just this purpose. As Duncan and Fitzpatrick note, "This lent a stylistic continuity to the camera moves, since the same compositional eye and operating style were in both places. It was hoped that this would help create a seamless blend of the live-action and CG realms."[62] In other words, the film's discursive collapsing of real and virtual was tied to a technofetishistic vision of the directorial author, an evocation of the film auteur that allows us to tie *Avatar* back to *Gone with the Wind*—two films that set a cinematic precedence for a new era of popular screen culture, buttressed by extrafilmic narratives of creative control, technical innovation, and unrivaled spectacle.

Shooting on the virtual camera or "swing camera," a lens-free collapse between external live-action actors and internal CGI sets, demanded two phases: one that included the cast and subsequently one that involved an isolated process in which Cameron would spend days in the Volume using the virtual camera to create complex camera movements that would then be algorithmically processed to mimic handheld motions. Once approved, these movements were uploaded into Avid and stored for the Weta team's CGI postproduction work.[63] Far from magical conjuration, these components were part of the digital hardware chain and reliant on constant streams of energy—but this information is not part of the *Avatar* myth, which like many blockbusters of the digital age claims an immaterial base while also delighting in the exaggerated material excess of big-budget studio filmmaking.

When the principle motion-capture and virtual photography was complete, this "digitally made film"—which utilized a dozen electrical cameras, hundreds of crew members, fabric costumes, plastic props, and an analog set—then moved to New Zealand for further filming. Not on location in one of New Zealand's pristine natural environments, mind you, but on Weta soundstages that included a forty-thousand-square-foot "Shack" and an annex—once a Mitsubishi car factory, in which ten thousand square feet of "practical rain forest" would be constructed, the filming of which would ultimately end up on the cutting-room floor.[64] Not only were the sets of this CGI world constructed in analog, but the basic units for the partial sets had to be manufactured specifically for the film, a meticulous attention to detail that was integral to the film's myth of directorial brilliance. Discussing the construction of a half-set of the circular Link Room, Mario Flaure testifies to the film's unique material demand:

> Jim decided that it was better to build half the set with great quality and design than have the whole set half-built. There was just an unbelievable amount of detail in the sets—railings and supports and the fasteners on the link beds—all these specific little elements. It wasn't simply showing up at the hardware store and picking out the parts. All the details, all the bolts and screws, all the locks on the doors were designed specifically for the film. I've never seen anything as thoroughly designed in any Hollywood film I've worked on.[65]

We can easily discern a cognitive and discursive dissonance running through the film's production and the crew's self-reflection: a glorification at once of the anthropological integrity and material extensiveness involved in the story's representations, countered by an ongoing romanticization of the technological acumen and complexity at the heart of the film's digital innovations.

The film's final phase took place in the hands of "the trick department," or Weta's CGI postproduction team. Letteri and the Weta crew employed the speed and storage potential of new computing techniques in what proved to be a truly transnational flow of digital information between Venice, California; Montreal; France; and New Zealand. The majority of the work, though, fell to Weta, which in the end provided 110 minutes of CG animation—about two-thirds of the film's total screen time. This work required enormous computing power, hardware, and energy. The film's digital postproduction became a subject of tech lore, captured by John Rath in a piece for *Data Center Knowledge* titled "The Data-Crunching Powerhouse Behind 'Avatar.'" After explaining Weta's complex server architecture, with mostly praise for its unprecedented hardware count and activity, Rath notes: "For the last month or more of production those 40,000 processors were handling 7 or 8 gigabytes of data per second, running 24 hours a day. A final copy of *Avatar* equated to 17.28 gigabytes per minute of storage."[66]

This is where *Avatar*'s ballooning production—just like that of *Titanic* a decade earlier—became part of the film's publicity campaign, again raising the bar for the technological excess so glamorized by our mainstream film culture. This excess would not be as noteworthy if it were not such a central part of *Avatar*'s advertising and release campaign, which embraced the most recent marketing strategies of spreadable media, dead-end environmental click bait, and multiformat saturation exhibition.[67] The making of *Avatar* is truly the essence of contradiction: a master class in American ideology and in the growing disconnect between real and virtual provided by our mythologization of environmental anxieties in the age of digital screen media.

THE "SEDUCTION OF REALITY"

We can understand the film on all levels—from its aesthetic mission to its environmental allegory to its various interactive platforms—according to Cameron's own description: "the seduction of reality."[68] There is no question that the director wanted to create an experience so detailed and textured that audiences could surrender completely to it. This experience was not limited to the balance between photorealism and fantasy in the film's visual and narrative world but also extended to its attempt to draw potential audiences into the myth of its environmental message. Yet *Avatar* was deeply embedded in the unacknowledged contradictions of a doubled analog-digital production that used extratextual discourse to maintain an illusion of immateriality for the digital image. Two months after the film's release, the Visual Effects Society honored Cameron with a Lifetime Achievement Award. In his speech, Cameron referenced previous special-effects films such as *Jason and the Argonauts* (Don Chaffey, 1963) and *The 7th Voyage of Sinbad* (Nathan Juran, 1958), attaching himself to a genealogy of both cinematic innovation and science fiction genius: "Arthur C. Clarke had these laws, and his third law said, 'Any sufficient advanced technology is indistinguishable from magic.' Well, to me, when I was a kid, what Ray Harryhausen did was magic. And now, what we're doing is absolute magic to the average person. We could sit down with them for ten hours and try to explain it, and they wouldn't get it. But that's OK. It doesn't matter."[69]

Beyond being horribly condescending, this moment of public self-congratulation is in line with the film's confirmation of the popular sociocultural contract of film spectacle: we want to view it as the magic of the silver screen and not as the fabricated product of labor and the exploitation of finite natural resources. Similarly, accounts of *Avatar*'s release and reception are grandiose in both profit and affect. Cameron's description glosses over the digital marketing campaign, the film's range of merchandising tie-ins, and its carpet-bomb exhibition blitz—those things aren't *magic*, after all, and the practices and processes of our advertising culture aren't supposed to part of the film's experience. Blending Gaia nostalgia with virtuoso technical innovation, *Avatar* reveals the connection between cutting-edge digital practices and the gradual disappearance of Earth itself—a fantasy of apocalypse echoing the gradual commodification and conversion of natural habitat and resources into streaming images, thrill rides, and amusement parks.

This irony has been lost in the oceanic swell of film culture's machinery of legitimization (box-office records, Academy Awards, coffee-table books, planned sequels), but the lasting psychological print of *Avatar* is a telling one. "Avatar blues" became a mass psychological epidemic after the film's wildly successful release; this pop-clinical term was coined to describe a mode of human depression stemming from the desire to live on Pandora and the consequent disgust with the sight of *our* world, which triggered a desire, as Jo Piazza of CNN put it, "to escape reality."[70] More specifically, it was a desire to escape the material present for a virtual future. The crystallization of mainstream screen spectacle, *Avatar* offers us an escape from the responsibilities and consequences of our present actions, indulging us in the fantasy of a world where technology can transcend both crippling physical conditions and intercultural strife. The colors and clichés divert our attention away from the geopolitical and environmental impact of digital culture, protecting us from the here and now through a myth of reincarnation.

There is no myth that more convincingly allows us to take a rain check on accountability than the myth of eternal life—which *Avatar*, in 2009, offered as a gift to the anxious viewers of the era of accelerated climate change: a virtual escape from the consequences of the present. In a moment of severe environmental discord and rising anxiety that the forces of neoliberalism have outpaced the progress of alternative resistance, our willing merger with the digital belies an inherently languorous assumption built into our use of the name "Anthropocene": that we have squandered the planet we inherited, that we will lean with the sociocultural contract of entertainment spectacle and sacrifice the real altogether.

We may indulge in fantasies of time travel and space colonization, may send probes to other planets as we shift our social interactions to the digital ether, but we get only one Earth. We are living out our only role, many millennia into this film that we will not get to see the end of. We do not get to stand up and walk out, having cathartically exercised our anxieties and fears without consequence; there is no sequel. This chapter reveals just how deeply embedded the myths and the cognitive dissonance surrounding the digital transition may be; in the process, what began very much as an alternate history and industry study has moved steadily toward a production-culture study, an attempt to understand the human practices and attitudes involved in producing the payoff for this sociocultural contract. I will now turn fully to this topic, exploring the fifth element—humanity—in terms of how unique ecosystems determine human approaches to nature and culture and how both environmental characteristics and human-made ecosystemic dynamics shape and are shaped by film and media practices.

CHAPTER FIVE

The Fifth Element

Hollywood as Invasive Species and the Human Side of Environmental Media

The human artifice of the world separates human existence from all mere animal environment, but life itself is outside this artificial world, and through life man remains related to all other living organisms. For some time now, a great many scientific endeavors have been directed toward making life also "artificial," toward cutting the last tie through which even man belongs among the children of nature.

—HANNAH ARENDT, *THE HUMAN CONDITION*

The social system in which they [Hollywood films] are made significantly influences their content and meaning.

—HORTENSE POWDERMAKER, *HOLLYWOOD, THE DREAM FACTORY*

In the constellation of elemental theories across human cultures, many include a fifth element, a roamer that differs depending on each specific spiritual system's underlying philosophy and the goal of its elemental taxonomy. In Hinduism, for example, which casts souls as immortally woven into the universe through perpetual reincarnation, this fifth element is the Void or ether, a complement to the ostensive elements that provides a loophole through which our negation is at once present and a means to our return. Although I have tried whenever possible to avoid the name "Anthropocene" in this book—due to the problematic nature of its temporal framing and the inconsistency produced by its overuse—there can be no question that the flow of environmental change, like that of history, has entered an era in which the human species exerts a uniquely strong influence among the factors of change in this natural world. In order to give this book a finalized shape that closes in an arc but also opens onto future horizons of scholarship and reflection, I hazard the claim that humanity has imposed itself as the fifth element, at once within the natural and increasingly at odds with the stability and health of our planet's ecosystems.

Hannah Arendt's haunting words, written in the wake of World War II's mass murders and during the darkest hour of Cold War nuclear proliferation, hinge on two problems regarding artifice that thrive in the digital age: the growing divide between the real and the virtual and the belief that technological culture is what separates humanity from the rest of nature. The "tie" that Arendt laments is what is cut every time we accept the sacrifice of the real on the altar of screen entertainment, a tie that is rendered all the more fragile as digital screens shift our everyday interactions to a virtual space. This is the irony of *Avatar* that *Avatar* does not, perhaps *cannot*, acknowledge: that Jake must become fully virtual and his body artificial in order for him to connect to some romanticized primitivist notion of nature. That this contradiction rests unexplored and is resolved so easily indicates just how far our sociocultural contract has been shaped by the emergence of digital and virtual technologies. Although Arendt's warning is all the more poignant today for these reasons, the other relevant notion of artifice holds a dangerous fallacy at the center of it: that human culture is separate from the natural world. Conversely, I argue here that human culture grows from the natural environment, is guided by and affects the natural world at every turn.

Science fiction and its many offshoots (into which we must now include the ecodisaster genre) cast contemporary and seemingly universal human problems into otherworldly scenarios with not-quite-human entities, but we have seen how very focused they are on what J. P. Telotte summarizes as the "problematic nature of the human being and the difficult task of being human."[1] From Mary Shelley's *Frankenstein* to Fritz Lang's *Metropolis* (1927), to *Invasion of the Body Snatchers*, *Blade Runner*, and *Avatar*, this problem of being human is, like all questions of identity, also evocative of negation—a "deep-seated fear of all that is not the self."[2] Across Hollywood eras, the nonhuman natural world has been consistently defined as "not the self," and this fear has been contained by narrativizing nature to be something destructive but ultimately controllable, beautiful and wondrous but delicate and mysterious, sacred but in need of taming.

Conversely, the very problem of what it means to be human that rests at the heart of science fiction is connected to a trepid process by which humanity must come to terms with its naturalness, come to see itself as part of nature.[3] This is the immortality offered by Jake's resurrection at the end of *Avatar* and an implicit rhetorical claim guiding the green myth of digital production: recovering our awareness of the essential interconnectedness between humanity and the natural world will somehow restore humanity to a state of grace and our ecosystem to a state of healthy balance. However, this claim does not account for the actuality of human cultural practices, and it leapfrogs the real opposition to environmental responsibility entrenched over centuries of anthropocentric living. Instead of evacuating the real and looking for a virtual solution, a miraculous rebirth, or a pristine new planet to start over on, we should return to our own planet. And even in an era of globalization, let us consider the local nature of ecomaterialism and the diverse relationship between specific production cultures, global industries, and local ecosystems.

Humanity has always inextricably been part of nature, our daily behaviors and views shaped by immediate ecosystemic demands, behaviors, and views that in turn determine our acts, routines, and forms of communication. This book has up to now focused on how our screen practices shape and affect the environment and the sociocultural contract of those who demand and consume movies. But in order to fully understand the hidden environmental costs of screen culture, we must also turn the lens on those who make films and media, how the industry has an environmental narrative, and how specific locales and ecosystems are connected to the emergence and identity of local production cultures.

The previous chapter's analysis of *Avatar* hinted at a production-culture study of digital Hollywood, offering an environmental critique of the decision-making logic, external self-justification, and problematic practice whereby the film was made. Indeed, that could be said for every major case study in this book. But, to some extent, David O. Selznick, Gene Kelly, and James Cameron have been part of different production cultures, and in turn their film practices have composed different dynamics between screen spectacle and the natural environment. In this chapter, I look beyond southern California to consider other geographically specific ways in which local production cultures are defined by—and define—the relationship between human practice and natural environment.

What seems from the perspective of Hollywood to be just a basic practice of runaway or outsourced production is in fact a large-scale dynamic force in the influence of local politics across the world, a constant engine of human displacement and carbon emissions, and a hidden tension among migrant media practice, regional political structures, and local ecosystems into which Hollywood productions and professionals move. This production process entails an economic and cultural occupation that resembles colonialism so strongly that it has been referred to as "the para-industry," through which ancillary companies have invaded cities in the name of Hollywood, just as Blackwater and other military groups have in the name of American foreign policy.[4] In environmental studies terms, I liken such production practices to an invasive species, which moves into new biomes and destructively alters their uniquely balanced ecology. The local effects of such practices go well beyond the economic to social and environmental problems of public services, natural resources, social organization, and waste pollution. Consequently we really need to reframe studies of local (i.e., "outside of Los Angeles"), runaway, and incentivized production not only within economic and industry analysis but also within environmental and social science—and, if possible, ethnographic—perspectives.

Toward this end, I argue for the introduction into production-culture studies of a relational-values approach, a holistic and dialogic approach currently emerging in environmental and social sciences, which recasts ecosystem services according to the belief that cultural identity and core values are largely driven by our relationship to natural environments. Such a perspective insists that we understand the environment not only in terms of the instrumental value of what nature can provide for us or in terms of what innate value we may believe it holds but also in terms of how our interactions with the natural world—such as through long-term care and stewardship or through "worldviews that encompass kinship between people and nature"[5]—define our core values, quality of life, and cultural practices.

According to a recent Intergovernmental Platform on Biodiversity and Ecosystem Services, relational values "reflect elements of cultural identity, social cohesion, social responsibility and moral responsibility towards nature,"[6] which we can integrate into a larger understanding of the specific cultural values, economic dynamics, and industrial practices that inform local policies and cultures of media production. Focusing on the recent incentive program in Michigan and the underwater cinematography culture of South Florida, I explore the extension of mainstream screen-media practice to the social and environmental specificity of extremely different localities and analyze the tensions that arise between invasive Hollywood industry practices and local networks of social organization, policy formation, relational values, and media infrastructure. By applying environmental studies frameworks to production-culture studies and by bringing an ecomaterialist approach into the political economy of these practices, we may begin to assess the complex ways in which such productions affect local environments, exploit natural resources, and produce new channels of waste. Such a valuation, which insists that the social and relational environmental values of local communities be included in policy conversations regarding economics and cultural politics, could be of great future value for those local cities and states considering opening their gates to the Hollywood invasion.

SOCIAL SCIENCES, MEDIA, AND THE ENVIRONMENT

Much current growth in environmental media research has come out of the social sciences, asserting the importance of communications and anthropological approaches to how people understand environmental science and risk—and how they shape their own relationship to nature—through screen technologies and other media. Columbia University's Center for Research on Environmental Decisions and Yale University's Program on Climate Change Communications, for example, are heavily imbued with a combination of human behavior description, public-survey study, and quantitative analysis that comes from these fields.[7] Anthony Leiserowitz, whose study of climate change risk perception and *The Day After Tomorrow* I discussed earlier in this book, has been a central player in many such studies. And the group-authored article titled "Contribution of Anthropology to the Study of Climate Change" argues that "natural sciences research on the dynamics of climate change has overshadowed social scientists' work to understand its human dimensions. . . . It is now also clear that climate change mitigation and adaptation projects are unlikely to succeed without a close understanding of the societies in which they are implemented."[8]

The authors map out three major strengths that anthropology can bring to the study of climate change. First, the discipline draws attention to the cultural values and political dynamics that shape climate-change discourse, focusing on the production of environmental knowledge and the "circulation of this knowledge in everyday practice, policy realms, media discourse and popular culture." Second, anthropology builds from an awareness of the historical context underpinning contemporary climate debates, acknowledging the history of society–environment interactions as developed from archaeology and, more recently, environmental anthropology, which "has highlighted the reciprocal relations between culture and nature, and has drawn attention to the close intersections between the environment and social and economic systems." And, last, anthropological method is based on a broad, holistic view of human and natural systems and "draws attention to the fact that the new forms of production and consumption driving contemporary climate change are also altering people's livelihood strategies, modes of interaction and spatial horizons."[9]

I lay out these points meticulously because they so perfectly capture the arching goals of my own study of film culture's transition to the digital age—a wholesale technological, philosophical, and geopolitical shift that is concurrent with an accelerated awareness and experience of the effects of climate change. Our social positioning of nature justifies, reflects, and permits our ritualistic popular-cultural practices of spectacle and mythology, and these cultural practices in turn shape our relationship to the environment. I complement this approach to cultural ritual, spectacle, and the environment with an analysis of the "intersections between the environment and social and economic systems,"[10] in particular screen-media systems. As the authors of "Contribution of Anthropology to the Study of Climate Change" argue, because "climate change is increasingly becoming more prominent an explanation for a wide range of social and economic issues, from crop failure to transborder refugees, to issues of national and international security, . . .

focusing on climate change to the exclusion of, and in isolation from, other social, political, cultural and economic processes that shape landscapes and livelihoods is problematic."[11]

We cannot understand our relationship with the natural environment on its own, just as we must cease to view our cultural practices as removed from environmental materiality.

In order to approach such an inclusive and symbiotic analysis, it is necessary to connect the dots between screen media, relational values, and social science—or, more precisely, ethnography. Film and ethnography share a long and complicated osmosis, dating back to early cinematic shorts aimed at bringing the geographic and cultural Other to Western screens. From the racism of early "watermelon-eating contest" shorts to Robert Flaherty's salvage ethnographies of the 1920s, the postcolonial films of Jean Rouch and the *cinéma vérité* movement, and the emergence of digital memoir and video ethnography as a crucial site of feminist, nonwhite, and queer videographers, this genealogy has been threaded through a fine line between filmmakers attempting ethnography and ethnographers attempting screen documentation.

Conversely, many social sciences have over the past two decades moved from linguistic models to visual modes of documentation and, as we can see in recent surveys of the field, are increasingly aware of the growing ubiquity with which digital screen media permeate the global daily interface with the real. As a consequence of this permeation, a great responsibility rests with those who must navigate both unique communities' social uses of digital media and, both by extension and in complementarity, communicate such communities through new audiovisual and moving-image forms. Anthropology—like media studies and approaches to sociology and psychology—is adapting to the fact that twenty-first-century smart technologies make it possible for such media not only to reveal other cultures but also to enter us into the very experience of those cultures.[12]

The Janus-like aspect of media as both object and subject of the enterprise of social sciences is reflected in the ways in which images are not only part of how we experience, learn, know, and communicate but also integrally part of technological and industrial networks that reshape our ecosystems, our economies, and our daily behaviors. As such, there has been a recent interest in production ethnography of the ways that on-location film shoots interact with and impact local spaces and communities. In "Setting Up Roots, or the Anthropologist on the Set," Arne Schneider follows a major Argentinian production (*El Camino*, Javier Olivera, 2000) to its shoot in a Mapuche Reservation in order to analyze how a film that explicitly sets out to incorporate an indigenous community into its process and narrative does in fact interact with that community. The object of inquiry here is not the indigenous group but the production crew. Schneider's short essay reveals the contradictions and invasive nature of even well-intentioned runaway productions and demonstrates that anthropological method offers incredible value for assessing the material and political impact of screen production.[13]

Social sciences have largely influenced film and media studies in recent years, in conjunction with reception studies and production-culture studies, to describe and to analyze how people consume screen media and how decisions are made and exercised in order to produce films, series, commercials, webcasts, and video games. This influence has also found deep resonance with environmental media scholarship. Nicole Starosielski's exemplary book *The Undersea Network* (2016) uses first-hand photographs, advertisement prints, and various forms of mapping to pinpoint particular material examples of how the infrastructure of undersea and fiber-optic cabling has altered landscapes, influenced community dynamics, and shaped the global history of the past century.[14] Starosielski's study and my own book reflect a recent reemergence of the long-silenced insistence that film and media industries are not only industry formations but also social organizations of human beings and groups.

In 1946, the esteemed anthropologist Hortense Powdermaker turned her trained eye from the Melanesian society of Papua New Guinea to another social group of great uniqueness and curiosity: Hollywood. *Hollywood, the Dream Factory*, written after a year of on-the-ground observation and released in 1951, was the only full-length ethnography of Tinseltown produced during American cinema's nascent century, and its poignant critique of the entertainment community's social behaviors and core values left a bruise.[15] As Sherry Ortner would find in the late 2000s, and as would compel her exploration of independent cinema, *Not Hollywood* (2013), mainstream Hollywood is not open to the prying eyes of the social scientist.[16] I made this same discovery a few years ago when I approached the studios to inquire about emerging green practices for this book: I was granted an off-the-record interview and a studio tour, after which my follow-up emails were met by an ominous response from the studio's legal team that concluded any communication with my studio contact. (Similarly, most of the people I interviewed for this study asked for and were granted complete anonymity.)

As Powdermaker put it regarding Hollywood films, "The social system in which they are made significantly influences their content and meaning,"[17] and as this social system is exported across the United States and intermingles with localized production spaces, her legacy can be felt in the recent rise of on-site, off-Hollywood production studies. In "Bringing the Social Back In," the opening essay in the seminal collection *Production Studies* (2009), Vicki Mayer lays out the goal of production-culture studies as being to "'ground' social theories by showing us how specific production sites, actors, or activities tell us larger lessons about workers, their practices, and the role of their labors in relation to politics, economics, and cultures."[18] This goal allows for a dialectical view of the micro- and macroforces at play in screen culture, a framework I have argued to be necessary to understanding the link between individuals, screen-cultural practice, and the environment.

The major case studies and minor anecdotes of this book demonstrate that an ecomaterialist approach must take into consideration the material fact that films and other media texts are made not only out of natural resources but also out of human beings with specific cultural behaviors and rituals, who are guided and bound by certain worldviews, political economies, modes of communication, and relational values to the natural world. In the memos and letters of David O. Selznick, in the tie-in marketing campaigns surrounding *Singin' in the Rain*, in the mythologies of science at the heart of *Twister*, and in the discursive patterns employed across James Cameron's implementation of digital production, we find the morphing clauses and amendments of our sociocultural contract with Hollywood and the natural environment not only in the attitudes and behaviors of those who watch films but also in the culture surrounding films' production. How are the ideological foundations of Hollywood, so deeply grounded in entitlement and excess but so savvy with regards to the power of public image, adapting to the era of raised environmental awareness? What might an environmentally driven production-culture study look like? I propose here a synthesized analysis of the environmental concerns, political strategies, publicity aims, and economic logics that drive the formation of recent shifts in media practice, both within Hollywood and across the United States.

GREENING HOLLYWOOD

Environmental and weather-related factors have long been a part of the American cinematic narrative, beginning with how the pre-Hollywood studios' planning and architecture were shaped by the necessity for sunlight, steady electricity, and other resource dependencies.[19] Although the move to California was fueled in part by a desire to escape the monopolistic practices of Thomas Edison's Motion Pictures Patents Company and the pervasive anti-Semitism of grounded northeastern institutions, major industry histories have framed the transition out West as one of mostly environmental incentives. Today, the historical consensus relates a tale of southern California's allure as one of open spaces, long days with lots of sunlight, and a diverse topographical concentration of desert, mountains, and sea.[20]

Ever since that move, the film and television industry has had a deeply rooted relationship with local and global resource use and waste production. The studios themselves, which installed autonomous water tanks and utilities networks and relied heavily on surrounding resource flows, have long been an integral node in the environmental infrastructure of the region, not to mention the generator of a great carbon footprint and a frequent source of interruption to local ecosystems both within and beyond Los Angeles. Despite this history of problematic environmental impact, though, Hollywood has *also* recently emerged as an instrumental purveyor of green rhetoric, launching initiatives meant to reform its brand as a bastion of liberal politics and to streamline its economic model according to higher-efficiency sustainability practices.

In 1989, a small group of environmentally minded industry leaders formed the Environmental Media Association (EMA), a nonprofit group that works with studios and encourages green production methods and environmental messaging in television and film. Every studio has launched its own version of a green wing, and the Producer's Guild of America (PGA) introduced the Producers Guild Green Initiative and

PGA Green, a bicoastal directive that supplies a best-practices guide (Green Production Guide) and a list of vendors from among the cottage industry of sustainability groups—such as the ReUse People, who help to repurpose production materials[21]—that have sprung up around the film industry. Due to their role as big-picture logistics organizers, producers in particular hold great sway over this shift. PGA Green cochair Rachael Joy, an avid developer and producer of environmental programming, told me that since producers are with a project from beginning to end and are the driving force of production, it is natural for them to spearhead the green initiative. The Green Production Guide is paid for through a partnership with studios who are working together, a rare cooperation in an industry of sharks that could be achieved only through the producers' station.[22]

Yet the studios are using green discourse merely as a mode of rebranding, riding the wave of public sentiment but not really altering their profit motive and making minimal adjustments to their material practice. Paramount Pictures fell back on the somewhat unimaginative tagline "Green. It's paramount to us" to describe their Green Action Team, which is a cross-departmental initiative that includes e-waste and cell phone recycling, green volunteering, and electric-vehicle charging stations. Sony has adopted the slogan "A Greener World," an umbrella cliché for similar adjustments and calls for awareness, production, and operations. 21st Century Fox is probably, and shockingly, *the most* far-reaching in its green transition: Rupert Murdoch, cartoonish supervillain and owner of Fox's parent company, NewsCorp, declared in 2007 that all company operations would go carbon neutral. In 2011, Murdoch announced to the world that this was to be achieved through various infrastructural changes (energy-efficient lighting, discouraged air travel) as well as the offset programs of films such as *Avatar*, which pay to have trees planted in exchange for carbon-offset points. In an uncharacteristic nod to transparency, 21st Century Fox has also publicly disclosed its carbon-footprint data and environmental-management strategy through the Carbon Disclosure Project, a voluntary reporting system that assesses the management of greenhouse gas emissions and monitors sustainability activities of companies around the world.

Most studios, however, have limited their efforts to "greenwashing," a mode of corporate environmentalism that flashes the environmental card—replacing disposable water bottles with water coolers and paper memos with email—but continues with the business of capitalist excess as usual. The *Guardian* captured this transition in a piece on Disney in 2009, "Greenwash: Disney's Green Intentions Are Pure Fantasy," which addresses Disney's public announcement that action on climate change is "urgent" and requires "fundamental changes in the way society, including businesses, use natural resources, and Disney is no exception." But, per the industry norm, Disney was making only token gestures to sustainability without instituting industry-level changes, and the article concluded: "Disney are [sic] greening some of their activities, but they are not greening their business model."[23]

Moreover, unlike most major industries, the film industry is not environmentally regulated. Hollywood has historically done a good job of avoiding regulation on many fronts—such as content censorship—by erecting internal bodies and protocols, and environmental regulation appears to be no exception. Industrial initiatives are helping the industry to deflect any sort of imposed regulation, as are Fox's transparency process and the studios' and celebrities' public-relations efforts. The greening of Hollywood is therefore a multilayered strategy, rebranding and streamlining the industry while also shielding it from the eye of government and the disfavor of public opinion. To borrow the words of Richard Maxwell and Toby Miller. "This is all at once a business plan, an element of the company's environmental policy that markets its corporate responsibility, and an attempt to elude democratic regulation."[24]

As arguments against greenwashing point out, most of it is smoke and mirrors, surface nods to popular environmental messaging without actually changing the operations of film and media practice. Just as films once bragged about not harming any animals in their making, an EMA certification will now be slapped at the end of a film, an accreditation stamp among the final credits that acknowledges: "This production was carbon neutral." However, "carbon neutral" rarely means that great changes have been made to the production process; rather, it almost uniformly means that the production has offset its environmental impact via other means, usually by purchasing carbon offsets outright or funding an organization to plant trees or some other eco-friendly activity that, in exchange, provides the production with carbon-offset credits. Before being stonewalled by legal representatives, I had a fruitful ongoing exchange with a newly appointed environmental executive at a major studio. This source made it clear that this recent studio turn is in fact the result of two major external influences in 2006—the success of *An Inconvenient Truth* and the surprising visibility of Charles Corbett and Richard Turco's report *Sustainability in the Motion Picture Industry*,[25] which shifted the studios' stance on three fronts: messaging (including the creation of the EMA and, of course, the annual EMA awards), guilds and unions (including the formation of the PGA Green), and transparency (including through the Motion Picture Association of America and especially along lines of waste treatment).

Based on this course and on the online sales pitch of studios' green initiatives, waste is the key focus, which basically means moving from paper to electronic communication, recycling and repurposing, and shifting from disposable water bottles to water coolers on set. Although progress is being made on the production side, each studio department has a different value in relationship to the production chain, keeping systematic change from being possible—though such change will always be secondary because, to put it generously, the studios will "never mess around with the creative process." The environmental executive I talked to also noted that one of the great obstacles to any systematic change is the fluid nature of the production process: production companies are often formed specifically for one film, then disbanded after a few months when the shoot is over. This practice, coupled with the many stages of a film (development, shooting, postproduction, marketing), makes any uniformity—as well as any oversight, regulation, or accountability—nearly impossible.

Hollywood's production scope extends beyond Los Angeles, however, and for more than half a century various local industries connected to Hollywood and of different degrees of permanence have grown up across the United States and around the world. These industries mostly include translocal production structures, such as the incentivized pop-up communities in Detroit and other cities. They are not products of local natural and cultural specificity but are the manufactured result of tax-incentive programs that lead Hollywood professionals to move across the country—translocal in that they are locals in Los Angeles and connected to Hollywood's social value system but residentially and existentially local in a new city. South Florida's underwater cinematography group, in contrast, is quite unique in that it is specific to its ecosystem: the subtropical Atlantic is shallow, clear, and relatively warm for the entire year, while the proximity and eased regulations of the Bahamas, where most of Hollywood's underwater filming is done, have enticed productions for decades. Moreover, a generally shared casual environmentalism and love of the outdoors have helped cultivate a small media infrastructure that, bolstered by Hollywood productions in need of sunshine and underwater shots, acts as intermediary between industry interlopers and the increasingly fragile local reefs, beaches, and wildlife. Different production cultures have their own unique cultural, economic, and ideological drives toward adopting environmental practices, which must be understood in terms of both industry policy and local relational values to the natural world.

HOLLYWOOD PRODUCTION AS INVASIVE SPECIES

When viewed according to a "translocal" media architecture, Hollywood film culture both becomes rooted in spaces and transcends any fixed local or geographic identity. And although the turn to digital technology has reinforced the illusion that screen media is intangible, media and film practices must be understood to have great material impact on local spaces, social practices, and natural environments. A film itself may not have a geographical or regional identity, but the people who make it do (whether as Hollywood transplants or as local media professionals), as does the constructed and natural environment where the film is made. The conflict between these two—the translocal nature of the cultural product and the specific local impact of its production—requires our attention, and understanding it benefits from understanding the history, logic, and process of runaway productions, incentive programs, and local media cultures.

How do the strategies of incentive programs actually play out on the ground? How do local spaces, ecosystems, and relational values become part of the growth of media infrastructures and, ultimately, of a larger strategy of political economy? I begin with the Michigan incentive program as a case study for how incentives affect local media economy, human experience and spatial identity, and the environment. This case is then set against the unique monopolization of underwater cinematography in the South Florida area, through which film and television productions from Los Angeles and New York outsource a specific mode of film shoot to a particular ecosystem. This micro-industry, growing alongside the expanding southern Florida diving and fishing culture as well as the postwar boom in marine entertainment, sprouted from a fairly small pool of active participants whose pivotal position between film industry and local ecosystem has been fraught with contradiction, constantly balancing a fine line between environmental protection and entertainment media.

As pointed to earlier in this chapter, the popular narrative holds that Hollywood was invented as a destination for northeastern and midwestern companies in search of a blank sociocultural canvas and optimal environmental circumstances for shooting in natural light. Since then, runaway production has been refined as an important weapon in the Hollywood arsenal, in conjunction with the postwar proliferation of independent production. As decentralization moved productions to nonpermanent transitory locations (which may, depending on the demands of the film, mean anything from Oklahoma to Rome), the number of films shot outside of Hollywood rose 40 percent between 1950 and 1973, tipping nearly to half of all films by the mid-1980s.[26]

Runaway productions enjoy reduced production costs, low wages and rental rates, tax credits, and subsidies. However, there is also an aesthetic, stylistic, and ambient facet to runaway productions, which benefit from realistic outdoor locations, embrace new shooting methods, and sometimes specifically establish a connection to the location itself. What the location stands to gain is multifold, though slippery: the production acts as a tourist attraction, the process ideally helps to train and configure an infrastructure of semipermanent local media professionals, and the exhibited text helps to put the local landscape on screens worldwide. The production logic is simple: although the studios bear the travel costs,[27] it is less expensive to film in Thailand, Mexico, or Detroit than in Los Angeles, an incentive that has turned Hollywood into a roaming environmental hazard.

The real cost of production is to more than just the financiers. The economic capital saved comes at the cost of the natural environment: most simply, transport is one of the biggest factors in our emission of greenhouse gases. Moreover, it is a process that by its very nature alienates incoming crews from the local ecosystem and community. As production ethnographer Arnd Schneider writes, "Feature film production (at least on the set) because of its specific, almost ritualized working practices leads to a kind of alienation from the surrounding reality. . . . A self-focused crew, involved with routinized requirements of shooting, is largely cut off from any meaningful dialogue with indigenous people."[28] Although visiting productions help to buttress local service industries, stimulate word-of-mouth excitement, provide a virtual capital for the local area, and are mostly beholden to a degree of decorum that will allow them to return for subsequent productions, they tend not to step outside of their industrial routines—they remain, almost always, a Hollywood production, a traveling sideshow that disrupts local resources and leaves in the middle of the night.

The costs can be extreme, and the environmental consequences must not be neglected—though up to now they more or less have been. There are particularly egregious cases. James Cameron's filming of *Titanic* offered employment to the workers of a struggling Mexican film industry but also ruined the local marine ecosystem and decimated a fishing community. The making of Danny Boyle's *The Beach* (2000), which raised tourist awareness for its Thai setting, destroyed the on-location dunes that were naturally sculpted monsoon buffers for the local ecosystem and human population.[29] These are among the worst such cases in recent years, but they belie a larger systematic problem whereby Hollywood productions extend the sociocultural contract of screen spectacle to the actual destruction of specific local ecosystems in the name of moving-image culture. As such, we might view the runaway production as an invasive species: a kind of living organism that is not native to an ecosystem and causes harm—to the environment, to the economy, and even to human health.[30] Beyond this, though, it allows Hollywood's cultural value system to get under the hood of diverse social configurations and specific local ecosystems, spreading beyond the confines of what Powdermaker deemed a somewhat controlled laboratory.

Due to the national increase in incentive plans, growing attention has been given to these plans' political machinery, industrial logic, economic nuances, and connection to space, as we can see in Vicki Mayer's excellent book *Almost Hollywood, Nearly New Orleans* (2017) and the collection *Locating Migrating Media* (2010).[31] However, the environmental impact of these policies has been largely neglected. This may well be due to the short lifespan of the programs (most states over the past two decades have failed to maintain their incentive programs, a failure that often mirrors the rise of conservative political power on the state level), the difficulty in tracking relocation patterns, and the impossible quantification of the carbon impact of an industry so deeply enmeshed in a global cultural economy, a national film industry, and the constant circulation of human and material resources. In pursuit of an environmental component to complement the social perspective offered by emerging production-culture studies, I look here at two different cases, Michigan (2008–2016) and Florida (2010–2016), in terms of their incentive's political economy, their cultural goals, and their social and environmental impact.

IMPORTED TO DETROIT

The Michigan incentive program started with a meeting between Democratic governor Jennifer Granholm and Michigan-born actor-director Mike Binder in August 2007, which led to Granholm pursuing economic subsidies for film production in Michigan. Granholm's immediate aim was to build a state-of-the-art Hollywood blockbuster facility in the ruins of a GM complex in Pontiac, just outside of Detroit, with the end goal being a cultural and economic transformation she likened to "a phoenix."[32] Signed into law on April 7, 2008, the Michigan Film and Digital Media Incentive laid the legislative groundwork for a tax-incentive program that would bring film and television production to Michigan, prompt the development of local media infrastructure, help to rehabilitate the state economy, and complement the state's new tourism campaign.

The incentive bill actually stipulates only one primary regulation of applicants: to guarantee promotion of Pure Michigan, a large-scale campaign designed to offset the collapse of the auto industry and to market Michigan according to its relational values with the lake-strewn natural environment. However, despite the state's bid to enhance tourism around the concept of a "pure Michigan," the film incentive program offered no guidelines regarding responsible waste disposal, the minimization of pollution, or similar practices. There is no mention of media production's environmental ramifications: the two driving forces are instead economic (Does this program generate income and/or jobs?) and representational (Does it depict Michigan in the desired way?).

In May 2008, Raleigh Studios of Hollywood opened Motown Motion Pictures LLC, incorporated with city, state, and federal incentives. The 42 percent budget incentive offering brought in 229 approved projects over four years, of which 164 wrapped. $392 million was approved on $1 billion in qualified expenditures in Michigan during this time, with a $47 million outlay in the first year leading to the creation of nearly 2,800 jobs. Economist David Zin argues that the film incentives had a positive impact yet acknowledges that this impact was not necessarily tangible, closing his thirty-four-page issue paper with the comment, "As with other types of incentives and credits, whether the relationship of costs to benefits is acceptable is a decision for individual policy-makers."[33] This is the bottom line of incentive programs, and the policy makers have partisan loyalties and political agendas.

Cost and benefit underlie the logic of such incentives, but what is on the other side of the bottom line? Part of the goal is certainly boosted infrastructure and employment; as Steven Miller and Abdul Abdulhadi argue in a study for the Center for Economic at Michigan State University, "Michigan has created an incentive package to not only draw filming crews to Michigan, but also to attract a whole industry in one effort to offset Michigan's declining manufacturing base." This package was meant to attract fresh labor and to erect a foundation for media professionals in the area, an attempt to form a "deep local supply chain" countering the previous flight of Michigan's educated and creative workforce to states with better job prospects.[34] The filmmaker and Michigan native son Sam Raimi celebrated this craft base as part of the process of job mobility: "With time more people will move there . . . so talented they just need a chance to work their way up through the guilds and unions. It's just a question of the incentive sticking."[35] However, this logic ignores the natural-resource and social service demand placed upon a constructed and natural environment by such influx and does not include in its mandate the infrastructural updates necessary to accommodate them.

Michigan's effort to attract tourists to the state and to train a local media base, in part by attracting major productions to its key cities using incentives to create filmmaking infrastructure, is not unique. In *The Film Studio: Film Production in the Global Economy* (2005), Ben Goldsmith and Tom O'Regan discuss how cities such as Toronto and New York built studios as a central part of urban renewal—"stargates" or hubs for city regeneration that are connected to waterfront and other city-renewal projects.[36] The goals and impact of incentive programs are not limited to what is brought into the space, though—they also include how the space is exported, and as such the incentive in Michigan also aimed at popularizing the state's image on screens across the world. An extension of the Pure Michigan impetus for that state's incentive was an attempt to export what Miller and Abdulhadi refer to as Michigan's "diverse environment" to the film-viewing world.[37]

Beyond the concrete issues of employment and economics, this production mode also strives to render the local space virtual, uploading it to a visual realm bereft of accountability to environmental health and community ethics. Janet Ward frames the role of such studios and incentive programs as a way of launching a city's appearance and identity into the virtual realm; "studios are then vehicles to propel cities toward a competitive realm of the virtual in which image-city competes with image-city."[38] For Detroit, this virtualization mostly meant targeting its dilapidated urbanity as a virtual substitute for any dystopian urban space, as it was used in the *Transformers* films and in *Batman v Superman: Dawn of Justice* (Zack Snyder, 2016). There are countless anecdotes about how the financial incentives and postindustrial smattering of abandoned buildings and lots made it easy for big-budget action films such as the *Red Dawn* reboot (Dan Bradley, 2012) to go there to blow things up—literally.

The tendency to rely on Detroit's urban aesthetic as a space to be exploded is at once an environmentally negligent manifestation of Granholm's "phoenix" and also part of a city rebirth that included the proliferation of greenway bike paths and shared urban gardens.[39] As the incentives brought films to the city, they brought industry workers, restored a creative class, and generated word of mouth. Performance artists and film craftspeople moved to Detroit to be in the center of the action, and they bought and renovated the dilapidated houses. Local businesspeople such as Mike Ilych took notice of the groundswell, and they too purchased buildings and thus participated in the city's renewal.

The jobs surrounding the incentives altered the demographic of the city and thousands of families' lives, changing the city's identity, population, and natural environment in unaccounted ways as downtown Detroit rebranded itself with greenways, microbreweries, and Shinola pride. In a city historically marked by racial segregation and environmental injustice, this population influx cashed in on the "aura of Hollywood"[40] without concern for the local material dynamics of an area, now being snatched up for development, that was previously laced with public-service problems whereby poorer and nonwhite neighborhoods were being left without electricity for traffic lights and where utility companies were threatening to cut the water of poorer homes.

Incentive plans can thus be identified as lacking an important environmental and social component: how such productions and population shifts weigh upon natural resources and public services as well as how they produce unexpected forms and quantities of waste and infrastructural demand. This is the local flipside of sustainable production, which must also be included into an environmental study of localized production. Although incentivized productions in Michigan were completed far from the watchful eye of the Producers Guild of America, every person I spoke to who worked on the ground in Michigan notes that similar environmental and sustainability measures were taken on these productions as those currently used in Hollywood: in other words, just as in Hollywood, they were superficial, lax, and primarily meant as token symbols of environmental concern. However, as one producer and location scout who was based in Detroit for the five years of the incentive program points out (in a comment that came across as an extension of the calculated kindness for which Hollywood is notorious), it was important to leave places in better condition than you found them because you would likely need to return at some point.

Until you don't need to. My Detroit contact has since moved to a new city, as have most film workers who originally moved to Detroit and bought homes and started families there. The cost–benefit gauge of the incentive was constantly challenged by conservative politicians, who argued that the economic costs were high, but the benefits were somewhat difficult to assess. Resistance became far more vitriolic when Jennifer Granholm was replaced as governor by Republican venture capitalist Rick Snyder in 2010. In August 2012, Raleigh Studios defaulted on its bond and left town.[41] Raimi's film *Oz the Great and Powerful* (2013), which received $40 million from the state, left a series of debts that Pontiac struggled to collect from Disney. As Emergency Manager Louis Schimell pointed out, echoing Caldwell's concept of the colonialist *paraindustry*, "This is a glamorous industry if you want to talk about Hollywood, but it's not very glamorous for the municipality that wants to collect something."[42] Snyder fully eliminated the program in 2015.

This snapshot reveals Michigan to be very much a textbook case of film incentives: liberal policies coupled with economic optimism and a short-term blossoming of nationwide attention standing on the shoulders of local social and environmental disruption, with any long-term benefits cut short by the grinding contestation of conservative state politics. However, some incentive plans and local media infrastructures arise for different reasons, providing a uniquely dynamic relationship between local relational values, political economy, and the encroachment of Hollywood production. In the playing out of these incentive plans, the rapid construction and undoing of studios, location sets, and family homes become part of the environmental impact of the screen industry. This problem is part of a larger relationship between localized media production and relational values to the environment that must be further explored if we are to develop constructive and environmentally healthy relationships between screen culture and the rest of the natural world.

SOUTH FLORIDA UNDERWATER CINEMATOGRAPHY

Although Miami catapulted into the popular screen imaginary in the 1980s with the rampant success of Brian de Palma's *Scarface* (1983) reboot and the zeitgeist-defining television series *Miami Vice* (1984–1990), it did not transition this on-location success into a systematic policy until the late 1990s. By 2000, Miami-Dade County was responsible for half of the state's media production, having enticed popular franchises *Bad Boys* and *The Fast and the Furious*, TV's *Burn Notice* (2007–2013), and a number of other films and television series.[43] Preceded by the slow growth of a state rebate program initiated in 2003, the Entertainment Industry Economic Development Act was passed in 2010, allocating $242 million in tax rebates and credits over the following five years, which drew enough production to Miami to place it third in national media production behind Los Angeles and New York. Moreover, due to Miami's demographic diversity and proximity to the Caribbean, it also became the focal node for Latin American and Spanish-language media.[44]

Summarizing the capitalist model behind such politics, Toby Miller and Richard Maxwell refer to Miami as "a stunning example" of "pump-priming" fiscal-stimulus strategies meant to boost local economies through financial incentives.[45] As we saw with Detroit, though, the pump ran dry when conservative policy makers managed to push through a different understanding of the cost–benefit analysis of film incentives. And though state politicians even channeled additional funds into the Florida incentive due to its success, the Koch brothers managed in 2016 to lead a systematic strangulation of the program through their lobbying group Americans for Prosperity, a conservative front for donating money to state senators and representatives who were willing to block further support.[46] The Florida incentive program became collateral damage in the demonstration of conservative might on the state level in a national push to the extreme right.

Regardless, the South Florida coast, with the Florida Keys adjacent and the Bahamas within tight proximity, has long been a hub for underwater cinematography in film and television. Today, nearly all underwater shots and sequences are filmed in this area due to its year-round warm weather, clear water, and the economic and legal ease of the Bahamas' lowered regulations. Unbeknownst to many, though, the mecca of underwater cinematography has a long history—one that enwraps local social habits and relational values within the institutionalization of national ideological views justifying the exploitation of nonhuman nature. Florida native Ric O'Barry, a local diver who began his career by capturing and training dolphins for the Florida Seaquarium and subsequently emerged as one of the nation's most vocal activists for animal rights, is perhaps most illustrative of this tension. O'Barry translated his diving skills and knowledge of marine wildlife into popular entertainment, transitioning from the Seaquarium to television as the capturer and head trainer of the five dolphins that collectively played Flipper on the popular eponymous TV show in the 1960s (figure 5.1). However, in 1970, after production of the show had ended, Kathy—the dolphin that most often played Flipper—died in what O'Barry considered a suicide (she simply did not resurface for air), and that same year O'Barry founded

FIGURE 5.1 Ric O'Barry training one of the original dolphins that played the role of television's Flipper. O'Barry played a huge role in the screen visibility and exploitative performance of dolphins before founding the Dolphin Project and becoming arguably the most vocal international spokesperson for dolphin protection. *Source*: Photograph courtesy of the Dolphin Project.

the Dolphin Project, an organization for public education on the plight of dolphins in captivity and for the catch-and-release rehabilitation of dolphins in North and South America.

O'Barry's personal trajectory offers a microcosmic paradigm for how relational values with the natural world may be co-opted by anthropocentric cultural practices that exploit wildlife and the environment without regard for the long-term consequences—or, just as easily, for how these same relational values may flip back to an active struggle against such values.

Perhaps even more foundational for the local cinematographic community, though, was Ricou Browning, best known under the guise "Gillman," the costume he donned in the *Creature from the Black Lagoon* film series. Raised in Florida and getting early experience as an underwater stuntman for local novelty acts, Browning also worked as a writer for the

Flipper film and television series and moved on to directing the underwater scenes in *Thunderball* (Terence Young, 1965, which won an Oscar for special visual effects), *Caddyshack* (Harold Ramis, 1980), *Never Say Never Again* (Irvin Kirshner, 1983), and the television series *Boardwalk Empire* (2010). Browning was inducted into the Florida Artists Hall of Fame in 2012, and his son—Ricou Browning Jr.—has worked as marine coordinator and water-safety director for countless films and television series, from the big-screen *Miami Vice* reprise (Michael Mann, 2006) to Netflix's *Bloodline* (2015–2017), from blockbusters such as *I Am Legend* (Francis Lawrence, 2007) to dramas such as *Up in the Air* (Jason Reitman, 2009)—not all beach-based or aquatic-adventure films, but all films and series that, for whatever reason, required some form of underwater cinematography.

Ricou Jr. currently plays a central role in the area's busy location-filming infrastructure as marine coordinator—the South Florida variation of a major crew position that has popped up in some form in most major cities where incentives lure regular Hollywood production. Although the film companies have to bring in necessary environmental engineers or munitions experts in order to solve logistical problems, the marine coordinator acts as an intermediary between the production and local licensing offices and as an on-site supervisor to maintain production protocol. As such, he is the official line of defense between external productions, state and city regulations, and the local ecosystem. As both part of the film industry *and* part of the South Florida ecosystem, Browning often privately contracts familiar faces from the local media world, including the cinematographer Pete Zuccarini, an underwater director of photography whose credit sheet is far too long to cite but includes the recent films *Life of Pi* (Ang Lee, 2012), *All Is Lost* (J. C. Chandor, 2013), and *Jurassic World* (Colin Trevorrow, 2015). As Browning told me, because the area contains sensitive reefs and wildlife balance, he wants Zuccarini not just because he is an expert cameraperson but also because he is a locally born and raised diver who knows and cares about that specific ecosystem.

The logic behind such hiring practices has been complemented by a recent rise in the sense of environmental concern on set. Browning, Zuccarini, and others note the increase in environmental and sustainability measures as well as the general sensibility toward protecting the environment during on-location productions. As Browning told me, the

U.S. Environmental Protection Agency and the U.S. Army Corps of Engineers have even sent monitors to local sets in order to photograph how the film companies do set cleanup—and in order to set their own standards. More than anything, though, filmmakers' rising attentiveness to their on-site locale appears to be part of a delicate balance between invasive crews and local access: as Browning puts it, "to make movies you have to be welcome back the next year."[47]

Investors, accountants, and lawyers are running the studios today, and they realize that it is in their best interest to maintain a good public image and rapport with their satellite locations. Nevertheless, as a top environmental studio exec told me, although local environmental services are available on site for low impact, the studios aren't actually accountable to the local spaces, as can be seen by the excess displayed by big-budget productions in Miami, Detroit, and elsewhere. The impact of filming on such locations, Browning and others have noted, has progressively lessened, however, due to the advent of digital practices—if for no other reason than speed. With smaller equipment and bigger memory, the process is expedited, and the production minimizes its interruption of fragile coral reefs and native fauna, thus sparing the ecosystem as much disruption as possible. However, for large-scale blockbuster shoots, it remains business as usual, with vast fleets of boats, copious use of fuel, and rampant disturbance to the local ecosystem.

Due to the visibility offered in South Florida waters and the infrastructure of media production that has grown up there over decades, it is safe to say that we will continue seeing underwater shots from these subtropical waters. However, such waters can also be faked: the *Baywatch* reboot (Seth Gordon, 2017) was shot in Savannah, where river waters are much muddier, a choice made by producers to access Georgia's more liberal incentive program. It was more cost effective for the producers to build set tanks and use green-screen processes in order to simulate the effect of oceanic waters. The migration of productions away from Florida has been an increasing problem since the incentive spout was cut off by the state legislature, creating what has been referred to as a "brain drain" of creative professionals as they leave for more incentivized states.[48] The circulation of human lives and with it the reshaping of social communities, urban spaces, and ecosystems must not remain underappreciated and unexplored by scholars, and to assess it according to dynamic terms that include political economy and relational values would benefit policy makers and industry managers.

From Los Angeles to Miami, Miami to Georgia, state and city film incentives create demographic shifts and affect human lives in ways that are as difficult to quantify as the symbolic impact of having your communal space transformed into a nebulous screened "somewhere." More critically, though, we must consider the environmental consequences of this facet of our film and media culture. Film productions use power, water, bodies, cities and thus produce both material and virtual transformations. The production came, the local changed—changed materially in its constitution, culturally in its identity, compositionally in its ecosystem, and virtually as a fluctuating puzzle piece in the astral cosmos of flickering projectors. Buildings were erected, blown up, or abandoned; new forms of waste and pollution were introduced; the organization of energy and resources was reconfigured; the relational values of marine life and beautiful landscapes were challenged with the values of dystopian urbanity and exploited animals.

The economic, cultural, and partisan drives of incentive programs and local media infrastructures shape our world both onscreen and off, and the economic benefits of film industry circulation continues to have profound social and political impact on local space—just look at the unexpected political implications of Georgia's incentive plan on the state's attempted Religious Liberties bill of 2017. A popular conservative measure, the bill promised to legitimize discrimination and allow the violation of human rights based on store owners' religious beliefs. Conservative governor Nathan Deal vetoed the bill when Disney and Marvel—whose array of productions in 2015 accounted for an estimated $2 billion influx to the state thanks to the allure of film incentives—threatened to yank their productions from Georgia, thus setting the proposed law at odds with local financial and media industry interests.[49] A bill that would have allowed business owners to exercise bigotry against patrons was quashed, despite a rising groundswell of alt-right support across the country and a legislative precedent set shortly beforehand in North Carolina, thus drawing identity politics and social policy into the incentive model's already complicated cost–benefit analysis.

In this case, the invasive species stymied a native threat to human rights. As a consequence, we must acknowledge and attempt to understand the complexities of translocal, incentivized, and localized production cultures without categorically viewing them as negative or positive—these dynamic production cultures are too complex to be assessed as fully either. The proliferation of film incentives offered outside Los Angeles reveals a complex array of competing motivations and impacts. States and cities use them to shore up flagging industries, to promote tourism and encourage home buying, to develop local media infrastructures, and to export the image of their city, state, and natural environments as a virtual product—and they allow Hollywood studios and culture to engage with local politics and to permeate local social practices and values. Paradoxically, local politicians who champion incentives for economic and cultural reasons ignore the challenge these film productions and the studios they are connected to may pose for other political agendas as well as for the negative environmental impact of conventional screen production practices that they entail.

This discussion is not meant to discourage film incentive programs or to charge Hollywood with full responsibility for the priorities and practices of other cities, but rather to encourage more dynamic ways of understanding how such programs interact with human groups and the natural environment. As Florida currently debates legislation to renew the film incentive program, its policy makers would do well to consider the relational values of local communities not only as something that can be marketed to Hollywood but also as something that should be protected from the assembly line of the global marketplace. Without this protection, local values and spaces are merely props and backdrops in Hollywood's increasingly global machinery, and incentive programs are doomed to repeat the patterns of the past, failing local communities and traumatizing local ecosystems.

Conclusion

An Element of Hope

Just as water, gas, and electricity are brought into our houses from far off to satisfy our needs in response to a minimal effort, so we shall be supplied with visual- or auditory images, which will appear and disappear at a simple movement of the hand, hardly more than a sign. Just as we are accustomed, if not enslaved, to the various forms of energy that pour into our homes, we shall find it perfectly natural to receive the ultrarapid variations or oscillations that our sense organs gather in and integrate to form all we know. I do not know whether a philosopher has ever dreamed of a company engaged in the home delivery of Sensory Reality.

—PAUL VALÉRY, "THE CONQUEST OF UBIQUITY"

I would like to conclude by returning to the quote that opened this book, but restoring to it its oft excluded second half—often excluded but all the more relevant as with instant streaming, interactive reception and gaming modes, and the current proliferation of augmented and virtual reality technologies Paul Valéry's once vague notion of a home-delivered "Sensory Reality" is today taking a sharply defined shape. Through virtual images, sounds, and sensations, the material real is increasingly replaced by a plethora of screen devices and interfaces whose mediated input forms "all we know." Not only *can* this Sensory Reality easily be dreamed (and in fact must be reckoned with) by philosophers today, but it *is* also very much the hybridized experience of everyday life. Valéry's point that we "are accustomed, if not enslaved, to the various forms of energy that pour into our homes" is key because it indicates the type of

tacit agreement and customary behavior that form our sociocultural contract. Beyond taking this network of digital screens for granted, we
increasingly depend on it for a number of mythological, pleasure-driven,
social, psychological, and scientific purposes and in this silent agreement
are blinded to its environmental costs. This is why we need more cultural awareness and social and political policy on the matter, from studios' carbon-footprint transparency to governmental regulation of
e-waste recycling.

Hope comes in many forms: in the messages expressed on screens,
in the values and behaviors of new generations of human beings, in the
policy changes of local and global policy shapers, in the expansion of
institutions and individuals working on environmental communication
and justice. Just as Moore's Law has been and will continue to be replaced
by faster rates of processing acceleration, just as the law of obsolescence
and the culture of the newest upgrade will turn two years into one and
one phone per capita into two, so are solar panels going up around Google
and Apple server farms to power our archived immortality. In fact, in
2013 Apple announced that its data centers—which house the computing infrastructure for services such as iTunes, Siri, and Maps—are now
run entirely on renewable energies; Amazon has pledged similar steps.
A number of similar emerging proposals for "green electronics" or "green
ICT" (information and communications technology) and "sustainable
HCI" (human–computer interaction) are turning the future of virtual-
media technology into a green conversation.[1] Sun Center, a production
studio opened in 2011 just outside of Philadelphia, lined its roofs with
solar panels to make its films—including *Creed* (Ryan Coogler, 2015) and
After Earth (M. Night Shyamalan, 2013)—at least partially by use of solar
power.

And although influential industries such as automobile manufacturing are not directly involved in film culture, they are increasingly reliant
on screen technologies and are making similar turns toward sustainability: Tesla stands at the forefront of solar-technology development and
electric-car production, and in 2017 Volvo announced plans to completely
phase out gas-only automobiles by 2019, manufacturing exclusively
hybrid and electric cars thereafter. Many would understandably identify
car culture as the predominant icon of twentieth-century capitalism, the
driving force of mainstream material consumerism. I have argued in this

book that capitalism is, in fact, more clearly projected in the sociocultural contract of our film and digital media customs, increasingly so given the twenty-first-century transition from an analog industrial economy to a digital information economy. If Volvo can restructure its entire business model according to minimizing environmental impact, why can't Disney? Sony? AMC? Netflix? Samsung?

Such a shift fits in with the tech sector's ongoing self-branding as a source of innovative practice and progressive thinking as well as with Hollywood's cultivated public image as a bastion of liberal politics. The potential merger of environmentalist policy and smart technology is a realizable dream at the center of today's digital screen culture, which extends to nearly every American household, every room, every pocket and which has profound ramifications for our entire planet—a problem that requires more than efficient lightbulbs, household recycling, and carbon offsets. The sociocultural contract explored in this book is not meant to reiterate the neoliberal myths of green consumerism; solutions to global warming cannot simply be dumped upon the viewer. Consumer habits can encourage small adjustments, but for the most part we are reliant on what a limited handful of companies are providing to the marketplace, and corporations are not ethically or legally accountable to their customers or even to their shareholders. On an overpopulated planet that continues to grow and to develop in nations whose populations are ripe for digital modernity, the effects of climate change are unique and specific, and one person's or even one company's actions justifiably feel like just a drop in the bucket.[2] And yet, as Naomi Klein endorses quite convincingly in *This Changes Everything* (2014),[3] massive change usually comes at a grassroots level, and what is necessary for this grassroots change is a bottom-up shift in our conceptualization of capitalism.

The fundamental dyad of capitalism—the conversion of ostensible objects into exchange value and the alienation of exploited labor from its product and profit—crystallizes in our popular screen culture, and the everyday role of quotidian media has in a brief time altered the planet. Our ecosystems are no longer made solely of components thousands or even millions of years old but are littered with a rapidly evolved and discarded trail of metal, chemical, and plastic objects that have enabled the catapulting of our attention to the canvases of the virtual. From pagan and religious symbols to icon paintings to filmstrips to GIFs, we have simply accelerated—and monetized—an ancient drive of animals to live beyond themselves, be it as survival or as culture, to defy their mortality through spectacle.[4] This sensory play has always been central to the various desires and performances of the natural world—screen culture did not invent spectacle; it merely adjusted how spectacle defines the human relationship to the environmental costs of pleasure and communication. The dramatic change offered by capitalism and cinema is that this drive, in its industrialized form and its ideological inequities, has managed to disrupt the balance of a global ecosystem that was once sustainable.

Be it in the blockbusters on our big screens, the televisual series streamed on our laptops, or the social media operated from our phones—

Be it in the representations of the natural world, in the use of natural resources and production of waste in the lifespan of media apparatuses, or in the glorification of excess and the sacrifice of the real implied by red carpet premieres and online avatars—

Be it in the development of the hardware, the degree of habituation in its use, the maintenance of its seemingly invisible process, or the casual disposal of its by-products—

We are not only reconfiguring dynamics of social justice but also changing the consistency and composition of our planet, its atmosphere, and its various ecologies.

This book makes a plea for us to consider the environmental ramifications and role of screen culture, to direct environmentalists toward screen practices as a crucial battlefield for green resistance, and to urge the exploration of this intersection for those who work in political economy, environmental studies, anthropology, and science communication. Consumers need to become more aware of the environmental and social effects of screen use; institutions of cultural production need to be regulated toward more ecological responsibility; and climate scientists would benefit from better understanding the connotations and strategies of screen representation and messaging. I embrace MacKenzie Wark's critique of climate science for having a *communicative fetish*, "where what is communicated is severed from how it is communicated. Climate science requires a theory and a method of studying the means of production of its own data—a media theory."[5] As climate science is increasingly both produced and communicated through digital screen technologies, and as it is drawn more centrally into the partisan divide, it must be challenged by a theory of its epistemology and messaging. But theory must arrive here at the service of the material, so that awareness of the material might then shape a change in practice and, in turn, enact a shift in the worldviews that guide our moral systems, ethical choices, policy formation, and behavioral patterns.

As this book demonstrates, the call for materiality does not preclude the need for analyzing textual representation with regard to how individual films toe the line between progressive environmental messages and conventional social norms and cultural values. As Andrew Hageman argues, "Every film contains contradictions—points at which their ecological representations and messages break down. Such breaking points must not be read as signs of failures to be lamented, but as indices of the contradictions within the ideology that determines our current ability to think and represent ecology."[6] By teasing apart the contradictions of some of Hollywood's most celebrated texts, I insist that we hold up a mirror to the ideological contradictions, cognitive dissonances, and representational inabilities that set us on a collusion course with environmental degradation. Representation must always be held in connection to its materiality as well, and in drawing the curtain back on how we make, market, consume, and dispose of popular movies, I call for a change in how we view the viewing of the world—a world we must consider ourselves *a part of*, not *apart from*. Being an integral and influential part of our global environment while remaining apart from its costs and obligations is perhaps the most dangerous unspoken clause of our screen culture's sociocultural contract, which until recently has remained hidden: Hollywood's dirtiest secret, which we are finally ready to speak aloud.

Notes

INTRODUCTION: THE BIG PICTURE

1. Patrick Curry, *Ecological Ethics: An Introduction* (Cambridge: Polity Press, 2006), 47, my emphasis.
2. Herbert Marcuse, *The Aesthetic Dimension: Toward a Critique of Marxist Aesthetics* (New York: Beacon Press, 1979), 32.
3. Hunter Vaughan, *Where Film Meets Philosophy: Godard, Resnais, and Experiments in Cinematic Thinking* (New York: Columbia University Press, 2013).
4. Paul Valéry, "The Conquest of Ubiquity" (1928), in *Aesthetics*, translated by Ralph Mannheim (London: Routledge and Kegan Paul, 1964), 225–226.
5. Carolyn Merchant, *The Death of Nature: Women, Ecology, and the Scientific Revolution* (San Francisco: Harper, 1980), 99.
6. McKenzie Wark, *Molecular Red: Theory for the Anthropocene* (London: Verso, 2015), 18.
7. For the relatively recent bloom of environmental concerns across the humanities, see Cheryll Glotfelty and Harold Fromm, eds., *The Ecocriticism Reader* (Athens: University of Georgia Press, 1996); Laurence Coupe, ed., *The Green Studies Reader: From Romanticism to Ecocriticism* (London: Routledge, 2000); and Stephen Siperstein, Shane Hall, and Stephanie LeMenager, eds., *Teaching Climate Change in the Humanities* (London: Routledge, 2016). For environmental communication, see Alison Anderson, *Media, Culture, and the Environment* (London: UCL Press, 1997), and Anders Hansen and Robert Cox, eds., *The Routledge Handbook of Environment and Communication* (London: Routledge, 2015).

8. See Adrian Ivakhiv, *Ecologies of the Moving Image* (Waterloo, Canada: Wilfred Laurier University Press, 2013); Sean Cubitt, *Finite Media: Environmental Implications of Digital Technologies* (Durham, N.C.: Duke University Press, 2016); Nadia Bozak, *The Cinematic Footprint: Lights, Camera, Natural Resources* (New Brunswick, N.J.: Rutgers University Press, 2011); Richard Maxwell and Toby Miller, *Greening the Media* (Oxford: Oxford University Press, 2012); and Nicole Starosielski, *The Undersea Network* (Durham, N.C.: Duke University Press, 2015).

9. Naomi Klein, *This Changes Everything: Capitalism vs. the Climate* (New York: Simon and Schuster, 2014); for the social movement, see theleapblog.org.

10. Naomi Oreskes and Erik M. Conway, *The Merchants of Doubt: How a Handful of Scientists Obscured the Truth on Issues from Tobacco Smoke to Global Warming* (New York: Bloomsbury Press, 2010).

11. Stephanie LeMenager gives one example from among many: "Josh Fox's remarkable documentary about hydrolic fracturing, *Gasland*, offers a fine example of how a documentary that airs on a cable television channel such as HBO can snowball into a national *and* grassroots phenomenon through Internet citation and social networking" (*Living Oil: Petroleum Culture in the American Century* [New York: Oxford University Press, 2014], 46).

12. Rob Nixon, *Slow Violence and the Environmental Violence of the Poor* (Cambridge, Mass.: Harvard University Press, 2011), 2.

13. Sean Cubitt, "Everybody Knows This Is Nowhere: Data Visualization and Ecocriticism," in *Ecocinema Theory and Practice*, ed. Stephen Rust, Salma Monani, and Sean Cubitt (New York: Routledge, 2013), 279, original emphasis.

14. Paul Virilio, *War and Cinema*, trans. Patrick Camiller (London: Verso, 1989), 32.

15. For a discussion of "zombie" media, see Bozak, *The Cinematic Footprint*, 130.

16. See M. A. Chan Kai, P. Balvanera, K. Benessaiah, M. Chapman, S. Díaz, E. Gómez-Baggethun, R. Gould, N. Hannahs, K. Jax, S. Klain, et al., "Why Protect Nature? Rethinking Values and the Environment," *Proceedings of the National Academy of Sciences* 113, no. 6 (2016): 1462–1465, and U. Pascual, P. Balvanera, S. Díaz, G. Pataki, E. Roth, M. Stenseke, R. T. Watson, E. B. Dessane, M. Islar, E. Kelemen, et al., "Valuing Nature's Contributions to People: The IPBES Approach," *Current Opinion in Environmental Sustainability* 26–27 (2017): 7–16.

17. Jane Bennett, *Vibrant Matter: A Political Ecology of Things* (Durham, N.C.: Duke University Press, 2010), 112.

18. Jennifer Gabrys, *Digital Rubbish: A Natural History of Electronics* (Ann Arbor: University of Michigan Press, 2013), vi.

19. Jussi Parikka, *A Geology of Media* (Minneapolis: University of Minnesota Press, 2015), 103.

20. See, for example, Jason Moore, ed., *Anthropocene or Capitolocene? Nature, History, and the Crisis of Capitalism* (Oakland, Calif.: PM Press, 2016).

21. Jean-Jacques Rousseau, *Du contract social; ou Principes du droit politique* (Amsterdam: Chez Marc-Michel Rey, 1762).

22. There exists an increasing number of strong summaries of this scientific consensus; for one that is especially concise and clear, see Andrew J. Hoffman, *How Culture Shapes the Climate Change Debate* (Stanford, Calif.: Stanford University Press, 2015), 7–9.

23. This trend is evidenced in a number of recent works in international screen studies, such as Alessandro Nova's sweeping visual-culture history *The Book of the Wind: The Representation of the Invisible* (Montreal: McGill-Queen's University Press, 2011); Weihong Bao's dynamic work *Fiery Cinema: The Emergence of an Affective Medium in China, 1915–1945* (Minneapolis: University of Minnesota Press, 2015); and John Durham Peters's book *The Marvelous Clouds: Towards a Philosophy of Elemental Media* (Chicago: University of Chicago Press, 2015).

24. Ellen Elizabeth Moore, "Green Screen or Smokescreen? Hollywood's Messages About Nature and the Environment," *Environmental Communication* 10, no. 5 (2015): 5.

25. Vicki Mayer, Miranda J. Banks, and John Thornton Caldwell, "Introduction: Production Studies: Roots and Routes," in *Production Studies: Cultural Studies of Media Industries*, ed. Vicki Mayer, Miranda J. Banks, and John Thornton Caldwell (New York: Routledge, 2009), 2.

26. Charles J. Corbett and Richard P. Turco, *Southern California Environmental Report Card 2006: Sustainability in the Motion Picture Industry* (Los Angeles: Institute of the Environment, University of California, 2006).

27. Anthony A. Leiserowitz, "Before and After *The Day After Tomorrow*: A U.S. Study of Climate Change Risk Perception," *Environment* 46, no. 9 (2004): 22–44. Matthew Schneider-Mayerson performed a similar study titled "Disaster Movies and the 'Peak Oil' Movement': Does Popular Culture Encourage Eco-apocalyptic Beliefs in the United States?" *Journal for the Study of Religion, Nature, and Culture* 7, no. 3 (2013): 289–314.

28. Matthew Nisbet, "Evaluating the Impact of *The Day After Tomorrow*," *Skeptical Inquirer*, June 16, 2004, http://www.csicop.org/specialarticles/show/evaluating_the_impact_of_the_day_after_tomorrow.

29. E. Ann Kaplan, *Climate Trauma: Foreseeing the Future in Dystopian Film and Fiction* (New Brunswick, N.J.: Rutgers University Press, 2015).

1. BURNING DOWN THE HOUSE

1. See Jean-Louis Schefer, *L'homme ordinaire du cinema* (Paris: Cahiers du Cinema, 1980).

2. "Summer Movie Preview," *New York Times*, May 2, 2014.

3. Tom Gunning, "An Aesthetic of Astonishment: Early Film and the (In)Credulous Spectator," *Art and Text* 34 (Spring 1989): 31–45.

4. Quoted in Esther Leslie, *Synthetic Worlds: Nature, Art, and the Chemical Industry* (Middlesex, U.K.: Reaktion Books, 2005), 201–202.

5. Weihong Bao offers an excellent historical case study of this centrality of fire to film in *Fiery Cinema: The Emergence of an Affective Medium in China, 1915–1945* (Minneapolis: University of Minnesota Press, 2015): "The dream of the fiery and affective medium, carrying cinema's desire to overcome its historical self by self-induced medium violence—from generic and aesthetic crossing of the representation frame to endured obsession with images of fire and similar entities to physical destructions of film screens, prints, and sites of exhibition—has always been with us in international film history" (6).

6. Jared Greenhouse, "Eli Roth on Being 'Almost Killed' by Fire While Shooting 'Inglourious Basterds,'" *Huffington Post*, July 2, 2015, https://www.huffingtonpost.com/2015/07/02/eli-roth-inglourious-basterds_n_7716150.html.

7. Andrea Stulman Demett and Nina Warnke, "Disaster Spectacle at the Turn of the Century," *Film History* 4, no. 2 (1990): 105.

8. Stulman Demett and Warnke, "Disaster Spectacle at the Turn of the Century," 107.

9. John Kasson, *Amusing the Millions: Coney Island at the Turn of the Century* (New York: Hill and Wang, 1978), 72.

10. Stulman Demett and Warnke, "Disaster Spectacle at the Turn of the Century," 107.

11. Quoted in David Biello, *The Unnatural World: The Race to Remake Civilization in Earth's Newest Age* (New York: Simon and Schuster, 2016), 59.

12. Biello, *The Unnatural World*, 59.

13. Kevin B. Lee, "Kaboom!" *New York Times*, May 2, 2014.

14. Robin L. Murray and Joseph K. Heumann, *Ecology and Popular Film: Cinema on the Edge* (New York: State University of New York Press, 2009), 19.

15. Murray and Heumann, *Ecology and Popular Film*, 20.

16. Murray and Heumann, *Ecology and Popular Film*, 21.

17. Rahman Badalov, "Oil, Revolution, and Cinema," *Azerbaijan International* 5, no. 3 (Autumn 1997): 57–64, htttp://www.azer.com/aiweb/categories/magazine/53_folder/53_articles/53_revolution/html.

18. Thomas McIlvaine Jr., "Reducing Film Fires," *Annals of the American Academy of Political and Social Sciences* 128 (November 1926): 96–99.

19. David Bordwell, "Nitrate Days and Nights," David Bordwell's Website on Cinema, May 13, 2015, http://www.davidbordwell.net/blog/2015/05/13/nitrate-days-and-nights/.

20. In May 2015, the George Eastman House in Rochester, New York, hosted "The Nitrate Picture Show," which was billed as "the world's first festival of film

conservation" and showcased Roger Smither's edited volume *This Film Is Dangerous: A Celebration of Nitrate Film* (Brussels: International Federation of Film Archives, 2002), an anthology focusing on the legacy and legend of nitrate film. The festival included talks and screenings of nitrate films in the hallowed Dryden Theatre (including tours of its safeguarded projection room), one of the only theaters still equipped to project nitrate film.

21. Martin Scorsese, foreword to *This Film Is Dangerous*, ed. Smither, ix.
22. See Paolo Cherchi Usai, *The Death of Cinema* (London: BFI, 2001), 15–21.
23. Wheeler Winston Dixon, *Visions of the Apocalypse: Spectacles of Destruction in American Cinema* (London: Wallflower Press, 2003), 3.
24. Justice Stewart's argument, intended to defend the protection of free speech in what he contended was Louis Malle's not-obscene film *The Lovers* (1958), has become a benchmark for U.S. Supreme Court's subjective integrity.
25. Ben Brewster and Lea Jacobs, *Theatre to Cinema: Stage Pictorialism and the Early Feature Film* (Oxford: Oxford University Press, 1997), 8, cited in Sheldon Hall and Stephen Neale, *Epics, Spectacles, and Blockbusters: A Hollywood History* (Detroit: Wayne State University Press, 2010), 6.
26. Julian Stringer, introduction to *Movie Blockbusters*, ed. Julian Stringer (London: Routledge, 2005), 8.
27. Verena Andermatt Conley, *Ecopolitics: The Environment in Poststructuralist Thought* (New York: Routledge, 1997), 5.
28. For a powerful application of this notion of detachment from spectacle to contemporary warfare, see Jean Baudrillard, *The Gulf War Did Not Take Place*, trans. Paul Patton (Bloomington: University of Indiana Press, 1995).
29. Stringer, introduction to *Movie Blockbusters*, 8. Stringer is in fact appropriating James Naremore's description of film noir in *More Than Night: Film Noir in Its Contexts* (Berkeley: University of California Press, 1998), 11.
30. Geoff King, *Spectacular Narratives: Hollywood in the Age of the Blockbuster* (London: I. B. Tauris, 2009), 2–4.
31. In "The Cursed, Buried City That May Never See the Light of Day," *Outside*, October 8, 2015 (http://www.outsideonline.com/2023921/cursed-buried-city-may-never-see-light-day), David Ferry writes an excellent story of DeMille's eradication of the set and Peter Brosnan's quest to excavate it.
32. "*Hellfighters*," IMDb, n.d., http://www.imdb.com/title/tt0063060/?ref_=nv_sr_1.
33. Murray and Heumann, *Ecology and Popular Film*, 30–31.
34. David Ingram, *Green Screen: Environmentalism and Hollywood* (Exeter, U.K.: University of Exeter Press, 2000), 19–20.
35. King, *Spectacular Narratives*, 156.
36. Tom Schatz, foreword to David Alan Vertrees, *Selznick's Vision: "Gone with the Wind" and Hollywood Filmmaking* (Austin: University of Texas Press, 1997), ix.

37. Adrian Turner, *A Celebration of "Gone with the Wind"* (New York: Gallery Books, 1990), 15.

38. See Hall and Neale, *Epics, Spectacles, and Blockbusters*, 113.

39. Vivian Sobchack, "Surge and Splendour," in *Film Genre Reader II*, ed. Barry Keith Grant (Austin: University of Texas Press, 1995), 285, 282.

40. Schatz, foreword to Vertrees, *Selznick's Vision*, x.

41. Gavin Lambert, *GWTW: The Making of "Gone with the Wind"* (Boston: Little, Brown, 1973), 44.

42. "DOS memo to Mr. Russell Birdwell, cc: Mr. George Cukor," February 14, 1938, Folder 106—*GWTW*, George Cukor Collection, Academy of Motion Picture Arts and Sciences, Margaret Herrick Library, Beverly Hills, Calif.

43. Quoted in Rudy Behlmer, *Shoot the Rehearsal! Behind the Scenes with Assistant Director Reggie Callow* (Lanham, Md.: Scarecrow Press, 2010), 39.

44. Schatz, foreword to Vertrees, *Selznick's Vision*, xiii.

45. Vertrees, *Selznick's Vision*, 72.

46. Annie Laurie Fuller Kurtz, "Pre-viewing of 'Gone with the Wind,'" original emphasis, completed in Rudy Behlmer Papers, Folder 110, "GONE WITH THE WIND—Research on Production," Wilbur G. Kurtz Collection, Academy of Motion Picture Arts and Sciences, Margaret Herrick Library.

47. Vertrees, *Selznick's Vision*, 5.

48. Fuller Kurtz, "Pre-viewing of 'Gone with the Wind.'"

49. Vertrees, *Selznick's Vision*, 69–70.

50. Quoted in Behlmer, *Shoot the Rehearsal!*, 39–40.

51. See Clarence Slifer, "Creating Visual Effects for *GWTW*," *American Cinematographer* 63, no. 8 (1982): 838–839.

52. "Correspondence to DOS from Menzies," November 9, 1938, Haver b. 1, Vertical File Collection, Academy of Motion Picture Arts and Sciences, Margaret Herrick Library.

53. "By this date (11/21/38), Selznick himself had begun to question the economy of capturing the spectacle of this sequence by sacrificing his studio's exterior sets to the fire. On the previous day, he had confided to Ginsberg in a memo that MGM had warned that burning the backlot would prove to be an unnecessary extravagance" (Vertrees, *Selznick's Vision*, 74).

54. Memos from Selznick to Henry Ginsberg and Kenneth MacGowan discuss the technological innovations that Selznick and Menzies experimented with in the search for greater spectacle, including a multicamera and mirroring process that was meant to achieve a Cinerama effect. However, equipping theaters for this process would be a great expense and would delay the film's release by two years. So Selznick, Jock Whitney (then chairman of the board of Selznick International Pictures, Inc.), and Al Lichtman (head of distribution for Loew's, which was set

to release the picture) decided to drop the idea. See David O. Selznick to Mr. Henry Ginsberg, memo, November 20, 1938, and Selznick to Mr. Kenneth MacGowan, memo, October 14, 1955, David O. Selznick Collection, Harry Ransom Center, University of Texas, Austin.

55. Vertrees, *Selznick's Vision*, 74.

56. Quoted in Behlmer, *Shoot the Rehearsal!*, 40

57. "GWTW Final Shooting Script," January 24, 1939, pp. 101, 107, Gen. no. 496, Box 29, General Collection, Doheny Memorial Library, University of Southern California, Los Angeles.

58. Fuller Kurtz, "Pre-viewing of 'Gone with the Wind.'"

59. Wilbur G. Kurtz, "'Gone with the Wind' from Behind the Cameras," converted for publication into "How Hollywood Built Atlanta," *Atlanta Journal Sunday Magazine*, December 3, 1939.

60. Kurtz, "How Hollywood Built Atlanta."

61. Lambert, *GWTW*, 54–56.

62. Slifer, "Creating Visual Effects for *GWTW*," 838–839.

63. David O. Selznick to Mrs. David O Selznick, December 12, 1938, in David O. Selznick, *Memo from David O. Selznick*, ed. Rudy Behlmer (New York: Viking Press, 1972), 186; "DOS memo to Jock Whitney," December 10, 1938, Folder 184.8, Selznick Collection, full capitalization in the original.

64. The original film program reads: "The burning of the military supplies of Atlanta, one of the major spectacular scenes in the picture, was filmed on the night of December 15, 1938, at which time David O. Selznick met Vivien Leigh" ("GWTW Program," p. 8, Folder f.24, Kurtz Collection).

65. David Thompson, *Showman: The Life of David O. Selznick* (New York: Knopf, 1992), 279.

66. In "Memo from Howard Deitz—HOME OFFICE, to ADVERTSING–PUBLICITY EXPLOITATION DEPARTMENTS," sent to the Advertising Department at Selznick's behest on December 21, 1939, Deitz instructs: "Outlined below is a list of DON'TS . . . Don't refer to the BURNING OF ATLANTA as such. The scene in the picture is not the burning of Atlanta but rather burning of certain buildings containing war materials, burning of freight cars loaded with ammunition, etc. The city in general was not touched by these fires. To assure accuracy of reference on this item, use the phrase—'The Atlanta fire scene'" ("GONE WITH THE WIND (misc)," Folder 45, Vertical File Collection).

67. Lambert, *GWTW*, 147.

68. "Exhibitor's Campaign Book from MGM," GWTW Advertising Publicity Exploitation Folder 1, Pressbook Collection, Doheny Memorial Library.

69. "Publicity Service," GWTW Advertising Publicity Exploitation Folder 2, Pressbook Collection.

70. Vertrees, *Selznick's Vision*, 5–6.

71. "Reviews from Press Preview of GWTW," Selznick Collection.

72. "London Reviews," *Cinema*, April 19, 1940, Folder 185.5, Selznick Collection, ellipses and full capitalization in the original.

73. "Press Book," GWTW Advertising Publicity Exploitation Folder 1, Pressbook Collection, full capitalization in the original.

74. "Press Book," GWTW Advertising Publicity Exploitation Folder 1, Pressbook Collection.

75. "LIVE RADIO 60-Second Live Announcement Spot" and "One-Minute Live Announcement No. 1," GWTW Advertising Publicity Exploitation Folder 1, Pressbook Collection, all ellipses in the original.

76. Edna Lim, "Displacing 'Titanic': History, Spectacle, Hollywood," in "Titanica," special issue of *International Literary Studies* 5, no. 1 (2003): 59–60.

77. Quoted in Turner, *A Celebration of "Gone with the Wind,"* 15.

78. See Steve Neale, "Hollywood Blockbusters: Historical Dimensions," in *Movie Blockbusters*, ed. Stringer, 51; Tom Schatz, "The New Hollywood," in *Movie Blockbusters*, ed. Stringer, 18.

79. Lambert, *GWTW*, 159.

80. Matilde Nardelli, "'The Sprawl of Entropy': Cinema, Waste, and Obsolescence in the 1960s and 1970s," *European Journal of Media Studies* 2, no. 2 (2013): 433.

81. Michelangelo Antonioni, "Let's Talk About *Zabriskie Point*," in *The Architecture of Vision* (1970; reprint, Chicago: University of Chicago Press, 2007), 102, quoted in Nardelli, "'The Sprawl of Entropy,'" 433.

2. "FIVE HUNDRED THOUSAND KILOWATTS OF STARDUST"

1. Rachel Carson, *Silent Spring* (1962; reprint, Boston: Mariner Books, 2002).

2. McKenzie Funk, "Glaciers for Sale," *Harper's Magazine*, July 2013.

3. See "Index," *Harper's Magazine*, March 2015, which cites Bartow J. Elmore, *Citizen Coke: The Making of Coca-Cola Capitalism* (New York: Norton, 2014), page number not cited.

4. The article outlines the impact that Gore and Guggenheim's film *An Inconvenient Truth* (2006) and the popularization of the global-warming debate had on the trading world as well as the focus on trading water and speculating on water distribution over the past decade. As Funk notes, "A report from Goldman called water 'the petroleum for the next century' and speculated excitedly about the impact of 'major multi-year droughts' in Australia and the American West" ("Glaciers for Sale").

5. David Ingram, *Green Screen: Environmentalism and Hollywood* (Exeter, U.K.: University of Exeter Press, 2000), 29.

6. Ingram, *Green Screen*, 28.

7. Verena Andermatt Conley, *Ecopolitics: The Environment in Poststructuralist Thought* (New York: Routledge, 1997), 1.

8. Ingram, *Green Screen*, 29.

9. Marc Reisner, *Cadillac Desert: The American West and Its Disappearing Water* (London: Pimlico, 2000), 9.

10. For this water history of Owens Valley and Los Angeles, see Robert A. Sauder, *The Lost Frontier: Water Diversion in the Growth and Destruction of Owens Valley Agriculture* (Tucson: University of Arizona Press, 1994).

11. KCET's documentary *AgH2o: Silver and Water* (2013) captures the environmental photography project of Lauren Bon and the Optics Division of the Metabolic Studio. In part as an acknowledgment of the Los Angeles Aqueduct's centennial anniversary, Bon and the Optics Division set up a "liminal camera," a portable camera and darkroom housed in a shipping container that can produce large black-and-white images matching the size of the container itself. The goal of the project is to make images of Owens Valley by using the silver and water that are indigenous to the ecosystem and which were pilfered in the formation of Hollywood.

12. Robin L. Murray and Joseph K. Heumann, *Ecology and Popular Film: Cinema on the Edge* (Albany: State University of New York Press, 2009), chap. 2.

13. Murray and Heumann, *Ecology and Popular Film*, 38.

14. Murray and Heumann, *Ecology and Popular Film*, 40.

15. Murray and Heumann, *Ecology and Popular Film*, 38.

16. Ingram, *Green Screen*, 88.

17. Ingram, *Green Screen*, 5.

18. Richard Maxwell and Toby Miller, *Greening the Media* (Oxford: Oxford University Press, 2012), 73.

19. "U.S. Geological Survey," 2013, http://ga.water.usgs.gov/edu/mgd.html (no longer available), and U.S. Environmental Protection Agency, "Water Trivia Facts," n.d., http://water.epa.gov/learn/kids/drinkingwater/water_trivia_facts .cfm.

20. Maxwell and Miller, *Greening the Media*, 73.

21. U.S. Environmental Protection Agency, "Water Trivia Facts."

22. Maxwell and Miller, *Greening the Media*, 73.

23. Maxwell and Miller, *Greening the Media*, 69.

24. Ben Goldsmith and Tom O'Regan, *The Film Studio: Film Production in the Global Economy* (Oxford: Rowman and Littlefield, 2005).

25. Maxwell and Miller, *Greening the Media*, 70.

26. Sharon Buzzard, "The Do-It-Yourself Text: The Experience of Narrativity in *Singin' in the Rain*," *Journal of Film and Video* 40, no. 3 (1988): 21.

27. Robert Sklar, *Movie-Made America: A Cultural History of American Movies* (New York: Vintage, 1975), 262.

28. Though the authenticity of voice is so central to the commentary and moralism of *Singin' in the Rain*, the production's use of dubbing is well documented in secondary studies as well as in archived production notes. Most notably, there is a montage sequence in which the lovely voice of the heroine, Kathy Seldon (played by Debbie Reynolds), is used to dub over the scenes played by the shrill and tyrannical silent star who is stunting Kathy's success. This dub was in fact done using the voice of Betty Royce, not that of Debbie Reynolds (see Christopher Ames, *Movies About the Movies* [Lexington: University Press of Kentucky, 1997]).

29. Carol J. Clover, "Dancin' in the Rain," *Critical Inquiry* 21, no. 4 (1995): 725.

30. Kristi McKim, *Cinema as Weather: Stylistic Screens and Atmospheric Changes* (New York: Routledge, 2013), 54.

31. Peter Wollen's book-length study of the film, *Sing in' the Rain* (London: BFI, 1992), and Earl J. Hess and Pratibha A. Dabholkar's monograph *"Singin' in the Rain": The Making of an American Masterpiece* (Lawrence: University of Kansas Press, 2009) go into great detail on the production of this scene, as do a number of other articles and book chapters, but none of them asks the questions I ask here.

32. Hess and Dabholkar, *"Singin' in the Rain,"* 12, 81.

33. Quoted in Hess and Dabholkar, *"Singin' in the Rain,"* 126.

34. Peter N. Chumo II, "Dance, Flexibility, and the Renewal of a Genre in *Singin' in the Rain*," *Cinema Journal* 36, no. 1 (1996): 39–54.

35. Richard Rickitt, *Special Effects: The History and Technique*, 2nd ed. (New York: Billboard Books, 2007), 307, quoted in McKim, *Cinema as Weather*, 54.

36. Steve Galich, phone interview by the author, 2013.

37. Assistant director's report, July 17, 1951, Box 21, Folder 2, Arthur Freed Collection, Cinematic Arts Library, Doheny Memorial Library, University of Southern California, Los Angeles.

38. Hugh Fordin, *The World of Entertainment: Hollywood's Greatest Musicals* (New York: Doubleday 1975), 358.

39. Ames, *Movies About the Movies*, 66–67.

40. Bosley Crowther, "*Singin' in the Rain*," *New York Times*, March 28, 1952.

41. Ames, *Movies About the Movies*, 67.

42. "*Singin' in the Rain*," *Variety*, March 12, 1952.

43. Steven Cohan, *Incongruous Entertainment: Camp, Cultural Value, and the MGM Musical* (Durham, N.C.: Duke University Press, 2005), 219.

44. Quoted in Stephen M. Silverman, *Dancing on the Ceiling: Stanley Donen and His Movies* (New York: Knopf, 1996), 142.

45. Quoted in Silverman, *Dancing on the Ceiling*, 316.

46. Rick Altman, *The American Film Musical* (Bloomington: Indiana University Press, 1987), 223.

47. *Singin' in the Rain* playbill, Box 21, Folder 1, Freed Collection.

48. Exhibitor's Campaign Book, *Singin' in the Rain*, Pressbook Collection, Doheny Memorial Library, University of Southern California, Los Angeles.

49. "Mother's Day—May 11th," marketing tie-in, *Singin' in the Rain*, Box 22, Folder 2, Freed Collection.

50. For a systematic critique of gender and the environment in popular advertising, see Noël Sturgeon, *Environmentalism in Popular Culture: Gender, Race, Sexuality, and the Politics of the Natural* (Tucson: University of Arizona Press, 2008), 17–52.

51. Exhibitor's Campaign Book, *Singin' in the Rain*, Box 22, Folder 2, Freed Collection.

52. Release ad for *Singin' in the Rain*, *Exhibitor*, February 20, 1952, Box 21, Folder 1, Freed Collection.

53. Hess and Dabholkar, *"Singin' in the Rain,"* 188.

54. Based on calculations in "Top Grossing Movies of 1952," Ultimate Movie Rankings, n.d., http://www.ultimatemovierankings.com/top-grossing-movies -of-1952/.

55. F. R., *"Singin' in the Rain," New York Compass*, March 28, 1952.

56. Quoted in Fordin, *The World of Entertainment*, 361.

57. Fordin, *The World of Entertainment*, 316.

3. WIND OF CHANGE

1. According to a *USA Today* survey in 2018, 78 percent of Americans have a smartphone, and more than half own a tablet device (Leo Sun, "Foolish Take: Nearly 80% of Americans Own Smartphones," *USA Today*, February 24, 2018, https:// www.usatoday.com/story/money/markets/2018/02/24/a-foolish-take-nearly-80 -of-americans-own-smartphones/110342918/). A Pew Research Center study verifies the smartphone count, adding that as of 2016 nearly nine out of ten Americans used the Internet (Aaron Smith, "Record Share of Americans Now Own Smartphones, Have Home Abroad," *FactTank*, January 12, 2017, http://www .pewresearch.org/fact-tank/2017/01/12/evolution-of-technology/).

2. Charles Baudelaire, "The Generous Gambler," poem no. 29, in *Prose Poems*, trans. Rosemary Lloyd (Oxford: Oxford University Press, 1991), 76.

3. Codes such as point-of-view editing, as Daniel Dayan has argued, help to "suture" us, the spectators, into the screen text, connecting us to a viewing position within the diegesis, which then erases for us all marks of the constructed nature of the

film experience, to inure us to the act of enunciation that is speaking meaning to us ("The Tutor-Code of Classical Cinema." *Film Quarterly* 28, no.1 [1974]: 22–31).

4. See Thomas Schatz, *Hollywood Genres: Formulas, Filmmaking, and the Studio System* (New York: McGraw-Hill 1981).

5. Robin Wood, "Ideology, Genre, Auteur: *Shadow of a Doubt*," in *Hitchcock's Films Revisited* (New York: Columbia University Press, 1989), 288–302.

6. André Bazin, "The Western, or the American Film *par Excellence*," in *What Is Cinema?* trans. and ed. Hugh Gray, 2 vols. (Berkeley: University of California Press, 1971), 2:141–148, and "The Evolution of the Western," in *What Is Cinema?* 2:149–157.

7. For an excellent example of this contradiction, see Brian Henderson's analysis of John Ford's film *The Searchers* (1956), which pinpoints miscegenation between white settlers and native Americans as colonial frontiersmen's greatest possible fear and sees the film as an attempt to explore and even vindicate popular anxieties over the civil rights movement and, in particular, over the integration of American schools in 1954 through *Brown v. the Board of Education* ("'The Searchers': An American Dilemma," *Film Quarterly* 34, no. 2 [1980–1981]: 9–23).

8. Raymond Williams, *The Country and the City* (New York: Oxford University Press, 1973), 45.

9. Sheldon Hall and Steve Neale, *Epics, Spectacles, and Blockbusters: A Hollywood History* (Detroit: Wayne State University Press, 2010), 250.

10. Geoff King, *Spectacular Narratives: Hollywood in the Age of the Blockbuster* (London: I. B. Taurus, 2009), 22.

11. Anthony A. Leiserowitz, "Before and After *The Day After Tomorrow*: A U.S. Study of Climate Change Risk Perception," *Environment* 46, no. 9 (2004): 25.

12. Rory Carroll, "Hollywood and the Downwinders Still Grapple with Nuclear Fallout," *Guardian*, June 6, 2015.

13. See Justin Owen Rawlins, "This Is(n't) John Wayne: The Miscasting and Performance of Whiteness in *The Conqueror*," *Quarterly Review of Film and Video* 27 (2010): 25.

14. Carroll, "Hollywood and the Downwinders Still Grapple with Nuclear Fallout"; Carroll gives no specific publication information for the *People* article.

15. In January 1986, Gina Maranto's article "Are We Close to the Road's End?" was the first cover story on climate change for *Discover Magazine*, and in January 1989 "Endangered Earth" took the cover honor in *Time*'s "Man of the Year" issue.

16. United Nations, "Kyoto Protocol to the United Nations Framework Convention on Climate Change," December 11, 1997, Art. 2, https://unfccc.int/process/the-kyoto-protocol.

17. See Andrew Dobson, *Citizenship and the Environment* (Oxford: Oxford University Press, 2003), 47–52.

18. For a treatise on this argument, see Naomi Klein, *This Changes Everything: Capitalism vs. the Climate* (New York: Simon and Schuster, 2014), 1–38.

19. Steve Rust, "Hollywood and Climate Change," in *Ecocinema Theory and Practice*, ed. Stephen Rust, Salma Monani, and Sean Cubitt (New York: Routledge, 2013), 192.

20. Rust, "Hollywood and Climate Change," 194.

21. According to Box Office Mojo, for example, of the top environmentalist films ("movies concerned with the [environmentalist] cause or promoting it") since 1980, all top five were released after 2000, with the top three released in the past ten years ("Environmentalist: Movies Concerned with the Cause or Promoting It, 1980–Present," Box Office Mojo, n.d., https://www.boxofficemojo.com/genres/chart/?id=environment.htm).

22. Charles J. Corbett and Richard P. Turco, *Southern California Environmental Report Card 2006: Sustainability in the Motion Picture Industry* (Los Angeles: Institute of the Environment and Sustainability, University of California, 2006), 7. In the this analysis, "conventional" air pollutants are defined as the basic primary "criteria" pollutants, such as nitric oxide and carbon monoxide, which are emitted from a wide range of sources. It is generally these criteria pollutants whose concentrations are controlled by air-quality regulations. Note that each of the primary or criteria pollutants leads to different environmental impacts and health effects.

23. These metrics are based on fuel consumption, using various conversion factors to reduce carbon dioxide, methane, and nitric oxide emissions to a single global-warming potential value, expressed in metric tons of carbon dioxide equivalents (see Corbett and Turco, *Southern California Environmental Report Card 2006*, 13).

24. As can be discerned from the title, Siegfried Kracauer's book *Theory of Film: The Redemption of Reality* (Oxford: Oxford University Press, 1960) argues for film's unique ability to salvage and restore the inherent value of a reality—both human and nonhuman—that has been overlooked and undervalued in an era of technological obsession and heightened distraction.

25. Jean Epstein's seminal essay "On Certain Characteristics of Photogénie" (1924, reprinted in *French Film Theory and Criticism*, vol. 1: *1907–1935*, ed. Richard Abel [Princeton, N.J.: Princeton University Press, 1988], 315–320) sets out a poetic, if circular, argument of the film camera's unique ability to bring out—and to instill at the same time—the spiritual personality of everyday objects. The origins of Dziga Vertov's montage method lie in his theoretical essay "WE: Variant of a Manifesto" (1919, https://monoskop.org/images/6/66/Vertov_Dziga_1922_1984

_We_Variant_of_a_Manifesto.pdf) and can be seen exercised across the breadth of his film work.

26. Kristi McKim, *Cinema as Weather: Stylistic Screens and Atmospheric Changes* (New York: Routledge, 2013), 50.

27. Adrian Danks, "Open to the Elements: Surveying the Terrain of Victor Sjöström's *The Wind*," *Senses of Cinema*, May 2006, http://sensesofcinema.com/2006/cteq/wind/.

28. Alessandro Nova, *The Book of Wind: The Representation of the Invisible* (Montreal: McGill-Queen's University Press, 2011), 34.

29. Danks, "Open to the Elements."

30. Danks, "Open to the Elements."

31. Richard Dyer, *White: Essays on Race and Culture* (London: Routledge, 1997), 31.

32. Dyer, *White*, 33–38.

33. This sense of enterprise is actually very common in mainstream films about the environment, especially those—such as Robert Redford's film *A River Runs Through It* (1992), which was part of Redford's larger mission to protect the Montana rivers where the film was shot—that are driven by a conservationist ideology, viewing nature as something both sacred and the dominion of man.

34. Though practiced increasingly throughout the twentieth century, "education entertainment" has emerged over the past half-century, using screen culture for public enlightenment, persuasion, and social change. It is often attributed in large part to the *telenovelas* of Mexican television producer Miguel Sabido, whose "soap operas for social change" produced wide results regarding such topics as family planning and illiteracy among the elderly.

35. Nicole Seymour, "'It's Just Not Turning Up': Cinematic Vision and Environmental Justice in Todd Haynes' 'Safe,'" *Cinema Journal* 50, no. 4 (2011): 26.

36. Shoshana Felman, *Writing and Madness* (Ithaca, N.Y.: Cornell University Press, 1985), 210, emphasis in original.

37. Bill McKibben, *The End of Nature*, with a new introduction (1989; reprint, New York: Random House, 2006).

38. Former secretary of state Rex Tillerson (February 2017–March 2018) moved to the White House after forty years at Exxon, where he was CEO from 2006 to 2016. After a short-lived attempt at working harmoniously with the environmental sector, Exxon set out on a notorious decades-long systematic attempt to fund and support climate-science denial.

39. Alison Anderson, *Media, Culture, and the Environment* (London: Routledge, 1997), 82. For an excellent study of petroleum companies' film productions, see Brian R. Jacobson, "Big Oil's High-Risk Love Affair with Film," *Los Angeles Review of Books*, April 7, 2017.

40. Leiserowitz, "Before and After *The Day After Tomorrow*"; Matt Nisbet, "Evaluating the Impact of *The Day After Tomorrow*," *Skeptical Inquirer*, June 16, 2004, http://www.csicop.org/specialarticles/show/evaluating_the_impact_of_the_day_after_tomorrow.

41. Quoted in Nisbet, "Evaluating the Impact of *The Day After Tomorrow*."

42. Quoted in Nisbet, "Evaluating the Impact of *The Day After Tomorrow*."

43. As recounted by the *Los Angeles Times* reporter Elizabeth Jensen and confirmed by the producer of *An Inconvenient Truth*, Laurie David, the Gore–Guggenheim film was born at a New York City premiere party for *The Day After Tomorrow* hosted by liberal activist organization MoveOn.org, where David—realizing the power film might have in the battle over climate change—remarked in an aside to Gore: "We all know one disaster film is worth 1,000 environmental speeches" (quoted in Elizabeth Jensen, "Activists Take 'The Day After Tomorrow' for a Spin," *Los Angeles Times*, May 26, 2004).

44. Nisbet, "Evaluating the Impact of *The Day After Tomorrow*"; Leiserowitz, "Before and After *The Day After Tomorrow*," 27.

45. Leiserowitz, "Before and After *The Day After Tomorrow*," 30.

46. According to on-set accounts, de Bont initially attacked director of photography Don Burgess's crew. The breaking point came when a camera assistant walked into the frame and ruined a complicated shot involving noisy wind machines, leading de Bont to shove the man into a mud puddle. Burgess and twenty crew members walked. The film was only five weeks into production. De Bont replaced Burgess with the veteran cinematographer Jack N. Green. Unfortunately, Green was hospitalized with a back injury when a house rigged to collapse did so while Green was still inside it. With two days left to shoot, de Bont took over camera duties. For more information on *Twister*'s production history, see "'Twister': 10 Things You Probably Didn't Know About the Summer Blockbuster," *Moviefone*, May 5, 2016, http://www.moviefone.com/2016/05/10/twister-facts/.

47. The oil truck seen flying around in the tornado bears the same name, Benthic Petroleum, as the company in James Cameron's underwater epic *The Abyss*; the name of the instrument package, Dorothy, is the same as the leading character in *The Wizard of Oz*, the film that Aunt Meg is watching at the time the tornado hits the house; and Young Jo's Cairn Terrier is the same breed as Toto in the Judy Garland classic. To read more on these allusions, see Jon O'Brien, "*Twister* Is 20 Years Old! 15 Things You Might Not Know abut the Classic Disaster Movie," *Metro*, May 10, 2016, http://metro.co.uk/2016/05/10/15-things-you-might-not-know-about-twister-5853475/#ixzz4EyCNeZ29.

48. See Sean Cubitt, *Finite Media: Environmental Implications of Digital Technologies* (Durham, N.C.: Duke University Press, 2016), 8–15.

49. King, *Spectacular Narratives*, 18.

50. Keay Davidson, *"Twister": The Science of Tornadoes and the Making of an Adventure Movie* (New York: Pocket Books, 1996), x.

51. Davidson, *"Twister,"* xii.

52. David Wiener, "Chasing the Wind," *American Cinematographer* 77, no. 5 (1996): 36.

53. Tapestry Institute, *"Twister,"* n.d., http://www.tapestryinstitute.org/tornado /twister.html.

54. King, *Spectacular Narratives*, 19.

55. Despina Kakoudaki, "Spectacles of History: Race Relations, Melodrama, and the Science Fiction/Disaster Film," *Camera Obscura* 17, no. 2 (2002): 122.

56. For example, Green attests that the filmmakers hoped "to give the tornado in their film a living malevolence." David Wiener quotes Green at length: "It's almost as if it's luring the chasers into a situation where it can kill them. People who chase storms actually feel that tornadoes have personalities." Wiener extends this strategy to de Bont: "To capitalize on this [feeling], DeBont [*sic*] treated the twister like an actor playing the heavy." " 'The tornado is a character,' director DeBont explains. 'You have to direct it and you have to be very specific' " ("Chasing the Wind," 42–43).

57. Wiener, "Chasing the Wind," 44.

58. According to online behind-the-scene accounts, producers initially had the tagline "It sucks" in mind for the film's publicity campaign (O'Brien, *"Twister* Is 20 Years Old!"). Perhaps it was wise not to load the critics' gun for them.

59. Quoted in Davidson, *"Twister,"* 130, original emphasis.

60. Alexandre Astruc, "Du stylo à la caméra et de la caméra au stylo," *L'Écran Française*, no. 144 (March 30, 1948): 207–217.

61. Davidson, *"Twister,"* ix–x.

62. Davidson, *"Twister,"* x.

63. Davidson, *"Twister,"* x.

64. Wiener, "Chasing the Wind," 37.

65. Wiener, "Chasing the Wind," 38.

66. For more on this blinding of the two stars, see " 'Twister': 10 Things You Probably Didn't Know" and O'Brien, *"Twister* Is 20 Years Old!"

67. Davidson, *"Twister,"* x–xvii.

68. Quoted in Wiener, "Chasing the Wind," 38.

69. Davidson, *"Twister,"* xv.

70. Quoted in Wiener, "Chasing the Wind," 42.

71. Quoted in Wiener, "Chasing the Wind," 42.

72. Quoted in Wiener, "Chasing the Wind," 42.

73. Davidson, *"Twister,"* xvii.

74. King, *Spectacular Narratives*, 18.
75. Davidson, *"Twister,"* 126.
76. Davidson, *"Twister,"* 122.
77. Lev Manovich, *The Language of New Media* (Cambridge, Mass.: MIT Press, 2002), 177–205.
78. Quoted in Wiener, "Chasing the Wind," 43.
79. Quoted in Wiener, "Chasing the Wind," 124.
80. Tapestry Institute, *"Twister."*
81. O'Brien, *"Twister* Is 20 Years Old!"
82. Davidson, *"Twister,"* 125.

4. APOCALYPSE TOMORROW

1. See Alison Caruth, "The Digital Cloud and the Micropolitics of Energy," *Public Culture* 26, no. 2 (2014): 339. For more on server-based media, see Shane Brennan, "Making Data Sustainable: Backup Culture and Risk Perception," in *Sustainable Media: Critical Approaches to Media and Environment*, ed. Nicole Starosielski and Janet Walker (New York: Routledge, 2016), 56–77.
2. Tom Gunning, "An Aesthetic of Astonishment: Early Film and the (In)Credulous Spectator," *Art and Text*, no. 34 (Spring 1989): 31–45.
3. Cyndy Hendershot, "From Trauma to Paranoia: Nuclear Weapons, Science Fiction, and History," *Mosaic* 32, no. 4 (1999): 76.
4. Fredric Jameson, "Progress Versus Utopia: Or, Can We Imagine the Future?" *Science-Fiction Studies*, no. 9 (1982): 153.
5. Robert Torry, "Apocalypse Then: Benefits of the Bomb in Fifties Science Fiction Films," *Cinema Journal* 31, no. 1 (1991): 7. See also Annette Kuhn, "The Alien Messiah," in *Alien Zone: Cultural Theory and Contemporary Science Fiction*, ed. Annette Kuhn (New York: Verso, 1990), 32–38.
6. Susan Sontag, "The Imagination of Disaster," in *Against Interpretation* (New York: Picador, 1961), 224.
7. Georges Bataille, "Concerning the Accounts Given by the Residents of Hiroshima," trans. Alan Keenan, in *Trauma: Explorations in Memory*, ed. Cathy Caruth (Baltimore: Johns Hopkins University Press, 1995), 26, original emphasis.
8. E. Ann Kaplan, *Climate Trauma: Foreseeing the Future in Dystopian Film and Fiction* (New Brunswick, N.J.: Rutgers University Press, 2015), 3.
9. Jean-Louis Baudry, "Le dispositif: Approches métapsychologiques de l'impression de réalité," *Communications* 23, no. 1 (1975): 56–72.
10. Ellen Elizabeth Moore does an excellent job tracking this aesthetic as well as its origin in Steve Jobs's position as founder of Pixar and, as a consequence of Disney's purchase of Pixar, as a board member and the largest shareholder at

Disney ("Green Screen or Smokescreen? Hollywood's Messages About Nature and the Environment," *Environmental Communication* 10, no. 5 [2015]: 10–11).

11. See Noël Sturgeon, *Environmentalism in Popular Culture: Gender, Race, Sexuality, and the Politics of the Natural* (Tucson: University of Arizona Press, 2008), 80.

12. Sturgeon, *Environmentalism in Popular Culture*, 94.

13. See Samuel Greengard, *The Internet of Things* (Cambridge, Mass.: MIT Press, 2015).

14. Jennifer Gabrys, *Program Earth: Environmental Sensing Technology and the Making of a Computational Planet* (Minneapolis: University of Minnesota Press, 2016), 16.

15. See United Nations Security Council, *Report of the Panel of Experts on the Illegal Exploitation of Natural Resources and Other Forms of Wealth of the Democratic Republic of the Congo* (New York: United Nations, April 12, 2001), and The Hague Center for Strategic Studies, *Coltan, Congo, and Conflict*, case study (The Hague: Polinares, May 2013). The report by the Security Council condemned surrounding nations (Rwanda, Burundi, and Uganda) for using the instability of the Congolese civil war to pilfer Congo's natural resources, including its coltan reserves, which they sold to tech manufacturers such as Apple and Dell to help fund ongoing military exercises, thus positioning smart technology as a main culprit in perpetuating a cannibalistic civil war in one of the least-stable parts of Africa. Though many manufacturers publically declared that they would cease using coltan from this region (there are also large deposits of it in Australia, for example), the region remains highly mined and a cheap source of both human labor and natural resources.

16. According to a study done in 2018, Rwanda and the Democratic Republic of Congo accounted for 60 percent of tantalum production, the primary metal used in coltan, though due to the unofficial manner of this mineral's circulation it is impossible to track which nation it began in. Nigeria is third on the list, followed by Brazil and China. See Amanda Kay, "Top Tantalum-Mining Countries," *Investing News*, June 12, 2018, https://investingnews.com/daily/resource-investing /critical-metals-investing/tantalum-investing/2013-top-tantalum-producers -rwanda-brazil-drc-canada/.

17. In *The One Device: The Secret History of the iPhone* (New York: Little, Brown, 2017), the journalist Brian Merchant reveals the extreme conditions and harrowing reality of Foxconn and other labor campuses that helped to bring us what has arguably been the most influential technological breakthrough of the twenty-first century. Under scrutiny of international media—and, more pressing, Foxconn's tech contractors—Foxconn took certain measures: while considering altering base wages, it immediately installed a system of nets to catch

self-defenestrated workers and drew up a standard legal document that employees had to sign to guarantee that they and their descendants would not sue in the case of death, suicide, or self-injury.

18. Mark Mills, *The Internet Begins with Coal: A Preliminary Exploration of the Impact of the Internet on Electricity Consumption. A Green Policy Paper for the Greening Earth Society* (Bethesda, Md.: Mills-McCarthy, May 1999).

19. Peter Huber, "Dig More Coal—the PCs Are Coming," *Forbes*, May 31, 1999.

20. See Jan Mezurek, *Making Microchips: Policy, Globalization, and Economic Restructuring in the Semiconductor Industry* (Cambridge, Mass.: MIT Press, 1998), and Ted Smith, David A. Sonnefeld, David Naguib Pellow, and Jim Hightower, eds., *Challenging the Chip: Labor Rights and Environmental Justice in the Global Electronics Industry* (Philadelphia: Temple University Press, 2006).

21. From the *Second Life* website, n.d., http://secondlife.com/?campaignid=54644 670&adgroupid=29573980350&loc_physical_ms=9011924&placement=&key word=%252Bsecond%2520%252Blife%2520play&matchtype=b&creative=10100 6621550&utmsource=Google&creativeid=T002085&gclid=CjwKEAiAm8nCB RD7xLj-2aWFyz8SJAAQNalayB6qIU05Oj32LsLhGijw69J4hIpsRciBwUWEm qfc-BoCeBrw_wcB.

22. Max Cafard, "Intergalactic Blues: Fantasy and Ideology in *Avatar*," *Psychic Swamp: The Surre(gion)al Review* 1 (2010), http://www.academia.edu/4476636 /_Intergalactic_Blues_Fantasy_and_Ideology_in_Avatar_by_Max_Cafard_.

23. John Hiscock, "James Cameron Interview for *Avatar*," *Guardian*, December 3, 2009, http://www.telegraph.co.uk/culture/film/6720156/James-Cameron-interview-for -Avatar.html.

24. Quoted in Jody Duncan and Lisa Fitzpatrick, *The Making of "Avatar"* (New York: Abrams, 2010), 39.

25. Max Cafard calls *Avatar* "a whole *ontological dimension* ahead of the pack," appearing in some theaters in 4D (with moving seats, smell of explosives, sprinkling of water), a "totalizing of the imaginary experience, an increasing colonization or occupation of imaginary distance" ("Intergalactic Blues").

26. Stephen Prince, *Digital Visual Effects in Cinema* (New Brunswick, N.J.: Rutgers University Press, 2012), 12–13.

27. Duncan and Fitzpatrick, *The Making of "Avatar*,*"* 14–15.

28. Prince, *Digital Visual Effects in Cinema*, 16–18.

29. Jody Duncan, "The Seduction of Reality," *Cinefex* 120 (January 2010): 146.

30. Prince, *Digital Visual Effects in Cinema*, 18.

31. Cameron quoted in Duncan and Fitzpatrick, *The Making of "Avatar*,*"* 105.

32. Duncan and Fitzpatrick, *The Making of "Avatar*,*"* 37.

33. Quoted in Duncan and Fitzpatrick, *The Making of "Avatar*,*"* 57.

34. Quoted in Duncan and Fitzpatrick, *The Making of "Avatar*,*"* 57.

35. Quoted in Duncan and Fitzpatrick, *The Making of "Avatar,"* 58.

36. Paul Thomas Anderson's film *There Will Be Blood* (2007) is another excellent example of a renovated genre film (neo-Western) aimed at critiquing American petroimperialism, in particular by revealing the development of the American frontier as a brutal capitalist drive to exploit natural resources.

37. Sean Cubitt,, "*Avatar* and Utopia," *Animation* 7, no. 3 (2012): 234.

38. Slavoj Žižek, "*Avatar*: Return of the Natives," *New Statesman*, March 4, 2010, https://www.newstatesman.com/film/2010/03/avatar-reality-love-couple-sex.

39. Adrian Ivakhiv, *Ecologies of the Moving Image* (Waterloo, Canada: Wilfred Laurier University Press, 2013), 285.

40. Peter Jackson, preface to Lisa Fitzpatrick, *The Art of "Avatar": James Cameron's Epic Adventure* (New York: Abrams, 2009), 7.

41. Cubitt, "*Avatar* and Utopia," 234.

42. Quoted in Duncan and Fitzpatrick, *The Making of "Avatar,"* 173.

43. Mark Bartlett argues for the film's inspiring impact on indigenous groups around the world, continuing: "The response of indigenist peoples world-wide is surely sufficient to justify attributing this claim to *Avatar*. *Avatar* has demonstrated that the connection between its material (social) relations can in fact have quite real and effective political consequences" ("Going (Digitally) Native" *Animation* 7, no. 3 [2012]: 298). Any lasting political impact of the film, however, is empirically unsubstantiated.

44. Quoted in Duncan and Fitzpatrick, *The Making of "Avatar,"* 256.

45. Bartlett, "Going (Digitally) Native," 290. Whereas Bartlett describes a film that offers inverted religious history by elevating pagan over Christian values and motifs, David Brooks's *New York Times* op-ed "The Messiah Complex," January 7, 2010, and many other prominent, progressive analyses condemn the film's white-savior narrative.

46. Lev Manovich, "Synthetic Realism and Its Discontents," in *The Language of New Media* (Cambridge, Mass.: MIT Press, 2002), 184.

47. "Indigenous peoples globally have received *Avatar* not just favorably, but as an extraordinary activist manifesto, screened on their behalf, and which from their perspectives represents their political and cultural values and lives with a powerful authenticity" (Bartlett, "Going (Digitally) Native," 288).

48. See Sherry Turkle, *Reclaiming Conversation: The Power of Talk in a Digital Age* (New York: Penguin Press, 2015), *Alone Together: Why We Expect More from Technology and Less from Each Other* (New York: Basic Books, 2011), and *Simulation and Its Discontents* (Cambridge, Mass.: MIT Press, 2009). See also Maurice Merleau-Ponty, "Le cinéma et la nouvelle psychologie," in *Sens et nonsens* (Paris: Gallimard, 1996), 74.

49. Turkle, *Alone Together*, 16.

50. Bartlett, "Going (Digitally) Native," 289.

51. Jackson, preface to Fitzpatrick, *The Art of "Avatar,"* 7.

52. Bartlett, "Going (Digitally) Native," 304.

53. Bartlett, "Going (Digitally) Native," 300.

54. Bartlett, "Going (Digitally) Native," 300.

55. Bartlett, "Going (Digitally) Native," 299.

56. Duncan and Fitzpatrick, *The Making of "Avatar,"* 172.

57. Quoted in Duncan and Fitzpatrick, *The Making of "Avatar,"* 212.

58. Duncan and Fitzpatrick, *The Making of "Avatar,"* 212.

59. Duncan and Fitzpatrick, *The Making of "Avatar,"* 47.

60. Quoted in Duncan and Fitzpatrick, *The Making of "Avatar,"* 106.

61. Duncan and Fitzpatrick, *The Making of "Avatar,"* 106–126.

62. Duncan and Fitzpatrick, *The Making of "Avatar,"* 138.

63. Duncan and Fitzpatrick, *The Making of "Avatar,"* 139.

64. Duncan and Fitzpatrick, *The Making of "Avatar,"* 192.

65. Quoted in Duncan and Fitzpatrick, *The Making of "Avatar,"* 192.

66. John Rath, "The Data-Crunching Powerhouse Behind 'Avatar,'" *Data Center Knowledge*, October 22, 2009, http://www.datacenterknowledge.com/archives /2009/12/22/the-data-crunching-powerhouse-behind-avatar/.

67. Max Cafard notes that *Avatar*'s website promised an environmentally activist project that Cameron set up, the "Home Tree Initiative," with the professed goal of helping to "save Homeplanet" (see http://www.avatarmovie.com/hometree). The website claimed, "The time has come to stand up and be warriors for the earth," though the initiative was ultimately just another tree-planting project to offset a carbon-intensive film production. The site professed "that a million eco-warriors [are] willing to endure the perils of imaginary tree adoption" so that celebrities can partner with nation-states to plant trees and offers traditional online attractions such as a sweepstakes and eco-oriented virtual games through which players can get "badges." The site's "take action now" link, Cafard fairly scoffs, "only led to a 'page not found' message" ("Intergalactic Blues," 22).

68. Quoted in Prince, *Digital Visual Effects in Cinema*, 146.

69. Quoted in Duncan and Fitzpatrick, *The Making of "Avatar,"* 268.

70. Jo Piazza, "Audiences Experience 'Avatar' Blues," CNN.com, January 11, 2010, http://edition.cnn.com/2010/SHOWBIZ/Movies/01/11/avatar.movie.blues /index.html, cited in Cubitt, *"Avatar* and Utopia," 229.

5. THE FIFTH ELEMENT

1. J. P. Telotte, "Human Artifice and the Science Fiction Film," *Film Quarterly* 36, no. 3 (1983): 44.

2. Telotte, "Human Artifice and the Science Fiction Film," 47.

3. See Loren Eiseley, *The Firmament of Time* (New York: Athenaeum, 1966), 72.

4. See Bill Caldwell, "Para-industry: Researching Hollywood's Blackwaters," *Cinema Journal* 52 (2013): 157–165.

5. M. A. Chan Kai, P. Balvanera, K. Benessaiah, M. Chapman, S. Díaz, E. Gómez-Baggethun, R. Gould, N. Hannahs, K. Jax, S. Klain, et al., "Why Protect Nature? Rethinking Values and the Environment," *Proceedings of the National Academy of Sciences* 113, no. 6 (2016): 1463.

6. U. Pascual, P. Balvanera, S. Díaz, G. Pataki, E. Roth, M. Stenseke, R. T. Watson, E. B. Dessane, M. Islar, E. Kelemen, et al., "Valuing Nature's Contributions to People: The IPBES Approach," *Current Opinion in Environmental Sustainability* 26–27 (2017): 12.

7. Columbia University's Center for Research on Environmental Decisions released the powerful report *The Psychology of Climate Change Communication* (New York: Columbia University, 2009), and Yale's recently institutionalized Climate Change Communication Program brings together scientists and communications experts to facilitate the open popular exchange and visualization of environmental science and information.

8. Jessica Barnes, Michael Dove, Myanna Lahsen, Andrew Mathews, Pamela McElwee, Roderick McIntosh, Frances Moore, Jessica O'Reilly, Ben Orlove, Rajindra Puri, et al., "Contribution of Anthropology to the Study of Climate Change," *Nature Climate Change* 3 (May 29, 2013): 541, 543.

9. Barnes et al., "Contribution of Anthropology to the Study of Climate Change," 541–543.

10. Barnes et al., "Contribution of Anthropology to the Study of Climate Change," 543.

11. Barnes et al., "Contribution of Anthropology to the Study of Climate Change," 543.

12. Natalie M. Underberg and Elayne Zorn, *Digital Ethnography: Anthropology, Narrative, and New Media* (Austin: University of Texas Press, 203), 4–10.

13. Arnd Schneider, "Setting Up Roots, or the Anthropologist on the Set: Observations on the Shooting of a Cinema Movie in Mapuche Reservation, Argentina," in *Visualizing Anthropology: Experimenting with Vision-Based Ethnography*, edited by Anna Grimshaw and Amada Ravetz (Chicago: University of Chicago Press, 2004), 100–115.

14. Nicole Starosielski, *The Undersea Network* (Durham, N.C.: Duke University Press, 2016).

15. Hortense Powdermaker, *Hollywood, the Dream Factory: An Anthropologist Looks at the Movie-Makers* (1950; reprint, Manfield Centre, Conn.: Martino, 2013).

16. Sherry Ortner, *Not Hollywood: Independent Film at the Twilight of the American Dream* (Durham, N.C.: Duke University Press, 2013).

17. Powdermaker, *Hollywood, the Dream Factory*, 3.

18. Vicki Mayer, "Bringing the Social Back In: Studies of Production Cultures and Social Theory," in *Production Studies: Cultural Studies of Media Industries*, ed. Vicki Mayer, Miranda J. Banks, and John Thornton Caldwell (New York: Routledge, 2009), 16.

19. Brian Jacobson, *Studios Before the System: Architecture, Technology, and the Emergence of Cinematic Space* (New York: Columbia University Press, 2015).

20. Kristi McKim, *Cinema as Weather: Stylistic Screens and Atmospheric Changes* (New York: Routledge, 2013), 51–52.

21. *The Matrix* sequels offer a perfect example of this repurposing, as documented in Mark E. Ferguson and Gilvan C. Souza, *Closed-Loop Supply Chains: New Developments to Improve the Sustainability of Business Practices* (Boca Raton, Fla.: CRC Press, 2016). The sets, built in Oakland and Alameda Point, were broken down by Re-Use People, and all of the materials—including lumber, steel, cement, and polystyrene—were sold or sent off to Mexico for use as insulation, decorative moldings, and other purposes in building low-income housing.

22. Rachael Joy, phone interview by the author, June 1, 2013.

23. Fred Pearce, "Greenwash: Disney's Green Intentions Are Pure Fantasy," *Guardian*, March 19, 2009, https://www.theguardian.com/environment/2009/mar/19/disney-greenwash-fred-pearce.

24. Richard Maxwell and Toby Miller, *Greening the Media* (Oxford: Oxford University Press, 2012), 84.

25. Charles J. Corbett and Richard P. Turco, *Southern California Environmental Report Card 2006: Sustainability in the Motion Picture Industry* (Los Angeles: Institute of the Environment, University of California, 2006).

26. Allen Scott, *On Hollywood: The Place, the Industry* (Princeton, N.J.: Princeton University Press, 2014), 49.

27. Scott, *On Hollywood*, 54.

28. Schneider, "Setting Up Roots," 114.

29. Maxwell and Miller, *Greening the Media*, 70.

30. The definition of an invasive species is taken from National Wildlife Federation, "Invasive Species," n.d., https://www.nwf.org/Educational-Resources/Wildlife-Guide/Threats-to-Wildlife/Invasive-Species.

31. Vicki Mayer, *Almost Hollywood, Nearly New Orleans: The Lure of the Local Film Economy* (Berkeley: University of California Press, 2017); Greg Elmer, Charles H. Davis, Janine Marchessault, and John McCullough, eds., *Locating Migrating Media* (Lanham, Md.: Lexington Books, 2010).

32. Quoted in Louise Story, "Michigan Town Woos Hollywood, but Ends Up with Bit Part," *New York Times*, December 3, 2012.

33. David Zin, "Film Incentives in Michigan," issue paper, Michigan Senate Fiscal Agency, September 2010, 2.

34. Steven R. Miller and Abdul Abdulhadi, *The Economic Impact of Michigan's Motion Picture Production Industry and the Michigan Motion Picture Production Credit* (Ann Arbor: Center for Economic Analysis, Michigan State University, 2009), 1, 8.

35. Quoted in Angela King, "Hollywood in Michigan," *Oakland Press*, February 2, 2009.

36. Ben Goldsmith and Tom O'Regan, *The Film Studio: Film Production in the Global Economy* (Oxford: Rowman and Littlefield, 2005).

37. Miller and Abdulhadi, *The Economic Impact of Michigan's Motion Picture Production Industry*, 10.

38. Janet Ward, "Berlin, the Virtual Global City," *Visual Culture* 3, no. 2 (2004): 250.

39. Journalist Mark Binelli catalogs these manifestations of a rebirth in *Detroit Is the Place to Be* (New York: Picador, 2013).

40. In her study of the problematic social dynamic of Hollywood filmmaking in New Orleans, Vicki Mayer uses the phrase "aura of Hollywood" to describe that intangible value offered to incentivized locations by the presence of Hollywood productions, "an ephemeral and affective sense that a film economy will resolve long-standing social ills and economic disparities," roundly used to justify and support incentive plans (*Almost Hollywood, Nearly New Orleans*, 103).

41. Story, "Michigan Town Woos Hollywood, but Ends Up with Bit Part."

42. Quoted in Story, "Michigan Town Woos Hollywood, but Ends Up with Bit Part."

43. Associated Press, "More Productions Are Using Florida as a Backdrop," *Gainesville Sun*, October 17, 2002, http://www.gainesville.com/news/20021017/more -productions-are-using-florida-as-a-backdrop.

44. See, for example, John Sinclair, " 'The Hollywood of Latin America': Miami as Regional Center in Television Trade," *Television & New Media* 4, no. 3 (2003): 211–229.

45. Toby Miller and Richard Maxwell, "Film and Globalization," in *Communications Media, Globalization, and Empire*, ed. Oliver Boyd-Barrett (London: John Libbey, 2016), 44.

46. David Robb, "How the Power-Broker Koch Brothers Are Killing the Florida Film Business," *Deadline Hollywood*, October 21, 2016, http://deadline.com /2016/10/koch-brothers-florida-film-industry-tax-incentives-lobbying-1201 838246/.

47. Ricou Browning Jr., interviewed by the author, Miami, March 31, 2017.

48. James Deruvo, "Film Companies Leave Florida—Tax Breaks Expire," *Doddle News*, March 18, 2016, http://www.doddlenews.com/news-room/film-companies-leave-florida-tax-breaks-expire/.

49. Niraj Choksi, "Disney and Marvel Fire Warning Shot as Georgia's Culture War Spreads to Hollywood," *Washington Post*, March 24, 2016, https://www.washingtonpost.com/news/post-nation/wp/2016/03/24/disney-marvel-threaten-to-pull-business-from-georgia-over-religious-liberty-bill/?utm_term=.7bfbe072eacd.

CONCLUSION: AN ELEMENT OF HOPE

1. Jennifer Gabrys, *Digital Rubbish: A Natural History of Electronics* (Ann Arbor: University of Michigan Press, 2013), 152–153.

2. See Douglas Rushkoff, interview of Richard Maxwell on "Greening the Media," episode 2 of *Team Human*, podcast, August 1, 2016, https://itunes.apple.com/us/podcast/ep-47-richard-barbrook-its-capitalism-mate/id1140331811?i=1000390323949&mt=2.

3. Naomi Klein, *This Changes Everything: Capitalism vs. the Climate* (New York: Simon and Schuster, 2014).

4. On this drive, see André Bazin, "Ontologie de l'image photographique," in *Qu'est-ce que le cinéma?* (1952; reprint, Paris: Editions du Cerf, 2002), 9–17.

5. McKenzie Wark, *Molecular Red: Theory for the Anthropocene* (London: Verso, 2015), 179.

6. Andrew Hageman, "Ecocinema and Ideology: Do Ecocritics Dream of a Clockwork Green?" in *Ecocinema Theory and Practice*, ed. Stephen Rust, Salma Monani, and Sean Cubitt (New York: Routledge, 2013), 65.

Bibliography

ARCHIVAL SOURCES

Arthur Freed Collection. Cinematic Arts Library, Doheny Memorial Library. University of Southern California, Los Angeles.

David O. Selznick Collection. Harry Ransom Center. University of Texas, Austin.

General Collection. Doheny Memorial Library. University of Southern California, Los Angeles.

George Cukor Collection. Academy of Motion Picture Arts and Sciences. Margaret Herrick Library, Beverly Hills, Calif.

Pressbook Collection. Doheny Memorial Library. University of Southern California, Los Angeles.

Vertical File Collection. Academy of Motion Picture Arts and Sciences. Margaret Herrick Library, Beverly Hills, Calif.

Wilbur G. Kurtz Collection. Academy of Motion Picture Arts and Sciences. Margaret Herrick Library, Beverly Hills, Calif.

PUBLISHED SOURCES

Altman, Rick. *The American Film Musical*. Bloomington: Indiana University Press, 1987.

Ames, Christopher. *Movies About the Movies*. Lexington: University Press of Kentucky, 1997.

Anderson, Alison. *Media, Culture, and the Environment*. London: Routledge, 1997.

Antonioni, Michelangelo. "Let's Talk About *Zabriskie Point.*" In *The Architecture of Vision*, 94–106. 1970. Reprint. Chicago: University of Chicago Press, 2007.

Arendt, Hannah. *The Human Condition.* Chicago: University of Chicago Press, 1958.

Associated Press. "More Productions Are Using Florida as a Backdrop." *Gainesville Sun*, October 17, 2002. http://www.gainesville.com/news/20021017/more-produc tions-are-using-florida-as-a-backdrop.

Astruc, Alexandre. "Du stylo à la caméra et de la caméra au stylo." *L'Écran Fran-çaise*, no. 144 (March 30, 1948): 207–217.

Badalov, Rahman. "Oil, Revolution, and Cinema," *Azerbaijan International* 5, no. 3 (Autumn 1997): 57–64. http://www.azer.com/aiweb/categories/magazine/53 _folder/53_articles/53_revolution/html.

Bao, Weihong. *Fiery Cinema: The Emergence of an Affective Medium in China, 1915–1945.* Minneapolis: University of Minnesota Press, 2015.

Barnes, Jessica, Michael Dove, Myanna Lahsen, Andrew Mathews, Pamela McEl-wee, Roderick McIntosh, Frances Moore, Jessica O'Reilly, Ben Orlove, Rajindra Puri, et al. "Contribution of Anthropology to the Study of Climate Change." *Nature Climate Change* 3 (May 29, 2013): 541–544.

Bartlett, Mark. "Going (Digitally) Native." *Animation* 7, no. 3 (2012) : 287–307.

Bataille, Georges. "Concerning the Accounts Given by the Residents of Hiroshima." Translated by Alan Keenan. In *Trauma: Explorations in Memory*, edited by Cathy Caruth, 21–35 . Baltimore: Johns Hopkins University Press, 1995.

Baudelaire, Charles. "The Generous Gambler," poem no. 29. In *Prose Poems*, trans-lated by Rosemary Lloyd, 76. Oxford: Oxford University Press, 1991.

Baudrillard, Jean. *The Gulf War Did Not Take Place.* Translated by Paul Patton. Bloomington: University of Indiana Press, 1995.

Baudry, Jean-Louis. "Le dispositif: Approches métapsychologiques de l'impression de réalité." *Communications* 23, no. 1 (1975): 56–72.

Bazin, André. "The Evolution of the Western." In *What Is Cinema?* 2 vols., trans-lated and edited by Hugh Gray, 2:149–157. Berkeley: University of California Press, 1971.

——. "Ontologie de l'image photographique." In *Qu'est-ce que le cinéma?*, 9–17. 1952. Reprint. Paris: Editions du Cerf2002.

——. "The Western, or the American Film *par Excellence.*" In *What Is Cinema?* 2 vols., translated and edited by Hugh Gray, 2:141–148. Berkeley: University of Cal-ifornia Press, 1971.

Behlmer, Rudy. *Shoot the Rehearsal! Behind the Scenes with Assistant Director Reg-gie Callow.* Lanham, Md.: Scarecrow Press, 2010.

Bennett, Jane. *Vibrant Matter: A Political Ecology of Things.* Durham, N.C.: Duke University Press, 2010.

Biello, David. *The Unnatural World: The Race to Remake Civilization in Earth's Newest Age*. New York: Simon and Schuster, 2016.

Binelli, Mark. *Detroit Is the Place to Be*. New York: Picador, 2013.

Bordwell, David. "Nitrate Days and Nights." David Bordwell's Website on Cinema, May 13, 2015. http://www.davidbordwell.net/blog/2015/05/13/nitrate-days-and-nights/.

Bozak, Nadia. *The Cinematic Footprint: Lights, Camera, Natural Resources*. New Brunswick, N.J.: Rutgers University Press, 2011.

Brennan, Shane. "Making Data Sustainable: Backup Culture and Risk Perception." In *Sustainable Media: Critical Approaches to Media and Environment*, edited by Nicole Starosielski and Janet Walker, 56–77. New York: Routledge, 2016.

Brewster, Ben, and Lea Jacobs. *Theatre to Cinema: Stage Pictorialism and the Early Feature Film*. Oxford: Oxford University Press, 1997.

Brooks, David. "The Messiah Complex." *New York Times*, January 7, 2010.

Buzzard, Sharon. "The Do-It-Yourself Text: The Experience of Narrativity in *Singin' in the Rain*." *Journal of Film and Video* 40, no. 3 (Summer 1988): 18–26.

Cafard, Max. "Intergalactic Blues: Fantasy and Ideology in *Avatar*." *Psychic Swamp: The Surre(gion)al Review* 1 (2010). http://www.academia.edu/4476636/_Intergalactic_Blues_Fantasy_and_Ideology_in_Avatar_by_Max_Cafard_.

Caldwell, Bill. "Para-industry: Researching Hollywood's Blackwaters," *Cinema Journal* 52 (2013): 157–165.

Carroll, Rory. "Hollywood and the Downwinders Still Grapple with Nuclear Fallout." *Guardian*, June 6, 2015.

Carson, Rachel. *Silent Spring*. 1962. Reprint. Boston: Mariner Books, 2002.

Caruth, Alison. "The Digital Cloud and the Micropolitics of Energy." *Public Culture* 26, no. 2 (2014): 339–364.

Center for Research on Environmental Decisions. *The Psychology of Climate Change Communication*. New York: Columbia University, 2009.

Chan Kai, M. A., P. Balvanera, K. Benessaiah, M. Chapman, S. Díaz, E. Gómez-Baggethun, R. Gould, N. Hannahs, K. Jax, S. Klain, et al. "Why Protect Nature? Rethinking Values and the Environment." *Proceedings of the National Academy of Sciences* 113, no. 6 (2016): 1462–1465.

Choksi, Niraj. "Disney and Marvel Fire Warning Shot as Georgia's Culture War Spreads to Hollywood." *Washington Post*, March 24, 2016. https://www.washingtonpost.com/news/post-nation/wp/2016/03/24/disney-marvel-threaten-to-pull-business-from-georgia-over-religious-liberty-bill/?utm_term=.7bfbeo72eacd.

Chumo, Peter N., II. "Dance, Flexibility, and the Renewal of a Genre in *Singin' in the Rain*." *Cinema Journal* 36, no. 1 (1996): 39–54.

Clover, Carol J. "Dancin' in the Rain." *Critical Inquiry* 21, no. 4 (995): 722–747.

Cohan, Steven. *Incongruous Entertainment: Camp, Cultural Value, and the MGM Musical*. Durham, N.C.: Duke University Press, 2005.

Conley, Verena Andermatt. *Ecopolitics: The Environment in Poststructuralist Thought*. New York: Routledge, 1997.

Corbett, Charles J., and Richard P. Turco. *Southern California Environmental Report Card 2006: Sustainability in the Motion Picture Industry*. Los Angeles: Institute of the Environment, University of California, 2006.

Coupe, Laurence, ed. *The Green Studies Reader: From Romanticism to Ecocriticism*. London: Routledge, 2000.

Crowther, Bosley. "*Singin' in the Rain*." *New York Times*, March 28, 1952.

Cubitt, Sean. "*Avatar* and Utopia." *Animation* 7, no. 3 (2012): 227–237.

——. "Everybody Knows This Is Nowhere: Data Visualization and Ecocriticism." In *Ecocinema Theory and Practice*, edited by Stephen Rust, Salma Monani, and Sean Cubitt, 279–296. New York: Routledge, 2013.

——. *Finite Media: Environmental Implications of Digital Technologies*. Durham, N.C.: Duke University Press, 2016.

Curry, Patrick. *Ecological Ethics: An Introduction*. Cambridge: Polity Press, 2006.

Danks, Adrian. "Open to the Elements: Surveying the Terrain of Victor Sjöström's *The Wind*." *Senses of Cinema*, May 2006. http://sensesofcinema.com/2006/cteq /wind/.

Davidson, Keay. "*Twister*": *The Science of Tornadoes and the Making of an Adventure Movie*. New York: Pocket Books, 1996.

Dayan, Daniel. "The Tutor-Code of Classical Cinema." *Film Quarterly* 28, no.1 (1974): 22–31.

Deruvo, James. "Film Companies Leave Florida—Tax Breaks Expire." *Doddle News*, March 18, 2016. http://www.doddlenews.com/news-room/film-companies-leave -florida-tax-breaks-expire/.

Dixon, Wheeler Winston. *Visions of the Apocalypse: Spectacles of Destruction in American Cinema*. London: Wallflower Press, 2003.

Dobson, Andrew. *Citizenship and the Environment*. Oxford: Oxford University Press, 2003.

Duncan, Jody. "The Seduction of Reality." *Cinefex* 120 (January 2010): 68–146.

Duncan, Jody, and Lisa Fitzpatrick. *The Making of "Avatar."* New York: Abrams, 2010.

Dyer, Richard. *White: Essays on Race and Culture*. London: Routledge, 1997.

Eiseley, Loren. *The Firmament of Time*. New York: Athenaeum, 1966.

Elmer, Greg, Charles H. Davis, Janine Marchessault, and John McCullough, eds. *Locating Migrating Media*. Lanham, Md.: Lexington Books, 2010.

Elmore, Bartow J. *Citizen Coke: The Making of Coca-Cola Capitalism*. New York: Norton, 2014.

"Environmentalist: Movies Concerned with the Cause or Promoting It, 1980–Present." Box Office Mojo, n.d. https://www.boxofficemojo.com/genres/chart/?id=environment.htm.

Epstein, Jean. "On Certain Characteristics of Photogénie" (1924). Reprinted in *French Film Theory and Criticism*, vol. 1: *1907–1935*, edited by Richard Abel, 315–320. Princeton, N.J.: Princeton University Press, 1988.

Felman, Shoshana. *Writing and Madness*. Ithaca, N.Y.: Cornell University Press, 1985.

Ferry, David. "The Cursed, Buried City That May Never See the Light of Day." *Outside*, October 8, 2015. http://www.outsideonline.com/2023921/cursed-buried-city-may-never-see-light-day.

Ferguson, Mark E., and Gilvan C. Souza. *Closed-Loop Supply Chains: New Developments to Improve the Sustainability of Business Practices*. Boca Raton, Fla.: CRC Press, 2016.

Fitzpatrick, Lisa. *The Art of "Avatar."* New York: Abrams, 2009.

Fordin, Hugh. *The World of Entertainment: Hollywood's Greatest Musicals*. New York: Doubleday, 1975.

F. R. *"Singin' in the Rain." New York Compass*, March 28, 1952.

Frost, Robert. "Fire and Ice." In the selection "A Group of Poems by Robert Frost." *Harper's Magazine*, December 1920.

Funk, McKenzie. "Glaciers for Sale." *Harper's Magazine*, July 2013.

Gabler, Neil. *An Empire of Their Own: How the Jews Invented Hollywood*. New York: Crown, 1988.

Gabrys, Jennifer. *Digital Rubbish: A Natural History of Electronics*. Ann Arbor: University of Michigan Press, 2013.

——. *Program Earth: Environmental Sensing Technology and the Making of a Computational Planet*. Minneapolis: University of Minnesota Press, 2016.

Glotfelty, Cheryll, and Harold Fromm, eds. *The Ecocriticism Reader*. Athens: University of Georgia Press, 1996.

Goldsmith, Ben, and Tom O'Regan. *The Film Studio: Film Production in the Global Economy*. Oxford: Rowman and Littlefield, 2005.

Greengard, Samuel. *The Internet of Things*. Cambridge, Mass.: MIT Press, 2015.

Greenhouse, Jared. "Eli Roth on Being 'Almost Killed' by Fire While Shooting 'Inglourious Basterds.'" *Huffington Post*, July 2, 2015. https://www.huffingtonpost.com/2015/07/02/eli-roth-inglourious-basterds_n_7716150.html.

Gunning, Tom. "An Aesthetic of Astonishment: Early Film and the (In)Credulous Spectator." *Art and Text* 34 (Spring 1989): 31–45.

Hageman, Andrew. "Ecocinema and Ideology: Do Ecocritics Dream of a Clockwork Green?" In *Ecocinema Theory and Practice*, edited by Stephen Rust, Salma Monani, and Sean Cubitt, 63–86. New York: Routledge, 2013.

The Hague Center for Strategic Studies. *Coltan, Congo, and Conflict.* Case study. The Hague: Polinares, May 2013. https://www.hcss.nl/sites/default/files/files/reports /HCSS_21_05_13_Coltan_Congo_Conflict_web.pdf.

Hall, Sheldon, and Steve Neale. *Epics, Spectacles, and Blockbusters: A Hollywood History.* Detroit: Wayne State University Press, 2010.

Hansen, Anders, and Robert Cox, eds. *The Routledge Handbook of Environment and Communication.* London: Routledge, 2015.

"Hellfighters." IMDb, n.d. http://www.imdb.com/title/tt0063060/?ref_=nv_sr_1.

Hendershot, Cyndy. "From Trauma to Paranoia: Nuclear Weapons, Science Fiction, and History." *Mosaic* 32, no. 4 (1999): 73–90.

Henderson, Brian. "'The Searchers': An American Dilemma." *Film Quarterly* 34, no. 2 (1980–1981): 9–23.

Hess, Earl J., and Pratibha A. Dabholkar. *"Singin' in the Rain": The Making of an American Masterpiece.* Lawrence: University of Kansas Press, 2009.

Hiscock, John. "James Cameron Interview for *Avatar." Guardian,* December 3, 2009. http://www.telegraph.co.uk/culture/film/6720156/James-Cameron-interview -for-Avatar.html.

Hoffman, Andrew J. *How Culture Shapes the Climate Change Debate.* Stanford, Calif.: Stanford University Press, 2015.

Huber, Peter W. "Dig More Coal—the PCs Are Coming." *Forbes,* May 31, 1999.

"Index." *Harper's Magazine,* March 2015.

Ingram, David. *Green Screen: Environmentalism and Hollywood.* Exeter, U.K.: University of Exeter Press, 2000.

Ivakhiv, Adrian. *Ecologies of the Moving Image.* Waterloo, Canada: Wilfred Laurier University Press, 2013.

Jackson, Peter. Preface to Lisa Fitzpatrick, *The Art of "Avatar": James Cameron's Epic Adventure,* 7. New York: Abrams, 2009.

Jacobson, Brian R. "Big Oil's High-Risk Love Affair with Film." *Los Angeles Review of Books,* April 7, 2017.

——. *Studios Before the System: Architecture, Technology, and the Emergence of Cinematic Space.* New York: Columbia University Press, 2015.

Jameson, Fredric. "Progress Versus Utopia: Or, Can We Imagine the Future?" *Science-Fiction Studies,* no. 9 (1982): 147–158.

Jensen, Elizabeth. "Activists Take 'The Day After Tomorrow' for a Spin." *Los Angeles Times,* May 26, 2004.

Kakoudaki, Despina. "Spectacles of History: Race Relations, Melodrama, and the Science Fiction/Disaster Film." *Camera Obscura* 17, no. 2 (2002): 109–153.

Kaplan, E. Ann. *Climate Trauma: Foreseeing the Future in Dystopian Film and Fiction.* New Brunswick, N.J.: Rutgers University Press, 2015.

Kasson, John. *Amusing the Millions: Coney Island at the Turn of the Century.* New York: Hill and Wang, 1978.

Kay, Amanda. "Top Tantalum-Mining Countries." *Investing News,* June 12, 2018. https://investingnews.com/daily/resource-investing/critical-metals-investing /tantalum-investing/2013-top-tantalum-producers-rwanda-brazil-drc-canada/.

King, Angela. "Hollywood in Michigan." *Oakland Press,* February 2, 2009.

King, Geoff. *Spectacular Narratives: Hollywood in the Age of the Blockbuster.* London: I. B. Tauris, 2009.

Klein, Naomi. *This Changes Everything: Capitalism vs. the Climate.* New York: Simon and Schuster, 2014.

Kracauer, Siegfried. *Theory of Film: The Redemption of Reality.* Oxford: Oxford University Press, 1960.

Kuhn, Annette. "The Alien Messiah." In *Alien Zone: Cultural Theory and Contemporary Science Fiction,* edited by Annette Kuhn, 32–38. New York: Verso, 1990.

Kurtz, Wilbur G. "'Gone with the Wind' from Behind the Cameras." Converted for publication into "How Hollywood Built Atlanta." *Atlanta Journal Sunday Magazine,* December 3, 1939.

Lambert, Gavin. *GWTW: The Making of "Gone with the Wind."* Boston: Little, Brown, 1973.

Lee, Kevin B. "Kaboom!" *New York Times,* May 2, 2014.

LeMenager, Stephanie. *Living Oil: Petroleum Culture in the American Century.* New York: Oxford University Press, 2014.

Leiserowitz, Anthony A. "Before and After *The Day After Tomorrow*: A U.S. Study of Climate Change Risk Perception." *Environment* 46, no. 9 (2004): 22–44.

Leslie, Esther. *Synthetic Worlds: Nature, Art, and the Chemical Industry.* Middlesex, U.K.: Reaktion Books, 2005.

Lim, Edna. "Displacing 'Titanic': History, Spectacle, Hollywood." In "Titanica," special issue of *International Literary Studies* 5, no. 1 (2003): 45–69.

Manovich, Lev. *The Language of New Media.* Cambridge, Mass.: MIT Press, 2002.

Maranto, Gina. "Are We Close to the Road's End?" *Discover Magazine,* January 1986.

Marcuse, Herbert. *The Aesthetic Dimension: Toward a Critique of Marxist Aesthetics.* New York: Beacon Press, 1979.

Maxwell, Richard, and Toby Miller. *Greening the Media.* Oxford: Oxford University Press, 2012.

Mayer, Vicki. *Almost Hollywood, Nearly New Orleans: The Lure of the Local Film Economy.* Berkeley: University of California Press, 2017.

——. "Bringing the Social Back In: Studies of Production Cultures and Social Theory." In *Production Studies: Cultural Studies of Media Industries,* edited by Vicki

Mayer, Miranda J. Banks, and John Thornton Caldwell, 15–24. New York: Routledge, 2009.

Mayer, Vicki, Miranda J. Banks, and John Thornton Caldwell. "Introduction: Production Studies: Roots and Routes." In *Production Studies: Cultural Studies of Media Industries*, edited by Vicki Mayer, Miranda J. Banks, and John Thornton Caldwell, 1–12. New York: Routledge, 2009.

McIlvaine, Thomas, Jr. "Reducing Film Fires." *Annals of the American Academy of Political and Social Sciences* 128 (November 1926): 96–99.

McKibben, *The End of Nature*. With a new introduction. 1989. Reprint. New York: Random House, 2006.

McKim, Kristi. *Cinema as Weather: Stylistic Screens and Atmospheric Changes*. New York: Routledge, 2013.

Merchant, Brian. *The One Device: The Secret History of the iPhone*. New York: Little, Brown, 2017.

Merchant, Carolyn. *The Death of Nature: Women, Ecology, and the Scientific Revolution*. San Francisco: Harper, 1980.

Merleau-Ponty, Maurice. "Le cinéma et la nouvelle psychologie." In *Sens et nonsens*, 61–74. Paris: Gallimard, 1996.

Mezurek, Jan. *Making Microchips: Policy, Globalization, and Economic Restructuring in the Semiconductor Industry*. Cambridge, Mass.: MIT Press, 1998.

Miller, Steven R., and Abdul Abdulhadi. *The Economic Impact of Michigan's Motion Picture Production Industry and the Michigan Motion Picture Production Credit*. Ann Arbor: Center for Economic Analysis, Michigan State University, 2009.

Miller, Toby, and Richard Maxwell. "Film and Globalization." In *Communications Media, Globalization, and Empire*, edited by Oliver Boyd-Barrett, 33–52. London: John Libbey, 2016.

Mills, Mark. *The Internet Begins with Coal: A Preliminary Exploration of the Impact of the Internet on Electricity Consumption. A Green Policy Paper for the Greening Earth Society*. Bethesda, Md.: Mills-McCarthy, May 1999.

Moore, Ellen Elizabeth. "Green Screen or Smokescreen? Hollywood's Messages About Nature and the Environment." *Environmental Communication* 10, no. 5 (2015): 1–17.

Moore, Jason, ed. *Anthropocene or Capitolocene? Nature, History, and the Crisis of Capitalism*. Oakland, Calif.: PM Press, 2016.

Murray, Robin L., and Joseph K. Heumann. *Ecology and Popular Film: Cinema on the Edge*. New York: State University of New York Press, 2009.

Nardelli, Matilde. "'The Sprawl of Entropy': Cinema, Waste, and Obsolescence in the 1960s and 1970s." *European Journal of Media Studies* 2, no. 2 (2013): 431–446.

Naremore, James. *More Than Night: Film Noir in Its Contexts*. Berkeley: University of California Press, 1998.

National Wildlife Federation. "Invasive Species." n.d. https://www.nwf.org/Educa
tional-Resources/Wildlife-Guide/Threats-to-Wildlife/Invasive-Species.

Neale, Steve. "Hollywood Blockbusters: Historical Dimensions." In *Movie Blockbusters*, edited by Julian Stringer, 47–60. London: Routledge, 2005.

Nisbet, Matt. "Evaluating the Impact of *The Day After Tomorrow*." *Skeptical Inquirer*,
June 16, 2004. http://www.csicop.org/specialarticles/show/evaluating_the_impact
_of_the_day_after_tomorrow.

Nixon, Rob. *Slow Violence and the Environmental Violence of the Poor*. Cambridge,
Mass.: Harvard University Press, 2011.

Nova, Alessandro. *The Book of the Wind: The Representation of the Invisible*. Montreal: McGill-Queen's University Press, 2011.

O'Brien, Jon. "*Twister* Is 20 Years Old! 15 Things You Might Not Know About the
Classic Disaster Movie." *Metro*, May 10, 2016. http://metro.co.uk/2016/05/10/15
-things-you-might-not-know-about-twister-5853475/#ixzz4EyCNeZ29.

Oreskes, Naomi, and Erik M. Conway. *The Merchants of Doubt: How a Handful of
Scientists Obscured the Truth on Issues from Tobacco Smoke to Global Warming*.
New York: Bloomsbury Press, 2010.

Ortner, Sherry. *Not Hollywood: Independent Film at the Twilight of the American
Dream*. Durham, N.C.: Duke University Press, 2013.

Parikka, Jussi. *A Geology of Media*. Minneapolis: University of Minnesota Press,
2015.

Pascual, U., P. Balvanera, S. Díaz, G. Pataki, E. Roth, M. Stenseke, R. T. Watson, E. B.
Dessane, M. Islar, E. Kelemen, et al. "Valuing Nature's Contributions to People:
The IPBES Approach." *Current Opinion in Environmental Sustainability* 26–27
(2017): 7–16.

Pearce, Fred. "Greenwash: Disney's Green Intentions Are Pure Fantasy." *Guardian*,
March 19, 2009. https://www.theguardian.com/environment/2009/mar/19/disney
-greenwash-fred-pearce.

Peters, John Durham. *The Marvelous Clouds: Towards a Philosophy of Elemental
Media*. Chicago: University of Chicago Press, 2015.

Piazza, Jo. "Audiences Experience 'Avatar' Blues." CNN.com, January 11, 2010. http:
//edition.cnn.com/2010/SHOWBIZ/Movies/01/11/avatar.movie.blues/index
.html.

Powdermaker, Hortense. *Hollywood, the Dream Factory: An Anthropologist Looks
at the Movie-Makers*. 1950. Reprint. Manfield Centre, Conn.: Martino, 2013.

Prince, Stephen. *Digital Visual Effects in Cinema*. New Brunswick, N.J.: Rutgers University Press, 2012.

Rath, John. "The Data-Crunching Powerhouse Behind 'Avatar.'" *Data Center Knowledge*, October 22, 2009. http://www.datacenterknowledge.com/archives/2009
/12/22/the-data-crunching-powerhouse-behind-avatar/.

Rawlins, Justin Owen. "This Is(n't) John Wayne: The Miscasting and Performance of Whiteness in *The Conqueror.*" *Quarterly Review of Film and Video* 27 (2010): 14–26.

Reisner, Marc. *Cadillac Desert: The American West and Its Disappearing Water.* London: Pimlico, 2000.

Rickitt, Richard. *Special Effects: The History and Technique.* 2nd ed. New York: Billboard Books, 2007.

Robb, David. "How the Power-Broker Koch Brothers Are Killing the Florida Film Business." *Deadline Hollywood*, October 21, 2016. https://deadline.com/2016/10/koch-brothers-florida-film-industry-tax-incentives-lobbying-1201838246/

Rousseau, Jean-Jacques. *Du contract social; ou Principes du droit politique.* Amsterdam: Chez Marc-Michel Rey, 1762.

Rushkoff, Douglas. Interview of Richard Maxwell on "Greening the Media." Episode 2 of *Team Human*, podcast, August 1, 2016. https://itunes.apple.com/us/podcast/ep-47-richard-barbrook-its-capitalism-mate/id1140331811?i=1000390323949&mt=2.

Rust, Steve. "Hollywood and Climate Change." In *Ecocinema Theory and Practice*, edited by Stephen Rust, Salma Monani, and Sean Cubitt, 191–211. New York: Routledge, 2013.

Sauder, Robert A. *The Lost Frontier: Water Diversion in the Growth and Destruction of Owens Valley Agriculture.* Tucson: University of Arizona Press, 1994.

Schatz, Tom. Foreword to David Alan Vertrees, *Selznick's Vision: "Gone with the Wind" and Hollywood Filmmaking*, ix–xii. Austin: University of Texas Press, 1997.

——. *Hollywood Genres: Formulas, Filmmaking, and the Studio System.* New York: McGraw-Hill, 1981.

——. "The New Hollywood." In *Movie Blockbusters*, edited by Julian Stringer, 15–44. London: Routledge, 2005.

Schefer, Jean-Louis. *L'homme ordinaire du cinema.* Paris: Cahiers du Cinema, 1980.

Schneider, Arnd. "Setting Up Roots, or the Anthropologist on the Set: Observations on the Shooting of a Cinema Movie in Mapuche Reservation, Argentina." In *Visualizing Anthropology: Experimenting with Vision-Based Ethnography*, edited by Anna Grimshaw and Amada Ravetz, 100–115. Chicago: University of Chicago Press, 2004.

Schneider-Mayerson, Matthew. "Disaster Movies and the 'Peak Oil' Movement': Does Popular Culture Encourage Eco-apocalyptic Beliefs in the United States?" *Journal for the Study of Religion, Nature, and Culture* 7, no. 3 (2013): 289–314.

Scorcese, Martin. Foreword to *This Film Is Dangerous: A Celebration of Nitrate Film*, edited by Roger Smither, ix. Brussels: International Federation of Film Archives, 2002.

Scorpions. "Wind of Change." On *Crazy World*. Vertigo, Mercury, 1990.

Scott, Allen. *On Hollywood: The Place, the Industry*. Princeton, N.J.: Princeton University Press, 2014.

Selznick, David O. *Memo from David O. Selznick*. Edited by Rudy Behlmer. New York: Viking Press, 1972.

Seymour, Nicole. "'It's Just Not Turning Up': Cinematic Vision and Environmental Justice in Todd Haynes' 'Safe.'" *Cinema Journal* 50, no. 4 (2011): 26–47.

Silverman, Stephen M. *Dancing on the Ceiling: Stanley Donen and His Movies*. New York: Knopf, 1996.

Sinclair, John. "'The Hollywood of Latin America': Miami as Regional Center in Television Trade." *Television & New Media* 4, no. 3 (2003): 211–229.

"*Singin' in the Rain*." *Variety*, March 12, 1952.

Siperstein, Stephen, Shane Hall, and Stephanie LeMenager, eds. *Teaching Climate Change in the Humanities*. London: Routledge, 2016.

Sklar, Robert. *Movie-Made America: A Cultural History of American Movies*. New York: Vintage, 1975.

Slifer, Clarence. "Creating Visual Effects for *GWTW*." *American Cinematographer* 63, no. 8 (1982): 833–848.

Smith, Aaron. "Record Share of Americans Now Own Smartphones, Have Home Abroad." *FactTank*, January 12, 2017. http://www.pewresearch.org/fact-tank/2017/01/12/evolution-of-technology/.

Smith, Ted, David A. Sonnefeld, David Naguib Pellow, and Jim Hightower, eds. *Challenging the Chip: Labor Rights and Environmental Justice in the Global Electronics Industry*. Philadelphia: Temple University Press, 2006.

Smither, Roger, ed. *This Film Is Dangerous: A Celebration of Nitrate Film*. Brussels: International Federation of Film Archives, 2002.

Sobchack, Vivian. "Surge and Splendour." In *Film Genre Reader II*, edited by Barry Keith Grant, 280–307. Austin: University of Texas Press, 1995.

Sontag, Susan. "The Imagination of Disaster." In *Against Interpretation*, 209–225. New York: Picador, 1961.

Starosielski, Nicole. *The Undersea Network*. Durham, N.C.: Duke University Press, 2015.

Story, Louise. "Michigan Town Woos Hollywood, but Ends Up with Bit Part." *New York Times*, December 3, 2012.

Stringer, Julian. Introduction to *Movie Blockbusters*, edited by Julian Stringer, 1–14. London: Routledge, 2005.

——, ed. *Movie Blockbusters*. London: Routledge, 2005.

Stulman Demett, Andrea, and Nina Warnke. "Disaster Spectacle at the Turn of the Century." *Film History* 4, no. 2 (1990): 101–111.

Sturgeon, Noël. *Environmentalism in Popular Culture: Gender, Race, Sexuality, and the Politics of the Natural*. Tucson: University of Arizona Press, 2008.

"Summer Movie Preview." *New York Times*, May 2, 2014.

Sun, Leo. "Foolish Take: Nearly 80% of Americans Own Smartphones." *USA Today*, February 24, 2018. https://www.usatoday.com/story/money/markets/2018/02/24 /a-foolish-take-nearly-80-of-americans-own-smartphones/110342918/.

Tapestry Institute. "*Twister.*" n.d. http://www.tapestryinstitute.org/tornado/twister .html.

Telotte, J. P. "Human Artifice and the Science Fiction Film." *Film Quarterly* 36, no. 3 (1983): 44–51.

Thompson, David. *Showman: The Life of David O. Selznick*. New York: Knopf, 1992.

"Top Grossing Movies of 1952." Ultimate Movie Rankings, n.d. http://www.ultimate movierankings.com/top-grossing-movies-of-1952/.

Torry, Robert. "Apocalypse Then: Benefits of the Bomb in Fifties Science Fiction Films." *Cinema Journal* 31, no. 1 (1991): 7–21.

Turkle, Sherry. *Alone Together: Why We Expect More from Technology and Less from Each Other*. New York: Basic Books, 2011.

——. *Reclaiming Conversation: The Power of Talk in a Digital Age*. New York: Penguin Press, 2015.

——. *Simulation and Its Discontents*. Cambridge, Mass.: MIT Press, 2009.

Turner, Adrian. *A Celebration of "Gone with the Wind."* New York: Gallery Books, 1990.

" 'Twister': 10 Things You Probably Didn't Know About the Summer Blockbuster." *Moviefone*, May 5, 2016. http://www.moviefone.com/2016/05/10/twister-facts/.

United Nations. "Kyoto Protocol to the United Nations Framework Convention on Climate Change." December 11, 1997. https://unfccc.int/process/the-kyoto -protocol.

United Nations Security Council. *Report of the Panel of Experts on the Illegal Exploitation of Natural Resources and Other Forms of Wealth of the Democratic Republic of the Congo*. New York: United Nations, April 12, 2001.

Underberg, Natalie M., and Elayne Zorn. *Digital Ethnography: Anthropology, Narrative, and New Media*. Austin: University of Texas Press, 2013.

Usai, Paolo Cherchi. *The Death of Cinema*. London: BFI, 2001.

U.S. Environmental Protection Agency (EPA). "Water Trivia Facts." N.d. http://water .epa.gov/learn/kids/drinkingwater/water_trivia_facts.cfm.

"U.S. Geological Survey." 2013. http://ga.water.usgs.gov/edu/mgd.html (no longer available).

Valéry, Paul. "The Conquest of Ubiquity" (1928). In *Aesthetics*, translated by Ralph Mannheim, 225–226. London: Routledge and Kegan Paul, 1964.

Vaughan, Hunter. *Where Film Meets Philosophy: Godard, Resnais, and Experiments in Cinematic Thinking*. New York: Columbia University Press, 2013.

Vertov, Dziga. "WE: Variant of a Manifesto." 1919. https://monoskop.org/images/6/66/Vertov_Dziga_1922_1984_We_Variant_of_a_Manifesto.pdf.

Vertrees, David Alan. *Selznick's Vision: "Gone with the Wind" and Hollywood Filmmaking*. Austin: University of Texas Press, 1997.

Virilio, Paul. *War and Cinema*. Translated by Patrick Camiller. London: Verso, 1989.

Ward, Janet. "Berlin, the Virtual Global City." *Visual Culture* 3, no. 2 (2004): 239–256.

Wark, McKenzie. *Molecular Red: Theory for the Anthropocene*. London: Verso, 2015.

Wiener, David. "Chasing the Wind." *American Cinematographer* 77, no. 5 (1996): 36–44.

Williams, Raymond. *The Country and the City*. New York: Oxford University Press, 1973.

Wollen, Peter. *Sing in' the Rain*. London: BFI, 1992.

Wood, Robin. "Ideology, Genre, Auteur: *Shadow of a Doubt*." In *Hitchcock's Films Revisited*, 288–302. New York: Columbia University Press, 1989.

Zin, David. "Film Incentives in Michigan." Issue paper. Michigan Senate Fiscal Agency, September 2010.

Žižek, Slavoj. "*Avatar*: Return of the Natives," *New Statesman*, March 4, 2010. https://www.newstatesman.com/film/2010/03/avatar-reality-love-couple-sex.

Filmography

All Is Lost (J. C. Chandor, 2013),
Avatar (James Cameron, 2009)
Bambi (Disney, 1942)
Batman v Superman: Dawn of Justice (Zack Snyder, 2016)
Baywatch film (Seth Gordon, 2017)
Beach, The (Danny Boyle, 2000)
Beavis and Butthead series (MTV, 1993–1997)
Black Mirror series (Channel 4 2011–2015, Netflix 2016–)
Blade Runner (Ridley Scott, 1982)
Bloodline series (Netflix, 2015–2017)
Boardwalk Empire series (HBO, 2010–2014)
Burn Notice series (USA Network, 2007–2013)
Caddyshack (Harold Ramis, 1980)
Chasing Coral (Jeff Orlowski, 2017)
Citizen Kane (Orson Welles, 1941)
Clockwork Orange, A (Stanley Kubrick, 1971)
Conqueror, The (Dick Powell, 1956)
Cove, The (Louis Psihoyos, 2009)
Crude (Joe Berlinger, 2009)
Daily Show, The (Comedy Central, 1996–)
Day After Tomorrow, The (Roland Emmerich, 2004)
Everything's Cool (Daniel Gold and Judith Helfand, 2007)

Feeding the Baby (Lumière brothers, 1895)

Fighting the Flames (1908)

Gasland (Josh Fox, 2010/2013)

Godfather, The (Francis Ford Coppola, 1972)

Gone with the Wind (Victor Fleming, 1939)

Golden Compass, The (Chris Weitz, 2007)

Hellfighters (Andrew McLaglen, 1968)

I Am Legend (Francis Lawrence, 2007)

Inconvenient Truth, An (David Guggenheim, 2006)

Inglourious Basterds (Quentin Tarantino, 2009)

Interstellar (Christopher Nolan, 2014)

Invasion of the Body Snatchers (Don Siegel, 1956; Philip Kaufman, 1978)

Jason and the Argonauts (Don Chaffey, 1963)

Jaws (Stephen Spielberg, 1975)

Jurassic Park (Steven Spielberg, 1993)

Jurassic World (Colin Trevorrow, 2015)

King Kong (Ernest B. Schoedsack and Merian C. Cooper, 1933)

King Kong (Peter Jackson, 2005)

King of Kings (Cecil B. DeMille, 1927)

Last Week Tonight with John Oliver series (HBO, 2014–)

Life of an American Fireman, The (Edwin S. Porter, 1903)

Life of Pi (Ang Lee, 2012)

Lord of the Rings (Peter Jackson, 2001–2003)

Mad Max: Fury Road (George Miller, 2015)

Merchants of Doubt (Robert Kenner, 2014)

Miami Vice (Michael Mann, 2006)

Miami Vice series (NBC, 1984–1990),

Moonlight (Barry Jenkins, 2016)

Nature Is Speaking (Conservation International, 2014–)

Never Say Never Again (Irvin Kirshner, 1983)

Racing Extinction (Louis Psihoyos, 2015)

Red Dawn (Dan Bradley, 2012)

River, The (Pare Lorentz, 1937)

River Runs Through It, A (Robert Redford, 1992)

Rebecca (Alfred Hitchcock, 1940,

Scarface (Brian de Palma, 1983)

7th Voyage of Sinbad, The (Nathan Juran, 1958)

Simpsons, The, series (Fox, 1987–)

Singin' in the Rain (Stanley Donan and Gene Kelly, 1952)

Snowpiercer (Joon-Ho Bong, 2013)

Soylent Green (Richard Fleischer, 1973)
Star Wars (George Lucas, 1977)
Survivor: The Australian Outback (CBS, 2001)
Thelma and Louise (Ridley Scott, 1991)
Ten Commandments, The (Demille, Cecil B., 1923)
Terminator 2: Judgment Day (James Cameron, 1992)
Thunderball (Terence Young, 1965)
Titanic (James Cameron, 1997)
Top Gun (Tony Scott, 1986)
Transformers: Dark of the Moon (Michael Bay, 2011)
Twister (Jan de Bont, 1996)
2001 (Stanley Kubrick, 1968)
Twilight Zone series (CBS, 1959–1964)
Up in the Air (Jason Reitman, 2009)
Wall-e (Andrew Stanton and Alan Barillaro, 2008)
Watermark (Jennifer Baichwal and Ed Burtynsky, 2013)
Waterworld (Kevin Reynolds, 1995)
Wedding Crashers (David Dobkin, 2005)
When the Levees Broke (Spike Lee, 2006)
Wild River (Elia Kazan, 1960)
Wind (Carroll Ballard, 1992)
Wind, The (Victor Sjöström, 1928)
Written on the Wind (Douglas Sirk, 1956)
Zabriskie Point (Michelangelo Antonioni, 1970)
Zero Dark Thirty (Kathryn Bigelow, 2012)

Index